THE HINDU CONCEPTION OF THE DEITY

AS CULMINATING IN RAMANUJA

THE HINDU CONCEPTION OF THE DEITY

AS CULMINATING IN RAMANUJA

BY

BHARATAN KUMARAPPA

GYAN

Published by

GYAN

Gyan Publishing House
5, Ansari Road
Daryaganj, New Delhi-110002
Phone: 011-47034999, 9811692060
E-mail: books@gyanbooks.com

Distribution Network
gyanbooks.com
India, USA, Canada, UK, Australia

ISBN: 978-93-6280-818-9 (HB)
First Published, 1934

2nd Impression 2024

Printed at: Gyan Press, Delhi.

THE HINDU CONCEPTION OF THE DEITY AS CULMINATING IN RAMANUJA

Author: BHARATAN KUMARAPPA

THE HINDU CONCEPTION OF THE DEITY

Thesis accepted by the University of London for the Ph.D. Degree in the Faculty of Arts

THE HINDU CONCEPTION OF THE DEITY

AS CULMINATING IN RĀMĀNUJA

By

BHARATAN KUMARAPPA
M.A. (Madras), Ph.D. (Edin.), Ph.D. (Lond.)
John S. Welles Fellow of the Hartford Theological Seminary, U.S.A.
Formerly Professor of Philosophy, Madras Christian College, Madras

LONDON
LUZAC & CO.
46 GREAT RUSSELL STREET, W.C. 1
1934

TO

MY MOTHER

WHOSE LIFE AND TEACHING
HAVE BEEN A SOURCE OF INSPIRATION
TO ME IN MATTERS PERTAINING
TO THE DEITY.

ABBREVIATIONS

Ahir. Saṁ—Ahirbudhnya Saṁhitā.
Ait.—Aitareya.
Ār.—Āraṇyaka.
A.V.—Atharva Veda.
Bhāg. P.—Bhāgavata Purāṇa.
Bhg.—Bhagavadgītā.
Bhg. Bh.—Bhagavadgītā Bhāṣya.
Bṛ.—Bṛhadāraṇyaka.
Chānd.—Chāndogya.
E.R.E.—Hastings' Encyclopædia of Religion and Ethics.
J.R.A.S.—Journal of the Royal Asiatic Society.
Ka.—Kaṭha.
Kauṣ.—Kauṣītaki.
Mah. Bh.—Mahābhārata.
Mait.—Maitri.
Māṇḍ.—Māṇḍukya.
Muṇḍ.—Muṇḍaka.
Nārāy.—Nārāyaṇīya.
O.R.L.I.—Outline of the Religious Literature of India (J. N. Farquhar).
R.V.—Ṛg Veda.
Śat. Br.—Śatapatha Brāhmaṇa.
S.B.E.—Sacred Books of the East.
Ś. Bh.—Śrī Bhāṣya.
Śvet.—Śvetāśvatara.
Taitt.—Taittirīya.
Up.—Upaniṣad.
Viśiṣṭ.—Viśiṣṭādvaitin.
Viṣ. P.—Viṣṇu Purāṇa.
Vs.—Vedānta sūtra.

CONTENTS

CONTENTS

CONTENTS

PART TWO

RĀMĀNUJA'S CONCEPTION OF THE DEITY

CONTENTS

PREFACE

A GREAT deal has been written in English on the monism of Śaṁkara, whose philosophy has been regarded as the highest product of the Indian intellect, and comparatively little on Rāmānuja, his philosophical rival, whose views represent the highest philosophical expression of religious thought in Hinduism down through the ages. Considering the philosophy of Śaṁkara as typical of Indian thought, Western critics have accused Hinduism of illusionism, i.e., of regarding the world of experience, the world of life and activity, as unreal; and on this ground, they have urged that Hinduism can in the end provide no basis for the living of life in this world. Even if such a criticism be true of Śaṁkara's philosophy, it certainly cannot claim to be true of all Hindu philosophy. Rāmānuja, at any rate, repudiates at every turn the doctrine of the illusoriness of the material world and the finite self, and postulates that ultimate Reality is one in which the material world and the finite self find a necessary place. Nay more, he claims that the ideals by which we live—the perfections of truth, goodness and love—are rooted in the very heart of the Eternal. Unlike Śaṁkara, who, as a stern metaphysician, follows the dictates of the intellect, even if it condemns the world of experience to ultimate unreality, Rāmānuja is primarily a realist, abiding by the data of physical, moral and religious experience and seeking to systematize them into a Whole in which they are not ultimately lost, but gain new meaning and value. To all those who construct their metaphysics on experience, who are not willing to dismiss the world of values as illusory,

Rāmānuja's conception of ultimate Reality must be of profound interest. Besides, in Rāmānuja Indian theism of several centuries attains its loftiest philosophical expression, and hence deserves greater attention than it has hitherto obtained.

The aim of this work is twofold—firstly, to deal with such conceptions of the Deity as led to Rāmānuja's views (thus excluding other Hindu conceptions such as the Śaivite, which had hardly any influence on him), and secondly, to deal with Rāmānuja's own conception of the Deity. Accordingly such important religious works of Hinduism as the Upaniṣads, the Bhagavadgītā, Vaiṣṇava portions of the Mahābhārata, the Viṣṇu Purāṇa, the Bhāgavata Purāṇa, and the Hymns of the Āḻvārs, all of which directly influenced Rāmānuja's view of the Deity, are dealt with in Part One, while Part Two gives an account of Rāmānuja's attempt to develop on the basis of these a systematic and consistent conception of the Deity. So far as one is aware there is no work on the subject along the lines of treatment here followed.

It is generally thought that the Upaniṣads tend finally to an abstract monism such as that of Śaṁkara. The view developed in the chapter on the Upaniṣads is opposed to this, and attempts to show that while no one type of thought is consistently adhered to in the Upaniṣads, abstract monism represents in the Upaniṣads an earlier view which gradually obtains its filling from moral and religious sources till it becomes transformed in the end into a monism of the type of Rāmānuja's. As against critics who think that morality finds no place in the philosophical and religious thought of India, the treatment of the writings here included aims to show the place that morality occupies in them.

Those who are not interested in Rāmānuja's criticism of Śaṁkara's monism will do well to omit the refutations of advaitism which are given as introductory to each chapter in Part Two of this work. For the rest, the Outline of Contents and the Index have been so framed as to guide the reader to select out of the book what he is most interested in.

In transcribing Sanskrit words I have followed the system now generally in vogue.

It is not easy to acknowledge my indebtedness to various scholars, for they are many. References in footnotes and the bibliography at the end of this work mention some of them. I am specially indebted to Dr. L. D. Barnett of the School of Oriental Studies, London, Keeper of Oriental Manuscripts at the British Museum, whose help in directing me to the relevant literature was invaluable. I am grateful to him for the Foreword he has written to this book. I must thank also the Library staff of the School of Oriental Studies, London, and more especially of the British Museum Reading Room and the Department of Oriental Manuscripts for the facilities they always willingly provided for my work.

This thesis was accepted by the University of London in June, 1930, under the title "Rāmānuja's Conception of the Deity." I have thought it best to alter the original title to its present form, as the latter seems to me more fully to indicate the scope of the work.

BHARATAN KUMARAPPA.

PART ONE

PRE-RĀMĀNUJA CONCEPTIONS OF THE DEITY

CHAPTER I

CONCEPTION OF THE DEITY IN THE UPANIṢADS[1]

1. *The Nature of the Deity*

THE earliest philosophic view with regard to the Supreme Being appears to have arisen out of an attempt to answer the question, Whence this Universe? Consequently the Upaniṣads abound in numerous creation-theories, each seeking to trace the universe to some First Cause, and describing how and why this First Cause created the universe. A very early creation-theory is to be found in Bṛhadāraṇyaka I (4). 1-5, which says that "In the beginning this world was Soul (*Ātman*) alone in the form of a Person (*Puruṣa*). Looking around, he saw nothing else than himself. . . . He desired a second. He was indeed as large as a woman and a man closely embraced. He caused that self to fall (√ *pat*) into two pieces. Therefrom arose a husband (*pati*) and a wife (*patnī*). He copulated with her. Therefrom human beings were produced." Such crude anthropomorphism where the Prime Being is conceived of on the analogy of a man, and the method of creation is regarded on the analogy of animal reproduction, stamps the theory as one of the oldest preserved for us in the Upaniṣads.

We rise to a distinctly higher level of philosophical thought when we pass from attempts to explain the universe in terms of a magnified man to explanations in terms of natural phenomena, such as Water, or Food (earth), and again from such obviously visible and particular elements to elements less visible and

[1] We limit ourselves to the thirteen chief Upaniṣads. References are to Dr. Hume's translation of them.

more universal, such as air, space, non-being, being and the Imperishable. Thus with regard to Water as the First Principle, it is said in the Bṛ. Up. V (5). 1, " In the beginning this world was just Water. That Water emitted the Real " . . . and in the Chānd. Up. VII (10). 1, " It is just Water solidified that is this earth . . . atmosphere . . . sky . . . gods and men, beasts and birds, grass and trees. . . . Reverence Water." The reason why Water was regarded as the source of all things seems to be that life is impossible without water. As the Chāndogya tells us, living beings perish if there is no rain (VII (10). 1). In a similar manner, it is argued that Food (earth)[1] is the source of all things, for without Food creatures perish (Taitt. II. 1 ; Mait. VI. 11-13 ; Praśna I. 14). Crude as these theories are, they mark a tremendous advance in philosophical thought, for here the thinker turns away from the anthropomorphism of an earlier day and all explanations in terms of gods and goddesses, and seeks to interpret the universe, not in terms of some creation of his imagination, but in terms of a principle known to him in everyday experience.

With Water and Food as the ultimate Principle, however, we still move in the realm of the particular and the sensible. Wind or Breath, being invisible and less sharply defined, tends to lead the mind away from attachment to the sensible—which again could not have been easy for these pioneer thinkers. The reason for regarding this as ultimate seems to have been derived chiefly from the observation that an individual dies when breath ceases, and also from the fact that it is breath alone which functions untiringly in the individual while other organs soon become exhausted and require rest. This is true of Air or Wind, the counterpart in the inorganic world of Breath in the living body, for Air never seems to require rest, unlike Fire, which soon exhausts itself, and the Sun and Moon,

[1] Rāmānuja points out that Food here should be taken to refer to Earth : Śrī-Bhāṣya, S.B E. Vol. 48, p. 536.

which daily set and thus take their rest (Bṛ. Up. I (5). 21 and 22). Moreover, just as all the other functions of the body disappear in sleep into Breath, and Breath alone remains, the elemental forces of nature such as fire, water, sun and moon are seen to disappear into Air or Wind. "The Wind (*vāyu*), verily, is a snatcher-unto-itself. Verily, when a fire blows out, it just goes to the Wind. When the sun sets, it just goes to the Wind. When the moon sets, it just goes to the Wind. When water dries, goes up, it just goes to the Wind. For the Wind, truly, snatches all here to itself. . . . Now with reference to oneself—Breath (*prāṇa*), verily, is a snatcher-unto-itself. When one sleeps, speech just goes to breath; the eye to breath, the ear to breath; the mind to breath; for the breath, truly, snatches all here to himself. Verily, these are two snatchers-unto-themselves" (Chānd. Up. IV (3). 1-4). And with regard to the supremacy of Breath among all the vital elements in the body, we have the dramatic portrayal of the rivalry among the five organs of the body, speech, sight, hearing, mind and breath, and the victory gained by Breath by its showing that without it none of the others can function, while without the other organs, it can still function (Bṛ. VI (1). 7-13; Chānd. V (1). 6-15; Kauṣ. III. 3; Praśna II. 3 and 4). It is primarily on the basis of the indispensability of Breath for living beings that it is acclaimed as Supreme. If so, it is obvious that while the philosopher who regarded Breath or Wind as the ultimate Principle made an advance over those who put forward a sensible element like Water or Food as ultimate, still he did not, any more than they, succeed in rising above anthropomorphism, if by anthropomorphism we mean the way of thinking which argues purely on the analogy of what is true in human experience. Whether the ultimately Real is conceived of as Water, Food, or Breath, it is precisely because these are absolutely essential to human life.

When, however, we pass to a comparatively universal and omnipresent element such as Space as the First Principle, we seem for the first time to pass to the level of abstract thought which has succeeded in dissociating itself from the sensible and the anthropomorphic. Thus in Chānd. I (9). 1, we have the question asked, "To what does this world go back?" and the answer is, "To space. . . . Verily, all things here arise out of space. They disappear back into space, for space alone is greater than these; space is the final goal." From this, the transition to such highly abstract conceptions such as that of Non-being, Being, or the Imperishable as ultimate was not very difficult, and we have these three principles put forward[1] as the source of all things. That by Non-being was not meant mere nothingness, but some form of characterless existence, appears from the fact that it is definitely asserted that non-being was "existent" and "developed" (Chānd. III (19). 1). If then by non-being was meant a primeval existence where all is as yet mere potentiality, it is not really affected by the criticism of a later thinker who ridicules the idea that the world could have come out of Non-being, understanding by non-being, as he does, mere nothingness. In advocating his own view that Being is ultimate, this critic argues, "To be sure, some people say: 'In the beginning this world was just non-being (*asat*), one only without a second; from that non-being, Being (*sat*) was produced.' But verily, my dear, whence could this be? How from non-being could Being be produced? On the contrary, my dear, in the beginning this world was just Being, one only, without a second. It bethought itself: 'Would that I were many! Let me procreate myself.' It emitted heat. . . . That heat bethought itself . . . 'Would that I were many! Let me procreate

[1] It must not be thought that these ideas arose for the first time during the period of the Upaniṣads, for we find many of them expressed in the philosophical portions of the Ṛgveda, Bk. x, in the Brāhmaṇas, and more especially in the Āraṇyakas.

myself.' It emitted water. . . . That water bethought itself . . . 'Would that I were many! Let me procreate myself.' It emitted food" (Chānd. VI. 2 f.); and we are told that the whole universe, including man, is nothing but a product of these three elements, heat, water and food, which have for their animating principle the Primal Being. It does not seem likely that this Being was conceived as characterised by consciousness.[1] The Thought that is ascribed to this Being in the passage above cited must not, it would seem, be taken literally, for the same word here translated 'thought' is also used in the case of heat and water as each of these differentiates itself. Further the very materialistic account that is given of man and his conscious faculties, as the product of heat, water and food, the thrice repeated maxim that "The mind consists of food," and the striking illustration of this truth in the fact that without food for 15 days Śvetaketu is unable to employ his mind, all seem to point to the view that consciousness was regarded by this philosopher as the result of non-conscious processes, and as therefore not ultimate. Then also the view that in sleep, where there is a total lack of consciousness, or in death, where we are told that the mind has passed into breath, and breath into heat one reaches Being, seems to indicate that Being was conceived as some primeval unconscious substance which underlies all things and which is best represented by the three elements of heat, water, and food (earth). This Being is also described as "finest essence" (VI (6). 6, 8-15), and seems as such to denote nothing more than some primeval stuff out of which everything in the universe, whether conscious soul or unconscious object, is ultimately constituted. The human soul ultimately dissolves into it, and so does the worm. 'Whatever they are in this world, whether

[1] As Max Müller in his translation suggests. See S.B.E. Vol. 1 p.93 footnote 2 (1879 edition); also Rāmānuja (Śrī Bhāṣya, S.B.E. Vol 48 pp. 200-206), arguing on the assumption that the Upaniṣads always mean to teach that the Supreme Being has personal qualities.

tiger or lion, or wolf or bear, or worm, or fly, or gnat, or mosquito, that they become. That which is the finest essence this whole world has that as its soul. That is Reality (*satya*). That is *Ātman* (Soul). That art thou, Śvetaketu' (Chānd. VI (9). 3 and 4). If then this ultimate essence which forms the stuff of all that exists is just the primeval substance out of which everything has come, it is not unlike that ultimate existence, called non-being, out of which an earlier philosopher had conceived the universe to have developed. Whether as Non-being or Being, then, ultimate Reality is some abstract potency or essence from which the universe has sprung and into which it will finally return. The reason for describing this ultimate Reality as merely Non-being or Being appears to be that, as the ultimate potentiality from which everything has sprung, it cannot have the qualities of the latter. It is that which exists prior to the development of qualities, and therefore cannot be described in terms of these qualities. It is true that our philosophers did not consciously argue thus, but it seems certainly to be implied in their view as well as in the view of those who taught that ultimate Reality or Brahman was to be described as the Imperishable (*akṣara*) and to be defined only negatively. Thus Yājñavalkya in answering Gārgī's question, "Across what, then, pray, is space woven, warp and woof?" states, "That, O Gārgī, Brahmans call the Imperishable (*akṣara*). It is not coarse, not fine, not short, not glowing (like fire), not adhesive (like water), without shadow and without darkness, without air and without space, without stickiness (intangible),[1] odourless, tasteless, without eye, without ear, without voice, without wind, without energy, without breath, without mouth (without personal or family name, unaging, undying, without fear, immortal, stainless, not uncovered, not covered),[1] without measure, without inside and without outside" (Bṛ. III (8). 8).

[1] A Mādhyaṁdina addition.

The doctrine of the Imperishable as put forward by Yājñavalkya is not, however, merely the doctrine of Being, with its negative tendencies coming to fuller expression. Yājñavalkya appears as one of the greatest expounders of the view that Brahman is the supreme Reality—Brahman, understood not as mere Being, but as a distinctly conscious principle.[1] Consequently Yājñavalkya means more by Brahman or the Imperishable than mere Being. "Verily, O Gārgī," he continues in answer to her question, "that Imperishable is the unseen Seer, the unheard Hearer, the unthought Thinker, the ununderstood Understander. Other than It there is naught that sees. Other than It there is naught that hears. Other than It there is naught that thinks. Other than It there is naught that understands. Across this Imperishable, O Gārgī, is space woven, warp and woof" (Bṛ. III (8). 11). In this thought of Yājñavalkya we reach the idea which is predominant in the Upaniṣads, that Brahman, the ground of all things, is a conscious principle.

The word Brahman itself does not appear always to have had this lofty meaning. Originally used in the sense of hymn, prayer, sacred knowledge or magic formula, it soon came to mean the power inherent in these, and from this the transition to the idea of cosmic power or the power that supports the worlds was not difficult.[2] But what distinguishes the concept of Brahman from concepts such as Water, Breath, or Space, is that, unlike these concepts, Brahman as cosmic power came to be thought of primarily as we have seen in the case of Yājñavalkya, as a conscious principle. It is thus implied that what underlies the external universe is one with what exists within one's own self; nay, more, that as conscious principle It is more akin to self than to not-self. The seeds of monistic idealism, which as we shall see characterises

[1] Cf. Bṛ. Up. III (4). 1 and 2.

[2] Cf. R. E. Hume—*Thirteen Principal Upaniṣads*, pp. 14 and 15.

the teaching of the Upaniṣads, as well as much of the later development of Indian thought, were sown, it would appear, by men like Yājñavalkya with their philosophic insight that Brahman, the ultimate ground of all things, is a conscious principle.

The development which we have so far traced in the view of Supreme Reality as some impersonal sensible element such as Water and Food (Earth) to more and more abstract and universal elements such as breath or air, space, non-Being, Being, the Imperishable, till finally we reach the view of Brahman as a conscious principle, represents only one among numerous lines of thought that came to development at this time.[1] Some philosophers, it would appear, conceived the Supreme Being as Self (*Ātman*) or Spirit[2] (*Puruṣa*). We have already referred to the creation-theory which speaks of the First Cause as *Ātman*, who existed in the form of a *Puruṣa*, and separating himself into male and female brings about all that exists in the universe. Another very primitive Ātman-theory is preserved for us in the Aitareya Upaniṣad, which begins with the words, "In the beginning *Ātman* (Self) verily, one only, was here—no other blinking thing whatever. He bethought himself: Let me now create worlds." He accordingly created the worlds, and deities to guard the worlds. Then he created man (I (1)-(3)). The method employed by *Ātman* in creating the worlds and man is significant. We are told that *Ātman* shaped a *Puruṣa* and drew him forth from the waters, and brooded upon him. From the mouth of this *Puruṣa* came Fire; from his nostrils, Air; from his eyes, the Sun; from his ears, the quarters of heaven; from his skin, plants and trees; from his heart, the moon; from his navel,

[1] Mythological ideas such as that of a giant *Puruṣa*, whom the gods sacrificed, and from whose body the universe came into being, and that of a cosmic egg, Hiraṇyagarbha, from which as it were the universe was hatched, come from Ṛgvedic times, and are also to be found in the Upaniṣads.

[2] I.e., as genius or guardian spirit of the universe, each individual and object of the universe likewise having its own presiding genius. See Dr. Barnett's article on "The Genius" in the J.R.A.S. for October 1929, esp. pp. 742-8.

death; and from his virile member, water. And in creating man, we are told that the Deity ordered those various elements in the external world to enter into man, and "fire became speech and entered the mouth. Wind became breath and entered the nostrils. The sun became sight and entered the eyes. The quarters of heaven became hearing and entered the ears. Plants and trees became hairs, and entered the skin. The moon became mind, and entered the heart. Death became the out-breath (*apāna*) and entered the navel. Waters became semen and entered the virile member" (I (2). 3 and 4). What is noteworthy is that both the self and the not-self, which seem so entirely different from each other, are here regarded as having a mutual correspondence, since both of them are permeated by the same forces which emanated from the Primeval *Puruṣa*. Further, the old Ṛgvedic idea[1] of a cosmic *Puruṣa*, from the parts of whose body various elements in the universe are regarded as emanating—an idea which occurs frequently in the Upaniṣads, as well as later Indian writings—is here assimilated by the Ātman-theory. The view that Ultimate Reality was *Puruṣa* or presiding Genius of the universe appears thus to have developed side by side with the view that It was *Ātman*. Nay more, as evidenced by these early Ātman-theories, it would appear that the distinction between *Puruṣa* and *Ātman* was not maintained, the two being freely identified with each other, and in some cases *Puruṣa* being subordinated to *Ātman*, when the latter came to be regarded as Ultimate Reality.

The idea that *Ātman* or Self created this universe naturally led philosophers to enquire in what *Ātman* or self-hood as known in their own experience consists. What they asked, is that permanent something which underlies all the changing experiences of an individual, and itself unchanging binds together his ever changing experiences? This is taught to Indra by Prajāpati.[2]

[1] Ṛg Veda X. 90. [2] Chānd, VIII (7)-(12).

The true self of the individual, he declares, is not (*a*) the bodily self, which undergoes changes, sickness and death, nor (*b*) the dream-self, which, though unaffected by the changes of the body (as, e.g., when the body is ill, the dreamer may be quite unaware of his illness and be supremely happy) still undergoes experiences as though it suffered change, sickness and death, nor (*c*), even the self in dreamless sleep, which neither suffers from the imperfection of the body nor undergoes experiences as though it suffered from these imperfections, and is thus truly above all change, but nevertheless suffers from the defect of lacking consciousness, but (*d*) that self which appears as the conscious principle in the body. Regarding this self, Prajāpati declares, "where the eye is directed thus toward space, that is the seeing person (*cākṣuṣa puruṣa*) ; the eye is (the instrument) for seeing. Now he who knows, 'Let me smell this'—that is, the Self (*Ātman*) ; the nose is (the instrument) for smelling. Now he who knows 'Let me utter this'—that is the Self ; the voice is (the instrument) for utterance. Now he who knows 'Let me hear this'—that is the Self ; the ear is (the instrument) for hearing. Now he who knows 'Let me think this'—that is the Self ; the mind (*manas*) is his divine eye (*daiva cakṣu*). He, verily, with that divine eye the mind, sees desires here, and experiences enjoyment" (Chānd. VIII (12). 4 and 5). The *Ātman* in the body is thus found to be the principle of consciousness which underlies all the experiences of an individual, and when it was postulated as the ground of the universe, there was very little to distinguish this from the view that Brahman as a conscious principle pervades the universe, and both theories are merged into one, *Ātman* being freely identified with Brahman, and Brahman with *Ātman*.[1] And since, as we have already pointed out, *Ātman* was also identified with *Puruṣa*, all three terms

[1] Cf. Bṛ II (5) ; IV, (4). 25 ; Chānd. III (14). 4 ; VIII (14). 1 ; Ait. (3). 13 ; (5). 3 ; Muṇḍ. II (2) ; Śvet. 1. 16 : Mait. II. 2 ; VI. 17.

are freely interchanged. "This, shining, immortal Person (*Puruṣa*) who is in this earth, and, with reference to oneself, this shining, immortal Person who is in the body—he indeed, is just this Soul (*Ātman*), this Immortal, this Brahma, this all" (Bṛ. II (5). 1 ff.). By the time of the Śvetāśvatara, it appears that these three terms were so generally used to designate one and the same Being, that the Śvetāśvatara uses all three terms to refer to the Supreme Reality, and passes from one to the other without the slightest hesitancy.[1] Whether, then, the Supreme Being was conceived of as Brahman, *Puruṣa* or *Ātman*, all theories meet in the end in the view that the ground of all things is an all-pervading conscious principle. What further attributes are ascribed to this Being, we must now enquire.

That Brahman is one without a second may be said to be the theme of all the Upaniṣads. "Verily, in the beginning this world was Brahman, one only" (Bṛ. I (4). 11).[2] All the gods and all the powers hitherto recognised are subordinate to Him. The gods Agni and Vāyu are unable respectively to burn or to blow away so much as a piece of straw without the power given to them by Brahman (Kena 14-23); and Yājñavalkya systematically reduces the number of gods from 3,306 to one, and proclaims Him to be Brahman (Bṛ. III (9). 1-9).

This unitary Being is described as infinite and limitless (Bṛ. II (4). 12; Taitt. II. 1). Its infinitude is

[1] Cf. Śvet. III. 7-12. Following this usage, we shall employ the term, Brahman, generally for the Supreme Being, even if in the text He is referred to by some other name.

Note.—Of other terms used in the Upaniṣads to refer to the Supreme Being, the more important are Prajāpati and Īśāna. Prajāpati rises to importance in the Brāhmaṇas as the Creator, and that is the significance which the term primarily has in the Upaniṣads also. Cf. Bṛ. I (5); VI (4). 2; Chānd. II (23). 2 and 3; IV (17). 1-3, etc. In his capacity as the source of all things Prajāpati is often addressed as Father: Cf. Bṛ. I (5). 1 and 2; V. 2. The references to the Supreme Being as Īśāna occur chiefly in the later Upaniṣads, e.g. Muṇḍ. III (1). 1-3; Śvet. I. 8; III. 7-9. The word means Lord, and of it, Mr. W. D. Hill writes, "the term approaches most nearly of all terms to the conception of the personal deity of monotheism." *The Bhagavadgītā*, p. 23. The significance of this conception will be considered later.

[2] Cf. also I (4). 1 and 17.

such that even if one removes the infinite from it, it still remains infinite. "The yon is fulness; fulness, this. From fulness, fulness doth proceed. Withdrawing fulness's fulness off, e'en fulness then itself remains" (Bṛ. V (1)).[1] Being infinite, temporal and spatial restrictions do not apply to it, for it transcends them. It is, therefore, ageless and deathless (Chānd. VIII (1). 5). "This Brahman is without an earlier and without a later, without an inside and without an outside" (Bṛ. II (5). 19); unborn and beyond space (Bṛ. IV (4). 20).

In this its infinite and transcendent form, it appears to be indescribable in terms of positive qualities, and hence, as we noted, Yājñavalkya could describe it only negatively. Yājñavalkya arrives at the same conclusion regarding the unknowability of the essential nature of Brahman on the ground that Brahman as conscious principle, is that whereby all knowing takes place, and as knower it can never become a known object. "You could not see the seer of seeing. You could not hear the hearer of hearing. You could not think the thinker of thinking. You could not understand the understander of understanding" (Bṛ. III (4). 2).

But while in its infinite and transcendent form and in its nature as knowing principle Brahman cannot be known, still as revealed in various elements in the universe, some at least of its attributes may, it would appear, be divined. Philosophers accordingly set themselves to this task. It is this epoch in Indian speculation that seems to be represented by the appearance of Yājñavalkya in the arena of philosophical discussion. Views similar to the one propounded in the Honey-Doctrine[2] seem for Yājñavalkya the starting-point. The Honey-Doctrine, which is expounded in fifteen paragraphs, is unable to say very much more regarding Brahman than that He is the Soul

[1] Cf. Atharva-veda X (8). 29, where this verse occurs with slight variations.
[2] Bṛ. II (5).

(*Ātman*), the Immortal One, who pervades the earth, the waters, fire, wind, sun, the quarters of heaven, moon, lightning, thunder, space, law, truth, mankind, and the soul, and corresponding with these, pervades also the body, the semen, speech, breath, eye, ear, mind, heat in the individual, sound, space in the heart, virtuousness, truthfulness, the human being, and the soul. Similarly, a philosopher proclaims that Brahman is in speech, breath, eye, and ear, and corresponding with these, in Fire, Wind, Sun and the quarters of heaven. But he is unable to say very much more about the nature of Brahman, than that he is the Brilliant One (Chānd. II (18). 2-6).[1] Yājñavalkya points out that though Brahman is in all these things, He is different from these, being the "unseen Seer, the unheard Hearer, the unthought Thinker, the ununderstood Understander" (Bṛ. III (7). 23). It is in possessing such knowledge of Brahman that Yājñavalkya considers himself superior to all the learned men of his day.[2] His contempt for Śākalya is precisely because the latter has failed to go beyond the traditional identifying of Brahman with the *Puruṣa* who abides in earth, desire, eye, space, darkness, water, semen and their corresponding counterparts (Bṛ. III (9). 10-18). He declares that it is necessary to pluck apart and to put together these *Puruṣas* and to pass beyond them (Bṛ. III (9). 26). So far as merely such identification of Brahman with various *Puruṣas* goes, he shows himself as expert as anyone else of his day (Bṛ. III (9). 19-26). But his own distinctive contribution lies in his penetrating behind the conventional view that Brahman is speech, life, breath, sight, hearing, mind, and heart, in order to discover the attributes of the Being who can be regarded in these various ways.

[1] For other similar identifications, see Bṛ. II (1); III (7); III (9). 10-17; IV (1); VI (1); Chānd. III (18); IV (5)-(10); V (12)-(18); VII; Kauṣ. II. 3 and 4; IV; and for similar classification of cosmic and corresponding personal phenomena, see Ait. I. 1 and 2; Chānd. III (13).

[2] Cf. Bṛ III (1). 1 and 2; III (9). 12.

Thus in his conversation with King Janaka he points out with great insight that, corresponding to these six principles, Brahman has the attribute of intelligence, which expresses itself in speech, the element of dearness which life has for all beings, the truthfulness of sight, the unlimitedness of the quarters of heaven (hearing), the blissfulness of mind, and the quality of being a steadfast support which is found in the heart (Bṛ. IV (1). The qualities deduced in each case are noteworthy, as being qualities which are the most significant of the qualities possessed by these objects, and suggest the view that if Brahman is to be described in terms of positive qualities, He must be described in terms of what is most significant in this universe, i.e., in terms of what makes various things in the world valuable and precious to us. This last appears, indeed, to be the gist of his classical eulogy of the Brahman-Ātman, where he declares that everything is dear, not for what it is in itself, but because of *Ātman.*[1] "Lo, verily, not for love of a husband is a husband dear, but for love of the soul (*Ātman*) a husband is dear. Lo, verily, not for love of the wife is a wife dear, but for the love of the soul, a wife is dear. Lo, verily, not for love of the sons are sons dear, but for love of the soul sons are dear. Lo, verily, not for love of the wealth is wealth dear, but for love of the soul wealth is dear . . . Lo, verily, not for love of all is all dear, but for love of the soul all is dear" Bṛ. II (4). 5). The supreme preciousness of Brahman is indicated by the immeasurable bliss which Yājñavalkya declares to belong to one who has attained the Brahma-world. He says that it is 100 x 100 x 100 x 100 x 100 x 100 times the highest bliss known in the world of men (Bṛ. IV (3). 33).[2] Brahman-Ātman is thus more

[1] The word *Ātman* is here used for the ultimate ground of all things (or Brahman) cf. "with the understanding of the soul (*Ātman*), this world-all is known" Bṛ. II (4). 5; see also the rest of this section (6)-(14).

[2] The same idea occurs in Taitt. II. 8, also in Śatapatha Brāhmaṇa XIV (7). 1, 31-39. The Taittirīya expounds the view that Brahman consists of four "persons" one inside the other, Food (earth), breath (*prāṇa*), mind (*mano-maya*), understanding (*vijñāna-maya*) and bliss (*ānanda-maya*); bliss

desirable than home, offspring or wealth (Bṛ. IV (4). 22). He is perfect bliss.

Brahman, then, according to Yājñavalkya, although unknown in His own essential nature, is as revealed in the universe that which gives significance and value to all things—Himself the most supremely valuable of all.

Yājñavalkya was not by any means the only one who sought to deduce the nature of Brahman from the traditional identifying of Him with various elements in the cosmos and the finite self. Records of four similar attempts by other philosophers have come down to us. Thus the philosopher-king, Ajātaśatru, systematically deduces from Gārgya's conception of Brahman as the Person (*Puruṣa*) in the sun, moon, lightning, space, wind, fire, water, mirror, sound, quarters of heaven, shadow, and the body, corresponding attributes in Brahman as the pre-eminent, white-robed, brilliant, full and non-active, unconquered, vanquisher, counterpart, the shining One, life, inseparable companion, death, the embodied and finally adds that He is the conscious principle within oneself (Bṛ. II (1).[1] Here again it is noteworthy that the attributes deduced are not equally every possible attribute which these elements may possess, but only what are most significant of them. Thus His pervading the sun reveals Him as the "pre-eminent, the head and king of all beings," His pervading space reveals Him as the full and non-active,[2] His pervading the wind reveals Him as the unconquered, the infinite in power, and so on with the rest.

So also in the instruction which Satyakāma receives, it is pointed out that Brahman is the shining One in

---

representing His inmost self (II. 1-5, III). As Food, He is the source of all creatures, as Breath He supports them, as Mind He is the source of all Vedas, as Understanding He is the source of *Sraddhā* (faith), *ṛta* (the right), *satya* (the true), *yoga* (discipline) and *mahas* (greatness); and as Bliss, He is the source of all delight.

[1] A similar account occurs in Kauṣ. IV.

[2] A sign possibly of perfection, for activity in Indian thought is usually associated with lack and finitude, and bondage to Karma.

the East, West, South and North, as the Endless or the infinite in the earth, air, sky, and ocean, as the Luminous in the fire, sun, moon, and lightning, and as Possessing a support in breath, eye, ear and mind. This discourse also ends by adding that above all Brahman is to be known as the conscious principle in oneself (Chānd. IV (4)-(15)). At this point the teacher breaks forth into a praise of Brahman as " 'Loveliness-uniter' (*samyadvāma*), for all lovely things come together unto it . . . 'Goods-bringer' *vāmanī*) for it brings all goods. . . . 'Light-bringer' (*bhāmanī*), for it shines in all worlds."

Kaikeya's instruction of the six Brahmans who come to him each with a different notion as to what Brahman is, viz., that He is heaven, sun, wind, space, water, and earth, is not only to show that Brahman is all these, but also to deduce from each of these partial definitions of Brahman, a corresponding attribute in Him. Thus, as heaven, He is the brightly shining One; as sun, the manifold one; as wind, one who possesses various paths; as space, one who is expanded; as water, one who is all wealth; as earth, one who is a support. Here again obviously the philosopher attempts to describe Brahman in terms of what is most striking and significant in each of these various elements with which He is identified, and concludes by pointing out that Brahman is the Soul which is within oneself (Chānd. V (11)-(18)).

The progressive instruction of Nārada by Sanatkumāra,[1] whereby Nārada is led from lower to higher and higher conceptions of Brahman—from Brahman as name, speech, mind, conception, thought, meditation, understanding, etc., to Soul (*Ātman*) as the highest—has for its characteristic the fact that each category, which is mentioned as descriptive of Brahman, is mentioned on the ground that it is important and indispensable; and if it is transcended it is only because there is a still higher category,

[1] Chānd. VII.

which is also important and indispensable, and which has the added merit of subsuming under itself the previous categories. Thus an effort is made to describe Brahman in terms of qualities, the most significant and all-inclusive.

In this way, it would seem, philosophers sought to go beyond the view that Brahman, the ultimate ground of all things, is a conscious principle, and to describe it in terms suggestive of value and pre-eminence. It is true that they do not tell us very much about the attributes of Brahman, beyond what has been mentioned above. Nevertheless, it is significant that Brahman, the all-pervading conscious principle, tended to be regarded as possessed of value.

While some sought thus to deduce the attributes of Brahman from the fact that He pervades this and that element in the universe, others, it would appear, with less discrimination, but greater zeal for the truth that Brahman is the unity which explains all this diversity, straightway identified Brahman with everything in the universe. To them the truth that nothing can exist without Brahman was all-engrossing, for was it not such a unitary principle which they so passionately sought after at this time? Exulting in their discovery, they therefore proclaim with blind enthusiasm, Lo, here, all is Brahman. "Verily, this whole world is Brahman. Tranquil, let one worship It as that from which he came forth, as that into which he will be dissolved, as that in which he breathes" (Chānd. III (14). 1). "Verily, what is called Brahman —that is the same as what the space outside of a person is. Verily, what the space outside of a person is—that is the same as what the space within a person is. Verily, what the space within a person is—that is the same as what the space here within the heart is" (Chānd. III (12). 7). "This Self, verily, is a world of all created beings" (Bṛ. I (4). 16). "Verily, this whole world is Brahman . . . containing all works, containing all desires, containing all odours, containing all tastes, encompassing this whole world, the unspeaking, the unconcerned—this is the Soul of mine within the heart, this is Brahman" (Chānd. III (14).

But this wholesale predication of everything found in the universe as being of Brahman, if it was intended seriously, and not meant merely in an exaggerated way to refer to the all-pervading power of Brahman, could not continue for very long, for a little reflection suffices to show that if Brahman is everything all over again, He is not the unity which philosophers were seeking. That which explains everything cannot be the same as everything. Accordingly philosophers were not long in perceiving that Brahman must be very different in character from the universe. Indeed so different it seemed to them He must be, that on the one hand, as already noted, they declared that He is essentially unknown, and on the other, that He is to be described only in terms of qualities which are most significant in the elements of this universe. This twofold tendency comes to fuller development in the later Upaniṣads,[1] as we shall presently see.

What is noticeable as we pass from the earlier Upaniṣads to the later is the growing conviction that Brahman must be very different from the universe, and therefore essentially unknown. "Him who is hard to see, entered into the hidden, set in the secret place, dwelling in the depth, primeval" (Kaṭha II. 12, Śvet. VI. 11). "Though He is hidden in all things, that Soul (*Ātman*) shines not forth. But He is seen by subtle seers with superior, subtle intellect" (Kaṭha III. 12, Śvet. IV. 15). "Not by speech, not by mind, not by sight can He be apprehended. How can He

[1] I assume, what scholars seem unanimously to believe, that the Bṛhadāraṇyaka and Chāndogya Upaniṣads to which I have confined myself so far, are older than other Upaniṣads, although it is not precluded that those two Upaniṣads have been subject to later interpolations. I have sought to confine my references to such passages as do not appear to be later interpolations. Bṛhadāraṇyaka, Chāndogya, Taittirīya, Aitareya, Kauṣītaki and the prose section of Kena are usually regarded as earlier than other Upaniṣads, and there seems little reason to question this view. (See, e.g., P. Deussen—*Philosophy of the Upaniṣads*, pp. 22-26.)

be comprehended otherwise than by one's saying 'He is'?" (Muṇḍ. III (1). 8; Kena 3; Kaṭha VI. 12). He is declared to have a transcendent nature which baffles human thought. "There the eye goes not, speech goes not, nor the mind. We know not, we understand not how one would teach It. Other, indeed, is It than the known, and moreover above the unknown.—Thus have we heard of the ancients who to us have explained It" (Kena 3). He possesses many marvellous and transcendent powers. "Sitting, He proceeds afar; lying, He goes everywhere . . . who is the bodiless among bodies, stable among the unstable, the great, all-pervading Soul" (Kaṭha II. 21 and 22). "Unmoving, the One (*ekam*) is swifter than the mind. The sense-powers (*deva*) reached not It, speeding on before. Past others running, This goes standing" (Īśā 4). "Eternal, all-pervading, omni-present, exceedingly subtle" (Muṇḍ. I (1). 6); "Brilliant is It the light of lights" (Muṇḍ. II (2). 9); "Vast, heavenly, of unthinkable form" (Muṇḍ. III (1). 7); "Having an eye on every side and a face on every side, having an arm on every side, and a foot on every side" (Śvet. III. 3). "The Person (*Puruṣa*) has a thousand heads, a thousand eyes, a thousand feet; He surrounds the earth on all sides, and stands ten fingers' breath beyond" (Śvet. III. 14).[1] "Without foot or hand, He is swift and a seizer! He sees without eye; He hears without ear" (Śvet. III. 19). "Not above, not across, nor in the middle has one grasped Him. There is no likeness of Him, whose name is Great Glory (*mahad yaśas*)" (Śvet. IV. 19). Brahman thus in His transcendent aspect has, it would seem, marvellous qualities beyond all thought and imagination.

Besides such qualities which make Brahman awful and incomprehensible, these later philosophers also

[1] These stanzas of the Śvetāśvatara are evidently taken from older sources. With Śvet. III 3, cf. Ṛgveda X (81). 3, and with Śvet. III. 14, cf. Ṛgveda X (90). 1.

ascribe to the Supreme Being numerous perfections which render Him an object of aspiration, and even of love. Thus he is described as the "best," the "supreme" (Kaṭha II. 17; Śvet. I. 7; III. 7; Mait. V. 2); "greater than the great" (Kaṭha II. 20; Śvet. III. 9); higher than whom there is nothing at all (Kaṭha III. 11; Muṇḍ. III (2). 8; Śvet. I. 12; III. 9); "a light without smoke" (i.e., the perfect One, Kaṭha IV. 13); "all-knowing, all wise" (Muṇḍ. I (1). 9; II (2). 7; Śvet. VI. 2 and 16; III. 19; Īśā 8); "lighted by His own intellect" (Śvet. VI. 18), the principle of intelligence (Mait. II. 4); "consisting of mind," "the blissful" (Muṇḍ. II (2). 7), "constant . . . stable" (Kaṭha III. 15; Muṇḍ. I (2). 11); "steadfast" (Mait. II. 4); "firm support" (Śvet. I. 7); "without equal or superior" (Śvet. VI. 8); "whose is this greatness on the earth" (Muṇḍ. II (2). 7); whom "all the gods reverence" (Kaṭha V. 3); "worthy to be worshipped day by day" (Kaṭha IV. 8); from whom one does not shrink away (Kaṭha IV. 5, 12 and 13); "who grants desires" (Kaṭha V. 13; Śvet. VI. 13); "the adorable God" (Śvet. VI. 18); "the object of desire" (Muṇḍ. II (2). 1).

While then it may be admitted that numerous perfections come to be ascribed to the Supreme Being in the later Upaniṣads, it remains to ask how far moral perfection is ascribed to Him. In the earlier Upaniṣads Brahman is proclaimed to be free from evil, and an early attempt to teach this occurs at the beginning of the Bṛhadāraṇyaka, where it is explained that Brahman is called *Puruṣa* "Since before *pūrva*) all this world, He burned up (√ *uṣ*) all evils" (I (4). 1). It is also asserted that one who becomes Brahman is freed from evil, for "Evil, verily, does not go to the gods" (Bṛ. I (5). 20). Similarly in the Chāndogya it is said of the Brahma-world, "All evils turn back therefrom, for that Brahma-world is freed from evil" (VIII (4). 1 and 2); and it is asserted that the Brahman-*Ātman* is "free from evil, ageless, deathless, sorrowless, hungerless, thirstless" (VII (1). 5). But in the absence of much positive teaching[1] regarding the moral nature of Brahman, and judging from the fact that being free from evil is associated with being ageless, deathless, sorrowless, hungerless and thirstless, one cannot be sure that more is meant by "evil" in these passages than sorrow, pain and death. It may be, therefore, that all that these Upaniṣads by saying that He is free from evil mean to teach is that Brahman is, as Yājñavalkya declares, "beyond hunger and thirst, beyond sorrow and delusion, beyond old age and death" (Bṛ. III (5). 1).

When, however, we turn to the later Upaniṣads, it seems likely that Brahman was regarded as free from "evil" understood also in its moral sense; for here, as we have tried to show, we find the thought emerging that Brahman is not merely the unknown conscious principle which He was predominantly conceived to be in the earlier Upaniṣads, but also One characterised by many perfections. Further, there is as we shall now see, also more definite teaching regarding the moral nature of the Supreme Being than is to be found in the ealier Upaniṣads. Thus when the Kaṭha declares, "As the sun, the eye of the whole world, is not sullied by the external faults of the eyes, so the one Inner Soul of all things is not sullied by evil in the world, being external to it" (V. 11), it is not unlikely that by evil is meant more than mere sorrow, pain and death, for in the passage preceding this it is said that Brahman is "pure" (V. 8), and it is part of the systematic teaching of the Kaṭha that only he attains Brahman, who has ceased from bad conduct (II. 24) and is ever "pure," holding his body

[1] The Honey-Doctrine mentions among other things that Brahman exists in *dharma* (virtue) and in *satyam* (truth), Bṛ. II (5). 11 and 12. The description of Brahman as *satyam* occurs frequently. Cf. Bṛ. II (1). 20; (3). 1, 6; IV (1). 4; V (5). 1; (14). 4; Chānd. VIII (1). 4; (3). 4; (7). 1; Taitt. II. 1; Kauṣ. I. 6, etc. As the source of the Vedas and sacrifices (cf. Bṛ. I (2). 5); II (4). 10; Chānd. I (6). 8; II (23). 2; IV. (17); VII (1) and (2); and as the origin of the castes Bṛ. I (4). 11-15; II (4). 6, Brahman may be regarded as the source of all that is binding on men in the way of duty.

in control (III. 3-9). Further it describes Brahman as one who with the soul drinks of righteousness (*ṛta*) in the world of good deeds, and as contrasted with the soul, which is called "shade," Brahman is called "light" (III. 1), which would seem to imply that Brahman does not "drink" of unrighteousness as the soul does. Besides it is taught that Brahman is "born in right (*ṛta*)" (V. 2). The teaching of the Īśā regarding the moral nature of Brahman is even more definite, for it describes Him as "the pure (*śuddha*), unpierced by evil (*a-pāpa-viddha*)," and adds, "Appropriately He distributed objects (*artha* through the eternal years" (Īśā 8). The Muṇḍaka exclaims, "pure is He whom the ascetics (*yati*) with imperfections done away, behold" (III (1). 5). In Him the best of Brahma-knowers delight (III (1). 4). From Him are produced "Faith *śraddhā*), truth, chastity, and the law (*vidhi*)" (II (1). 7). The Maitri likewise declares that Brahman is "pure, steadfast and unswerving, stainless . . . an enjoyer of righteousness" (II. 7). He abides in goodness (*sattva*) (VI. 38). All these visions of the moral nature of Brahman seem to reach their culmination in the Śvetāśvatara, where it is declared that Brahman is "the instigator of the highest being (*sattva*) unto the purest attainment" (III. 12), bountiful (*maghavan*), kindly (*śiva*) (III. 11), devoid of the quality of the senses (III. 17), the bringer of right (*dharma*), the remover of evil (*pāpa*) (VI. 6), "irreproachable, spotless" (VI. 19). It is true that in these Upaniṣads the teaching regarding the moral nature of Brahman appears only in scattered references and even then mingled with much else which tends to rob it of clarity and pointedness. Nevertheless it is significant that it does appear and appears much more definitely than in the earlier Upaniṣads.

It would seem, then, that Upaniṣadic thought regarding the nature of the Supreme Being passed from an earlier stage of speculation and investigation where the view that was reached was that Brahman was primarily an ultimate, all-pervading conscious principle, to a later stage, where Brahman, besides being conceived thus, came also to be regarded as possessing many transcendent qualities as well as several perfections.[1]

2. *The Relation of the Deity to the world.*

The earliest theories which we find in the Upaniṣads assume, as the cosmogonies already referred to abundantly testify, a naïve realistic attitude towards the world, and regard it when once created by the Deity as something real and external to Him. Thus most of these theories begin by saying that in the beginning the Primal Being alone existed, and desiring to be many He created the worlds. "In the beginning, this world was Soul (*Ātman*) alone in the form of a person. . . . Verily, He had no delight. He desired a second," and He created beings (Bṛ. I (4). 1 and 3).[2] The worlds which He created were external to Himself, and so He entered into them "even to the finger-nail tips" (Bṛ. I (4). 7).

While their realism led them thus to speak of the Supreme Being as something external to the world, from the beginning, as this early creation-theory shows, they also regarded the Deity as completely pervading the universe. The thought of Divine immanence is stressed to such an extent that it often leads them into thorough-going pantheistic utterances. "Having entered into it, He became both the actual (*sat*) and the yon (*tya*), both the defined (*nirukta*) and the undefined, both the based and the non-based, both the conscious

[1] The fact that the Śvetāśvatara shows the greatest development along these lines, and reveals sectarian tendencies, identifying the Deity Rudra with the Supreme Being (cf. III. 1-4), seems to suggest that the development which we have traced in thought regarding Brahman in the later Upaniṣads was chiefly due to the influence of religious ideas. This will become more evident when we consider the relation in which these thinkers regarded the Supreme Being as standing to the finite soul.

[2] Cf. also Bṛ. I (4). 11 and 17; Chānd. VI (2). 1 and 3, Taitt. II. 6; Praśna I. 4.

vijñāna) and the unconscious, both the real (*satya*) and the false (*anṛta*). As the real, He became whatever there is here" (Taitt. II. 6). "This Self, verily, is a world of created things" (Bṛ. I(4). 16). Generally, however, their realism appears to modify their pantheism and to lead them to the view that Brahman is not Himself the universe, but one who completely pervades the universe as its Soul. "He entered in here, even to the fingernail tips, as a razor would be hidden in a razor-case, or fire in a fire-holder" (Bṛ. I (4). 7). Thus when philosophers discussed the nature of Brahman, the conceptions of Brahman as the 'Person' in the sun, moon, lightning, space, wind, fire, water, earth, body and such like, we saw, were not denied but accepted (Bṛ. II (1); II (5); III (9); Kauṣ. 4). Kaikeya points out to the six Brāhmans who go to him for instruction that the Brahman-Ātman is not to be identified with the heaven, sun, wind, space, water and earth, for these form only various parts of His body, while He himself is Soul, similar to oneself (Chānd. V (18). 1 and 2). Śvetaketu is taught that "that which is the finest essence—this whole world has that as its Soul" (Chānd. VI (9)-(16), cf. also Chānd. VII (26)). The Honey-Doctrine declares that Brahman has made numerous dwelling-places for Himself in the world. "'Citadels with two feet He did make, citadels with four feet He did make. Into the citadels He, having become a bird—Into the citadels (*puras*) the Person (*puruṣa*) entered.' This, verily, is the Person (*puruṣa*) dwelling in all cities (*puriśaya*). There is nothing by which He is not covered, nothing by which He is not hid" (Bṛ. II (5). 18). Yājñavalkya systematically teaches in Bṛ. III (7)[1] that Brahman is "He, who dwelling in all things, yet is other than all things, whom all things do not know, whose body all things are, who controls all

[1] Cf. also Bṛ. III (4) and (5) where Yājñavalkya teaches that Brahman is "the Soul in all things," and (6) where he teaches that on Him everything is woven warp and woof.

things from within—He is your Soul, the Inner Controller (*antaryāmin*), the Immortal" (III (7). 15). It is asserted that He "has entered this conglomerate abode—He is the maker of everything, for He is the creator of all; the world is His" (Bṛ. IV (4). 13).

The same view appears also in the later Upaniṣads. "By the Lord enveloped must this all be—whatever moving thing there is in the moving world" (Īśā 1). "He who on all things looks as just in the Self (*ātman*), and on the Self as in all beings—He does not shrink away from Him" (Īśā 6). The Kaṭha (V. 9-13) proclaims that Brahman exists in the universe as its Inner Soul (*antarātman*). "As the one fire has entered the world and becomes corresponding in form to every form, so the one Inner Soul of all things is corresponding in form to every form, and yet is outside" (V. 9). The Muṇḍaka, in language reminiscent of the Ṛgvedic idea of the Primeval *Puruṣa*, from various parts of whose body the universe came into being, teaches that the universe forms the body of Brahman: "Fire is His head; His eyes, the moon and sun; the regions of space, His ears; His voice, the revealed Vedas; wind, His breath; His heart, the whole world; out of His feet, the earth. Truly, He is the Inner Soul of all." "From Him, the seas and mountains all. From Him roll rivers of every kind. And from Him all herbs, the essence too, whereby that Inner Soul dwells in beings" (II (1). 4 and 9). Similarly the Śvetāśvatara describes Brahman as "the Soul which pervades all things as butter is contained in cream" (I. 16); the "Inner Soul of all things" (VI. 11), and the Maitri asks the sacrificer to meditate upon the divinity as Him "who is the bird of golden hue, who dwells in both the heart and sun" (VI. 34). The predominant thought of the Upaniṣads seems therefore to be that Brahman pervades the world as its Soul.

As its Soul, it would appear, He is the power which makes it what it is. Hence it is that in the early theories the ultimate Principle was, as we noted, described as Breath and as Food, for it is by means of these that creatures live; cf. Taitt. II. 2 and 3. So the Kauṣītaki observes with regard to Wind as Brahman, "This Brahman, verily, shines when fire blazes. This Brahman, verily, shines when the sun is seen" (II. 12). The gods themselves, as we found, are powerless apart from Brahman, for the power of Agni to burn and of Vāyu to blow are given to them by Brahman (Kena 14-26). "On It all the worlds do rest" (Kaṭha V. 8); "founded on which the whole world shines radiantly" (Muṇḍ. III (2). 1). So completely is everything regarded as dependent on Brahman who resides in them as their inner power, that the Śvetāśvatara even proceeds to speak of Brahman poetically as Himself these various objects. "That surely is Agni (fire). That is Āditya (sun). That is Vāyu (wind), and that is the moon. That surely is the pure. That is the waters. That is Prajāpati (Lord of creation)." "Thou art woman. Thou art man. Thou art the youth and the maiden too. Thou as an old man totterest with a staff. Being born, thou becomest facing in every direction" (IV. 2 and 3).[1] Similarly the Kaṭha: "The swan

[1] It is to be noted that these passages are not original in these Upaniṣads, but quotations. Śvet. IV. 2 = Vājasaneyi Saṁhitā 32. 1; Śvet. IV 3 = Atharva-Veda X (8). 27; Kaṭha V. 2 = with the omission of the last word Ṛg. Veda IV (40). 5, and exactly as here = Vājasaneyi Saṁhitā 10. 24; 12. 14, Taittirīya Saṁhitā 3. 2. 10. 1; Śatapatha Brāhmaṇa 6. 7. 3. 11 (Hume).

It would appear that these passages, as they occur in these two Upaniṣads, are to be interpreted as suggested above, and not pantheistically, not only on the ground that the general trend of the Śvetāśvatara and the Kaṭha is to distinguish clearly between Brahman and the world (cf. Śvet. I. 7-12; III. 1 and 2; III 10, 14, 17 and 18; IV. 1, etc; Kaṭha II. 22; IV. 9, 12 and 13; V. 9-11; V. 13; VI. 2 and 3), but also for the reason that the Śvetāśvatara adds to the two stanzas quoted above a stanza which ends "Thou dost abide with immanence, wherefrom all beings are born"—which seems to imply that Brahman is immanent in these objects rather than identical with them; and the passage from the Kaṭha definitely, in its latter half, teaches that Brahman is born *in* these various objects.

Similarly, it is doubtful if many passages which seem to identify Brahman with the objects of the world are to be understood literally. One must always seek to understand them, it would appear, in the light of their context. Thus it is certain that when the Muṇḍaka exclaims, "The Person Himself is everything here" (II (1). 10), it means only to say in a forceful way that (i.e., sun) in the clear, the Vasu in the atmosphere, the priest by the altar, the guest in the house, in man, in broad space, in the right (*ṛta*), in the sky, born in water, born in cattle, born in the right, born in rock, is the Right, the Great" (V. 2).

The relation of body to soul, in terms of which relation, as we noted, these philosophers chiefly conceive the relation of the universe to Brahman, does not, however, express all that they teach regarding the relation of the world to Brahman, for while it has the merit of revealing the intimate manner in which Brahman pervades and energises the universe, it does not make explicit the fact that Brahman is not only the operative cause of the universe, but also its material cause; i.e., that the universe depends on Brahman not only for its energising power, but also for its very substance, as they no doubt believe. Thus the early cosmogonies always proceed, as we saw, by saying that Brahman, *Ātman* or *Puruṣa* existed alone at the beginning, and then created the world out of Himself.[1] They do not recognise a second principle existing side by side with the Creator and providing Him with the materials necessary for creation. Accordingly they picture creation predominantly as an emanation rather than as a construction out of given elements. "As a spider might come out with his thread, as small sparks come forth from the fire, even so from this Soul come forth all vital energies (*prāṇa*) all worlds,

---

everything is completely dependent on Brahman, not that Brahman is Himself everything, for the passage occurs at the end of nine stanzas which portray dramatically how everything in the universe comes *from* Brahman as its Supreme Source. Cf. also Ait. V. 3, where after identifying Brahman with the gods, the five gross elements, the creatures born from the four origins—viz., egg, womb, sweat and sprout—horses, cows, etc., all creatures moving and stationary, it is concluded that "all this is guided by Intelligence, is based on Intelligence. Brahman is Intelligence."

Scientific precision in the use of language being yet unknown, it would appear that by means of such exaggerated statements these men were seeking merely to teach in a striking manner the great truth that they had discovered, that Brahman is in all things as that which makes them what they are. It is too much to expect these early thinkers to observe strictly the sharp distinction which we make with centuries of philosophical thinking behind us, between pantheism and non-pantheism.

[1] Cf., e.g., Taitt. II. 6; Bṛ. (4). 1, 11, 17.

all gods, all beings" (Bṛ. II (1). 20). The Creator declares, "I, indeed, am this creation for I emitted it all from myself" (Bṛ. I (4). 5), and the created world is said to be the result of what originally was undifferentiated becoming differentiated by name and form (Bṛ. I (4). 7; Chānd. VI (2)). Creation therefore is the sending forth by Brahman of the worlds out of Himself. The universe with all its diversity depends for its matter[1] as well as its form on Him.

As knowledge of the material universe advanced in "Sāṁkhyan" fashion, as especially in the Śvetāśvatara and the Maitri, the tendency is to distinguish Brahman very sharply from the material universe, and to declare that He does not share in its nature, although he pervades it. "Seeming to possess the quality (*guṇa*) of all the senses, it is devoid of all the senses! The Lord (*prabhu*) the Ruler of all" (Śvet III. 17). "Higher and other than the world-tree, time, and forms is He from whom this expanse proceeds" (Śvet. VI. 6).[2] So different is the material world conceived to be from the nature of Brahman that it is said to be like a veil hiding His nature. "The one God . . . covers Himself, like a spider with threads produced from Primary Matter (*pradhāna*)" (Śvet. VI. 10).[3] "This whole world the illusion-maker (*Māyin*) projects out of this. And in it by illusion

[1] The later Upaniṣads, notably the Śvetāśvatara and the Maitri, envisage the material universe in Sāṁkhyan fashion as composed of Matter and its Qualities. There is no explicit reference in the earlier Upaniṣads to any such material principle The Chāndogya (vi (4)) explains all objects as composed of three elements—a procedure suggestive of the Sāṁkhyan account of all material objects as composed of the three *guṇas*. But besides this in the Śvetāśvatara and the Maitri, we meet with an enumeration of principles similar to those found in Sāṁkhya philosophy only in Kaṭha III. 10-13, VI. 7-8, and Praśna IV. 8. The Śvetāśvatara makes use of the doctrine of the three *guṇas* (cf. 14) and the Maitri refers to the *guṇas* by name and enumerates their effects, as in Sāṁkhyan philosophy. (Cf. III. 5). But the Sāṁkhyan system as we know it from the Kārikās of Īśvara Kṛṣṇa (date about 4th or 5th cent. A.D.), with its atheism and unqualified dualism, is not found in the Upaniṣads, for Matter with its *guṇas*, when it is recognised, is always regarded as existing in Brahman and as entirely subordinate to Him: cf., e.g., Śvet. I. 3; Mait. V. 2.

[2] Cf. Kaṭha III. 10 and 11; VI. 8.

[3] Cf. Kaṭha III. 12.

(*māyā*) the other (individual soul) is confined " (IV. 9). Similarly the Maitri, in speaking of Brahman as abiding in the body, declares " As an enjoyer of righteousness, He covers Himself (*ātmānam*) with a veil made of qualities " (II. 7).

Thus the view is maintained that though Brahman exists in the material world, His own true nature is not that of the material world. And if the world is thus different from Him and yet exists only in and through Him, Brahman cannot be a pure unity. The Śvetāśvatara declares that Brahman is a triad (I. 7 and 12). Symbolically the wheel which holds together diverse parts within its unity, or a river composed of several tributaries, best represents the nature of Brahman in relation to the universe (Śvet. I. 4 and 5; VI. 1).

This idea that Brahman in relation to the diversity of this universe must be conceived as a unity-in-diversity, or a One which holds together the many is not by any means peculiar to the Śvetāśvatara. On the other hand, the conception which we have indicated as predominant in the Upaniṣads, that Brahman is the all-pervading soul of the universe, is only another way of stating the truth that the multiplicity of this universe is held together in, and energised by, the Supreme Being. Even the thought that Brahman as pervading principle, remains hidden in all things, and that He is ultimately to be conceived as a triad, is not unknown in early Upaniṣadic philosophy. Thus in Bṛ. II (6) it is declared that the world is a triad of name, form, and work, and it is said " Although it is that triad, this Soul (*ātman*) is one. Although it is one, it is that triad. That is the Immortal, veiled by the real (*satya*). Life (*prāṇa*) verily is the Immortal. Name and form are the real. By them this life is veiled." The " real " by which the " Immortal " is veiled is obviously the world of multiplicity (or " name and form " as the passage explains).

Similarly the thought that Brahman is to be conceived as a wheel holding diverse parts within itself occurs frequently in the Upaniṣads.[1]

Thus it would appear that the instinctive realism of earlier thinkers and possibly the "Sāṁkhyan" tendencies of later philosophers prevented them in the main from reducing the diversity of the world to the characterless unity of a distinctionless Brahman. But it would be too much to claim that this was always done. The thought that Brahman is the Supreme Real could easily lead to the thought that He is the only real. This, as we shall see, is very often the position they adopt in regard to Brahman in relation to the finite soul. But the material world was too sensibly real to be dismissed as unreal, although with the development of abstract thought it would appear that some of them even succeeded in overcoming the assumptions of common-sense, and proclaimed that Brahman alone as Pure Thought is real, and all else, including the material world, is unreal. "Verily in the beginning this world was Brahman, the limitless One. Incomprehensible is that Supreme Soul, unlimited, unborn, not to be reasoned about, unthinkable. He assuredly awakes this world which is a mass of thought. It is thought by Him, and in Him it disappears" (Mait. VI. 17). With even greater definiteness, it is said, "*Saṁsāra* is just one's own thought; with effort he should cleanse it then" (Mait. VI. 34).

Nevertheless, we may conclude that the predominant thought of the Upaniṣads regarding the relation of Brahman to the material universe is that the latter in all its diversity is real and exists in Him. He is its soul, it is His body. He is both its material and operative Cause. He is different from it in nature, and controls it from within.

[1] Cf. Bṛ. I (5) 15; Bṛ. II (5). 15, "As all the spokes are held together in the hub and felly of a wheel, just so in this Soul all things, all gods, all worlds, all breathing things, all selves are held together;" also Kauṣ. III 8; Praśna II. 6; VI. 6.

3. *The Relation of the Deity to the finite self.*

As in the case of the material world, the earliest accounts found in the Upaniṣads regard the finite self when first created by the Deity, as something external to Him. But, it is said, He was not pleased that man should exist independently of Him. So "He bethought Himself, 'How now could this thing exist without me? . . . If with speech there is uttered, if with breath there is breathed, if with sight there is seen . . . then who am I?' So, cleaving asunder this very hair-part (*sīman*), by that door He entered" (Ait. III. 11-12).

So completely is He conceived as having entered into the finite self, that very early the view appears that Brahman Himself underlies all the activities of the individual. "When breathing, He becomes breath *prāṇa*) by name; when speaking, voice; when seeing, the eye; when hearing, the ear; when thinking, the mind; these are merely the names of His acts. . . . One should worship with the thought that He is just one's self (*ātman*), for therein all these become one" (Bṛ. I (4). 7).

The reason for regarding Brahman as Him who performs these various functions in the body is suggested in the last sentence of the passage just quoted, viz., that it is in Brahman that these functions become one, as for example in sleep. The fact that in sleep, quite unknown to oneself and hence involuntarily, one loses consciousness, and then again, unknown to the self and as not willed by it, one returns to consciousness after sleep, seems early to have impressed these thinkers. They could not account for it except by thinking that there must be something other than the self which performs these conscious functions in the body. Thus in the instruction of Gārgya by Ajātaśatru, Ajātaśatru declares that Brahman is best known as that into which one passes in sleep, and from which one returns in waking (Bṛ. II (1). 14-20). He conducts Gārgya to a sleeping man, in order to demonstrate this teaching with regard to Brahman, and waking the man, asks, "When this man fell asleep thus, where then was the person who consists of intelligence (*vijñāna*)? Whence did he thus come back?" Gārgya being unable to reply, Ajātaśatru declares, "When this man has fallen asleep thus, then the person who consists of intelligence, having by his intelligence taken to himself the intelligence of these senses (*prāṇa*), rests in that place which is the space within the heart. When that person restrains the senses, that person is said to be asleep. Then the breath is restrained. The voice is restrained. The eye is restrained. The ear is restrained. The mind is restrained. The mystic meaning (*upaniṣad*) thereof is 'the Real of the real' (*satyasya satya*). Breathing creatures, verily, are the real. He is their Real." Thus it is proclaimed on the basis of the phenomenon of sleep, that Brahman in His own nature exists in the heart of the individual, and as a conscious principle pervades the body and the sense-organs; sleep is the withdrawing of consciousness from the sense-organs by Brahman into Himself, and awaking from sleep is this conscious principle returning to the sense-organs, from where it rested.

In the light of such analysis of sleep, we are able to understand the passage, in the Chāndogya, which declares that it is That which lies in the small space of the heart that one should seek to know. "Now, what is here in this city of Brahman,[1] is an abode, a small lotus-flower.[2] Within that is a small space. What is within that, should be searched out; that, assuredly is what one should desire to understand. . . . As far, verily, as this world-space extends, so far extends the space within the heart. Within it are contained both heaven and earth, both fire and wind, both sun and moon, lightning and the stars, both what one possesses here and what one does not possess; everything here is contained within it. . . .

[1] Explained by Śaṁkara as body. [2] Explained by Śaṁkara as heart.

That is the Soul (*ātman*), free from evil, ageless, deathless, sorrowless, hungerless, thirstless, whose desire is the Real, whose conception is the Real" (Chānd. VIII (6). 5). That soul is Brahman and accordingly it is declared that daily in sleep one goes into the "Brahman-world" without realising it, "just as those who do not know the spot might go over a hid treasure of gold again and again, but not find it" (Chānd. VIII (3). 2). Similar teaching with regard to Brahman as resident in the body and as withdrawing all its vital energies into Himself during sleep is to be found in Kauṣ. III. 3, Praśna IV, and Māṇḍ. 3-7. Thus arises the view, which is predominant in the Upaniṣads, that Brahman is the conscious principle in the body. Nay more, it is advocated, as already pointed out, that it is Brahman who performs the functions of the finite self in the body. "He who breathes in with your breathing in is the Soul of yours, which is in all things. He who breathes out with your breathing out is the Soul of yours, which is in all things" (Bṛ. III (4). 1). He controls the breath, the speech, the eye, the ear, the mind, the skin, the understanding and the semen from within, and He is the one in the body who sees, hears, thinks and understands." "Other than He there is no seer . . . no hearer, no thinker . . . no understander. He is your Soul" (Bṛ. III (7). 16-23).[1] "In the space within the heart lies the Ruler of all" (Bṛ. IV (4). 22); "this soul of mine within the heart is greater than the earth, greater than the atmosphere, greater than the sky, greater than these worlds, containing all works, containing all odours, containing all tastes, encompassing this whole world, the unspeaking, the unconcerned—this is the Soul of mine within the heart, this is Brahman" (Chānd. III (14). 3-4).[2] And Prajāpati teaches Indra, "now, when the eye is directed thus toward space, that is the seeing person; the eye is (the instrument)

[1] Cf. also Ait. V. 1; Kauṣ. III. 3.
[2] Words to this effect are found in Chānd. VIII (1). 3-5.

for seeing. Now, he who knows 'Let me smell this'—that is the Self; the nose is (the instrument) for smelling. Now he who knows, 'Let me utter this'—that is the Self; the voice is (the instrument) for utterance. Now he who knows, 'Let me hear this'—that is the Self; the ear is (the instrument) for hearing. Now he who knows, 'Let me think this'—that is the Self, the mind (*manas*) is his divine eye. He, verily, with that divine eye the mind, sees desires here, and experiences enjoyment" (Chānd. VIII (12). 4 and 5). It is thus taught that when the individual sees, hears, thinks, desires, or enjoys himself, it is not he that does it, but Brahman, the all-pervading One.

When Brahman was thus identified with the self of the individual, it was only natural that the usual distinctions of father, mother, husband, wife, Brahman, Śūdra, thief and sage should cease, for ultimately all individuals are Brahman, "a unity without duality," such as exists, for example, in dreamless sleep, where "a father becomes not a father; a mother, not a mother; the worlds, not the worlds; the gods, not the gods; the Vedas, not the Vedas; a thief, not a thief. There the destroyer of an embryo becomes not the destroyer of an embryo; a Cāṇḍāla[1] is not a Cāṇḍāla, a Paulkasa[2] is not a Paulkasa; a mendicant is not a mendicant; an ascetic is not an ascetic" (Bṛ. IV (3). 22).[3]

But from this, it must not be thought that these thinkers carried their views to its logical consequences, and declared that the individual is unreal, Brahman alone being real. Their instinctive realism coupled with their monism leads them often as in the Honey Doctrine[4] to think that Brahman exists as a plurality of individuals.

[1] The son of a Śūdra father and a Brāhman mother.
[2] The son of a Śūdra father and a Kṣatriya mother
[3] Accordingly ethical distinctions cease to have meaning. Cf. Bṛ. IV (4). 22 and 23; Kauṣ. III. I, 8.
[4] See p. 26 above.

Since the individual is therefore nothing but Brahman Himself in the body, what is necessary is to realise this fact, and the individual becomes Brahman, for Brahman verily He is, although He does not realise it, when in the body. Consequently the departure from embodied existence of one who knows himself to be Brahman is described thus. "As a heavily loaded cart goes creaking, just so this bodily self, mounted by the intelligent Self, goes groaning when one is breathing one's last. When he comes to weakness—whether he comes to weakness through old age or through disease—this person frees himself from these limbs just as a mango, or a fig, or a berry releases itself from its bond. . . . As noblemen, policemen, chariot-drivers, village heads wait with food, drink and lodgings for a king who is coming, and cry: 'Here he comes! Here he comes!' so indeed do all things wait for him who has this knowledge and cry: 'Here is Brahman coming! Here is Brahman coming!" (Bṛ. IV (3). 35-38). But the individual who does not know himself to be Brahman passes from birth to birth according to his deeds, although even he, we are assured, is really Brahman (Bṛ. IV (4). 5).

Consequently what is all-important, and what is insisted upon throughout the Upaniṣads, as necessary for realising Brahman, is knowledge. In the period of the Brāhmaṇas knowledge of rituals was regarded as supremely important for it conferred extraordinary powers. The Upaniṣads substitute 'Brahman' in the place of 'rituals.' "Whoever thus knows 'I am Brahma' becomes this All; even the Gods have not power to prevent his becoming thus, for he becomes their self" (Bṛ. I (4). 10). So naïvely is this theory held at first that it is asserted that the gods who desire men as sacrificial animals, do not wish men to know this doctrine, for men by knowing that they are Brahman cease to be men, and become Brahman (Bṛ. I (4). 10). The supreme value of this knowledge is the theme of many a passage. "If a person knew the Soul (*ātman*) with the thought 'I am He,' with what desire, for love of what would he cling to the body?" "He who has found and has awakened to the Soul that has entered this conglomerate abode—He is the maker of everything, for he is the creator of all. The world is his: indeed, he is the world itself." "Verily, while we are here we may know this. If you have known it not, great is the destruction. Those who know this become immortal, but others go only to sorrow" (Bṛ. IV (4). 12, 13 and 14). Yājñavalkya teaches that works, however arduously performed, have very little effect, for it is knowledge that is all-important. "Verily, O Gārgī, if one performs sacrifices and worship, and undergoes austerity in this world for many thousands of years, but without knowing that Imperishable, limited indeed is that (work) of his. Verily, O Gārgī, he who departs from this world without knowing that Imperishable is pitiable. But O Gārgi, he who departs from this world knowing that Imperishable is a Brāhman" (Bṛ. III (8). 10). Yājñavalkya, however, does not appear to have held that mere intellectual apprehension of the fact that one is Brahman suffices to produce release, for desires play an important part in producing the sense of individuality. He accordingly recommends that desires should be renounced. "For desire for sons is desire for wealth, and desire for wealth, is desire for worlds, for both these are merely desires. Therefore let a Brahman become disgusted with learning and desire to live as a child. When he has become disgusted both with the state of childhood and with learning, then he becomes an ascetic (*muni*). When he has become disgusted both with the non-ascetic state and the ascetic state, then he becomes a Brāhman" (Bṛ. III (5). 1). "When are liberated all the desires that lodge in one's heart, then a mortal becomes immortal. Therein he reaches Brahman" (Bṛ. IV (4). 7).

Besides knowledge, yogic[1] discipline is therefore also recommended for the individual who would become Brahman, and when by these means he has overcome the sense of individuality, the consciousness of self ceases and he becomes one with Brahman in a unity without duality. "An ocean, a seer alone without duality becomes he whose world is Brahman" (Bṛ. IV (3). 32). "For where there is a duality, as it were, there one sees another; there one smells another; there one tastes another; there one speaks to another; there one hears another; there one thinks of another; there one touches another; there one understands another. But where everything has become just one's own self, then whereby and whom would one see . . . smell . . . taste . . . speak to . . . hear . . . think . . . touch . . . understand?" (Bṛ. IV (5). 15).

What is significant is that although these philosophers in the main regarded Brahman as Himself the self in the body their realism not only led them to believe in the plurality of individuals, but also to think that these individuals have, as we have just seen, still to become Brahman. In spite of the alleged identity of Brahman with the individual, a surreptitious distinction between the two is thus maintained. The more discerning among them tended, it would appear, to make this distinction very clear. Thus the instruction of Indra by Prajāpati was precisely that Brahman cannot be identified with either the embodied self or the dream-self, for the reason that these experience change and imperfection, while Brahman is above all such experience (Chānd. VIII (9) and (10)). Nay more, Prajāpati held that Brahman was different even from self in dreamless sleep, for in dreamless sleep there is complete absence of consciousness, while Brahman is a conscious principle. This was also the teaching of Yājñavalkya, who after identifying

[1] I do not mean that the Yoga system attributed to Patañjali was known at this time, but I employ the word here and elsewhere merely to refer generally to the method of repressing normal mental activity.

Brahman with the self in dreamless sleep, where all distinctions are lost, and there is complete cessation of consciousness of anything "within or without" goes on to add that Brahman is not to be mistaken for mere unconsciousness, such as we find in dreamless sleep, for He is in essence a conscious principle, and therefore remains conscious even when this self is unconscious in dreamless sleep. "Verily, while he does not there see [with the eyes][1], he is verily seeing, though he does not see (what is [usually] to be seen); for there is no cessation of seeing of a seer, because of his imperishability [as a seer]. It is not, however, a second thing, other than himself and separate, that he may see" (Bṛ. IV (3). 23). Thus, it is evident that if philosophers identified Brahman with the self, some of them came to think that He cannot be identified with the self, even in dreamless sleep, and the theory is formulated that He cannot be identified with any of the three usually recognised states of the self—viz., waking consciousness, dream, and dreamless sleep—but with a fourth state, specially invented for the purpose, and which because of its difference from anything known in the experience of the self is declared to be incomprehensible. "Not inwardly cognitive, not outwardly cognitive . . . not non-cognitive, unseen, with which there can be no dealing, ungraspable, having no distinctive mark, non-thinkable, that cannot be designated, the essence of the assurance of which is the state of being one with the Self, the cessation of development, tranquil, benign, without a second—[such] they think is the fourth. He is the Self (*ātman*). He should be discerned" (Māṇḍ. 7). Similarly the Maitri, in referring to these four states, proclaims, "He who sees with the eye, and he who moves in dreams, He who is deep sleep, and he who is beyond the deep sleeper—These are a person's four distinct conditions. Of these the fourth is greater

[1] The words in [ ] are Dr. Hume's words, and those in ( ) are an addition in the Mādhyaṁdina text.

[than the rest]. In the three a quarter Brahman moves; a three-quarter in the last" (VII. II (7) and (8)).

Thus it is certain that, although in the main the sages of the Upaniṣads tended to identify Brahman with the self in the body, some of them also tended to distinguish Him very clearly from the embodied self, as we know it in waking life, dream and dreamless sleep, and came to the conclusion that He is not to be identified with any of the known states of the embodied self. While their realism led them in this direction, their monistic bias was, it would appear, so strong that they could not imagine how a self can exist in the body beyond the One Brahman. Accordingly, as we have seen, they believe that though Brahman is very different in nature from the embodied self, nevertheless it is He who is undergoing experiences in the body.

While this appears to be the predominant view of the Upaniṣads, hints as to another view, whereby the individuality of the finite self is recognised and distinguished from the Universal Self, are not lacking. Significantly enough, the view appears definitely only in the later Upaniṣads, and seems to point to the direction in which the realistic distinction between the characteristics of the embodied self and those of Brahman finally led.[1] It was easy enough to maintain the doctrine of the identity of Brahman with the finite self, when only some striking phases of the self were considered, such as its capacity to speak, see, smell, hear, think and understand. But as the darker characteristics of the embodied self (such as imperfection, sorrow, pain, death and bondage in *saṁsāra*) came to be considered more fully, it became less possible it would seem, to identify the finite self with Brahman, and it is declared that Brahman and the finite self are not one and the same Self but two.

The view occurs explicitly, for the first time[2] in

[1] Religious influences may also have contributed to this end.

[2] Reasons for thinking that this is the earliest expression of the view in the Upaniṣads are given below.

the Upaniṣads in Kaṭha III. 1. "There are two that drink of righteousness (*ṛta*) in the world of good deeds; both are entered into the secret place (of the heart), and in the highest upper sphere. Brahma-knowers speak of them as 'light' and 'shade.'" The reason for distinguishing between them and speaking of them as two is that while both "drink of righteousness," one is characterised by evil, and is therefore said to be 'shade' in contrast to the other, which is 'light.' The view as it occurs in the Muṇḍaka shows a greater development, for while the passage in the Kaṭha regards both selves as enjoying good deeds, the Muṇḍaka quotes a stanza from the Ṛg Veda,[1] wherein it is declared that only one of the two partakes of deeds, while the other merely looks on. "Two birds, fastbound companions, clasp close the self-same tree. Of these two, the one eats sweet fruit, the other looks on without eating" (Muṇḍ. III (1). 1). Thus the Muṇḍaka goes further than the Kaṭha not only in separating the two selves, but also in setting off the greatness of the One against the weakness of the other. "On the self-same tree a person, sunken, grieves for his impotence, deluded; when he sees the Other, the Lord (*Īś*), contented, and His greatness, he becomes freed from sorrow' (III (1). 2).[2] It is noteworthy that in the stanza which is taken from the Ṛg Veda there is no reference to the disagreeable qualities of the finite self, and that those receive special mention in the stanza which is added in the Muṇḍaka. Brahman is powerful and great, the finite self is sunken, grieving, impotent and deluded. It is small wonder, then, that they should be distinguished as two distinct principles.

In a section of the Maitri, we find this theory in the process of making. The evil qualities of the

[1] Ṛg Veda I (164). 20.

[2] Both these stanzas of Muṇḍaka are repeated in Śvet. IV. 6 and 7. The Śvetāśvatara, with the advanced knowledge it reveals of several metaphysical theories regarding the ultimate Principle (cf. I. 1-3) its Sāṁkhyanism (I. 4-6) and its sectarianism (III. 1-6), is obviously later than the Muṇḍaka.

embodied self are set sharply in the foreground, and starting with the assumption that Brahman is the self in the body it progressively shows that He cannot be identical with the embodied individual. Thus it starts by describing the body as "ill-smelling, unsubstantial, a conglomerate of bone, skin, muscle, marrow, flesh, semen, blood, mucus, tears, rheum, feces, urine, wind, bile, and phlegm . . . afflicted with desire, anger, covetousness, delusion, fear, despondency, envy, separation from the desirable, union with the undesirable, hunger, thirst, senility, death, disease, sorrow and the like" (I. 3), and repeatedly asks itself "Who is its driver?" (II. 3). It begins by accepting the view that Brahman is the self (II. 1), but is careful to add that if He is the self, He does not share the evil nature of the body. "He assuredly, indeed . . . is reputed as standing aloof, like those among qualities, abstain from intercourse with them—He, verily, is pure, clean . . . eternal, unborn, independent. He abides in his own greatness. By him this body is set up in possession of intelligence; or in other words, this very one, verily, is its driver" (II. 4). This, however, does not satisfy the sage who has come to see the real nature of the finite individual, and the question is asked, 'How is this one its driver?' In reply, the view that Brahman is the self is further modified, and it is said that if He is the self, He abides here with only a "part" of Himself; and the philosopher, as though wishing that not even this part should be confounded with the evil nature of the embodied self, adds that this part is to be identified only with what appears as intelligence in the finite self (II. 5). Further, our sage goes on to say that Brahman, though existing in the body, is not bound by the deeds of the embodied individual, for with regard to them, He is not the agent (III. 7). And with the doctrine that Brahman is not the agent in the body, we have already reached the view that Brahman is not the same as the self which activates the body, and the philosopher who began with the conventional doctrine of Brahman as the self in the body, now declares " There is indeed another different soul, called the elemental soul (*bhūtātman*)—he who being overcome by the bright or dark fruits of action, enters a good or an evil womb . . . he, assuredly, indeed, who is said to be in the body is said to be 'the elemental soul.' Now, its immortal soul is like 'the drop of water on the lotus leaf.'[1] This (elemental soul) verily is overcome by nature's (*prakṛti*) qualities (*guṇas*). Now because of being overcome he goes on to confusedness; because of confusedness, he sees not the blessed Lord (*prabhu*) . . . who stands within oneself (III. 2). Thus systematically in the light of the evil which characterises the embodied individual, the doctrine that Brahman is the self in the body is examined and progressively modified, till at last it is concluded that Brahman is not the self in the body, but resides within this self as an Other, unaffected by its imperfections and the deeds which bind it to earthly existence. Our philosopher, however, does not wish his teaching to be understood in a way which is disruptive of monism, and accordingly, in seeking to reconcile the individuality of the self with the all-pervadingness and all-powerfulness of Brahman, he declares what is undoubtedly baffling, and appears to reflect the difficulty he had in conceiving of their relationship—that the finite self is the doer of action while Brahman is the causer of action (II. 3). He means by this to make the " doer " in the body ultimately subservient to Brahman who pervades it, and who drives it as a potter drives the wheel, and he assumes also the individuality of the soul, for he declares that the soul is in the miserable state in which it is because of its attachment to the Qualities (III. 3). It shows how difficult it was for some of these thinkers, who ever more clearly distinguished the finite self from Brahman, and yet also

[1] That is, it is unaffected (Hume).

believed with others at this time that Brahman is the supreme all-pervading principle, to reconcile the individuality of the self with the unity and supremacy of Brahman.

The Śvetāśvatara seems to reflect the furthest development which the theory of those who distinguished the embodied self from Brahman reached in Upaniṣadic philosophy; for while, like the Muṇḍaka, it regards the finite self and the Universal Self as two (IV. 6 and 7), it postulates the theory that Brahman, the ultimate One which philosophers had proclaimed, is a many-in-One. It is not that the One Brahman has become many and goes about in many forms—the view which, we have tried to show, is predominant in the Upaniṣads, and which seems to be disruptive of the ultimate reality of the individual—but that He always is a many-in-one, a view which suggests that the individual is always preserved and held together in the unity of the Absolute. "This has been sung as the supreme Brahman. In it there is a triad." "There are two unborn ones; the knowing (Lord) and the unknowing (individual soul), the Omnipotent and the impotent. She (i.e., Nature, *Prakṛti*), too, is unborn, who is connected with the enjoyer and objects of enjoyment. Now, the soul (*ātman*) is infinite, universal, inactive. When one finds out this triad, that is Brahman." "That Eternal should be known as present in the self (*ātmasaṁstha*). Truly there is nothing higher than that to be known. When one recognises the enjoyer, the object of enjoyment, and the universal Actuator, all has been said. This is the threefold Brahman" (I. 7, 9 and 12). In this way, the finite self, which, as we have tried to show, was growingly distinguished by some philosophers from the Universal Self, came finally, it would seem, to be regarded as an eternally distinct element held within the unity of the Supreme Being.

A point which must be noted in connection with the view of those who tended to distinguish the finite self more and more from Brahman who pervades it, is the tendency to describe Brahman as having glorious qualities as compared with the imperfections of the embodied self. Since the embodied self is distinguished from Brahman chiefly because of its imperfections, Brahman by contrast appears as the all-powerful and all-glorious One. Thus Yājñavalkya, who as we saw regarded Brahman as identifiable only with the conscious principle in the body and not with the individual as we know him in waking life, dream or dreamless sleep, says of Him, " In the space within the heart lies the Ruler of all, the Lord of all, the King of all. He does not become greater by good action nor inferior by bad action. He is the Lord of all, the Overlord of beings, the Protector of beings " (Bṛ. IV (4). 22). The greatness of the Supreme Being, His transcendent powers and His perfections are, as we have seen, described much more in the later Upaniṣads than in the earlier ones ; and, what is even more significant, the term *Iś* (Lord) together with its compounds comes to be applied systematically to the Supreme Being only in the Śvetāśvatara Upaniṣad, while, with one or two exceptions [1] it is not to be found in the earlier Upaniṣads, and occurs only in scattered references in the other Upaniṣads.[2] The reason for this is not far to seek. The term ' Lord ' implies among other things the essential distinctness of the Supreme Being from the finite soul, and in so far as this was only imperfectly conceived earlier, and was clearly conceived only in the Śvetāśvatara, it could be used freely of the Supreme Being only by the author of the Śvetāśvatara.

The term is essentially religious in significance and points to an unmistakable religious influence in the Śvetāśvatara. "The One who rules over every single source, in whom this whole world comes together

[1] E.g., The Bṛhadāraṇyaka passage cited above, which recurs with some additional words in Kauṣ. III. 8 ; see also Bṛ. V (6).

[2] Cf. Kaṭha VI. 5, 12, 13 ; Īśā I ; Muṇḍ. III (1). 2 and 3 ; Praśna II. 9 and 11.

and dissolves, The Lord (*īśāna*), the blessing-giver, God (*deva*) adorable " (IV. 11). " He who is the source and origin of the gods, the Ruler of all, Rudra, the great Seer . . . Who is the Overlord of the gods, on whom the worlds do rest, who is Lord of biped and quadruped here—To what God will we give reverence with oblations? " (IV. 12 and 13). " Him who is the supreme Mighty Lord (*maheśvara*) of lords, the Supreme Divinity of divinities, the Supreme Ruler of rulers, paramount, Him let us know as the Adorable God, the Lord (*īś*) of the world " (VI. 7). With the conception of Him as Lord, we thus seem finally to arrive at a religious view of the Supreme Being.

According to this view, the Deity is different from the finite soul, and at the same time pervades it without by this means losing His supreme and perfect nature. " The one God, hidden in all things, all-pervading, the Inner Soul of all things, the Overseer of deeds (*karman*), in all things abiding, the Witness, the sole Observer (*cetā*), devoid of qualities (*nir-guṇa*), the one Controller of the inactive many, who makes the one seed manifold. The wise who perceive Him as standing in one's self—They, and no others, have eternal happiness " (VI. 11 and 12). The view is thus maintained, in line with early Upaniṣadic speculation,[1] that though Brahman exists in the individual, He does not share in the latter's imperfections. He exists merely as Witness and is not responsible for the deeds which bind the individual to *saṁsāra* (worldly existence).

Besides, the religious world-view of the author of the Śvetāśvatara leads to the doctrine that the Supreme Being is related to the individual soul not only as the Perfect and adorable Lord who exists within the individual without destroying its individuality on the one hand, or His own essential greatness

[1] In so far as it held that Brahman exists in the individual merely as conscious Principle.

on the other, but also as the "Kindly One" who shows grace to the finite individual (Śvet. I. 6; III. 20).

The doctrine of grace in the Upaniṣads does not appear for the first time in the Śvetāśvatara. It occurs in Kaṭha II. 20, where it is declared that one becomes freed from sorrow, "when through the grace (*prasāda*) of the Creator (*dhātṛ*)[1] he beholds the greatness of the Soul (*ātman*)." It is also said, "This Soul (*Ātman*) is not to be obtained by instruction, nor by intellect, nor by much learning. He is to be obtained only by the one whom He chooses; to such a one that Soul (*Ātman*) reveals His own person (*tanūm svām*): Kaṭha II. 23. This verse is found also in Muṇḍ. III (2). 3. It is significant that the doctrine that the Supreme Being shows favour to the individual soul should be found precisely in these three Upaniṣads, which, as we saw, were the ones explicitly to express the view that Brahman and the individual are not one but two, for it seems to indicate in these Upaniṣads a tendency to conceive the Supreme Being and His relation to the finite soul in definitely religious terms. According to this, it would seem that the Supreme Being stands in personal relationship to finite souls—a view which is quite impossible so long as Brahman is not sufficiently distinguished from the individual soul.

Further, it must be noted that as the individuality of the soul is recognised, and as the Supreme Being tends to be thought of in personal and religious terms, ethical conditions are specially[2] emphasised as necessary to be fulfilled by one who wishes to attain Brahman. So long as Brahman was regarded as

[1] I.e., if we take the words here to be *dhātuḥ prasādāt* ("by the grace of the Creator"). There is a variant reading, viz. *dhātu prasādāt* ("by the clearness of the natural elements").

[2] Ethical teaching is not altogether absent in earlier Upaniṣads; cf., e.g., Chānd. VII (26). 2; VIII (4). 3; VIII (5); VIII (15). 1; Taitt. I (9) and (11). Although ethical distinctions are meaningless on the basis of a pure monism, many of these thinkers, as we noted, tacitly assume a distinction between Brahman and the embodied individual.

Himself the individual in the body, all that was chiefly thought to be necessary was, as we have noted, to realise this fact, and to suppress one's individuality, till one passes into the distinctionless unity of Brahman. But with the recognition of the individuality of the finite soul, and with the inflow of religious ideas regarding the Supreme Being, ethical requirements are specially emphasized, for obtaining release. "Not he who has not ceased from bad conduct . . . can obtain Him by intelligence" (Kaṭha II. 24). "He . . . who has not understanding, who is unmindful and ever impure, reaches not the goal, but goes on to transmigration (*saṁsāra*) Kaṭha III. 1). "This Soul is obtainable by truth, by austerity (*tapas*), by proper knowledge (*jñāna*), by the student's life of chastity (*brahmacārya*) constantly (practised). . . . Consisting of light, pure is He whom the ascetics (*yati*) with imperfections done away behold" (Muṇḍ. III (1). 5). The Śvetāśvatara teaches that it is "by knowing God, one is released from all fetters" (I. 8; II. 15; IV. 16; V. 13, etc.), but knowledge of God, according to it, is impossible apart from "highest devotion (*bhakti*) for God" and for teacher, and apart from Yogic practice whereby the individual becomes cleansed (II. 14). Similarly in the section of the Maitri above dealt with, it is asked, what the method for attaining release is, and it is replied, "The antidote, assuredly, indeed, for this elemental soul is this: study of the knowledge of the Veda, and pursuit of one's regular duty. Pursuit of one's regular duty, in one's own stage of the religious life—that, verily, is the rule! . . . If one does not practise austerity, there is no success in the knowledge of the Soul, nor perfection of works. For thus has it been said: ''Tis goodness (*sattva*) from austerity (*tapas*), and mind from goodness that is won; and from the mind the soul is won, on winning whom no one returns.'" It is by knowledge, by austerity whereby one "becomes free from evil," and by meditation that Brahman is apprehended and release is obtained (IV. 3 and 4). Thus in addition to knowledge which in the Upaniṣads is well nigh universally held to be necessary for obtaining release, ethical requirements come to be emphasized in these later Upaniṣads.

In addition to all this, what reveals the essentially religious view which those philosophers came to hold regarding the Supreme Being, is the doctrine, which we have already noted, that the knowledge which saves the soul from *saṁsāra* is not so much the product of one's own efforts as the gift of God's grace. If originally redeeming knowledge was something purely philosophical and intellectual, it is thus transformed in these Upaniṣads, into something religious, for which, as we have noted, according to the Śvetāśvatara, religious devotion (*bhakti*), and, according to the Maitri, performance of religious duty are necessary, and which in the last analysis must be conferred on the individual by the Deity Himself.

For these reasons, we may conclude that some of the later philosophers of the Upaniṣads tended to conceive of the Supreme Being as not identical with the self in the body, but as distinct from it though pervading it, as not sharing in its imperfections or in its deeds, and as standing to it in that personal relationship which religious experience demands.

One more point remains to be dealt with, and that is regarding the relation of the Supreme Being to the soul which has found Release. We have already seen that philosophers like Yājñavalkya, who held that Brahman is in the end identical with the individual self, regarded Release as becoming Brahman, in such a way that all consciousness disappears, and one has become a unity without duality (Bṛ. IV (5). 13-15). "Being very Brahman, he goes to Brahman" (Bṛ. IV (4). 6). "Whoever thus knows 'I am Brahman' becomes this all" (Bṛ. I (4). 10).

This doctrine is not by any means limited to early

thought, for throughout the Upaniṣads passages occur[1] capable of being interpreted to teach this doctrine, and it is clearly formulated in some sections of the Maitri. Thus, in the Maitri it is taught that by means of Yoga one should suppress individuality and consciousness and pass into the distinctionless unity of Brahman. "The precept for effecting this (unity) is this: restraint of the breath, withdrawal of the senses, meditation, concentration, contemplation, absorption (*samādhi*). Such is said to be the sixfold Yoga. By this means, when a seer sees the brilliant Maker, Lord, Person, the Brahma-source, then, being a knower, shaking off good and evil, he reduces everything to unity in the supreme Imperishable" (VI. 18). "When through self, by the suppressing of the mind, one sees the brilliant Self which is more subtle than the subtle, then having seen the Self through one's self, one becomes self-less (*nir-ātman*). Because of being self-less, he is to be regarded as incalculable (*a-saṁkhya*) without origin—the mark of liberation (*mokṣa*). This is the supreme secret doctrine (*rahasya*). . . . Because of selfishness, one becomes a non-experiencer of pleasure and pain; he obtains the absolute unity (*kevalatva*)." "Passing beyond this variously characterised, men disappear in the supreme, the non-sound, the unmanifest Brahma. There they are unqualified, indistinguishable, like the various juices which have reached the condition of honey" (VI. 20, 21 and 22). Where Release thus means the complete loss of individuality, it is obvious that the problem of the relation of the Supreme Being to the individual soul ceases to exist.

Side by side with, and indeed much more frequently than, this view which considers Release to be the passing of the soul into the characterless unity of Brahman

[1] Cf., e.g., Kena 2, 12 and 13; Kaṭha II. 12; III. 13; IV. 10 and 11, 15; VI. 10 and 11, 14; Īśā 7; Muṇḍ. II (1). 10; (2). 4; III (1). 3, (2) 4 f.; Praśna IV. 10 and 11; VI. 5; Māṇḍ. 12; Śvet. II. 14 and 15; III. 10, etc.

is to be found what no doubt is an older view[1], that the released soul continues to exist and enjoys personal immortality. Thus in the Chāndogya, besides this world, two other worlds are recognised, the world of the gods and the world of the fathers, and it is said that those who by Brahma-knowledge are qualified to go to the world of the gods " pass over into a flame; from a flame, into the day; from the day into the half-month of the waxing moon; from the half-month of the waxing moon, into the six months during which the sun moves northwards; from the months into the year; from the year into the sun; from the sun into the moon; from the moon, into lightning. There there is a Person (*puruṣa*) who is non-human (*a-mānava*). He leads them on to Brahma. This is the way to the gods, the way to Brahma. They who proceed by it return not to the human condition —yea, they return not " (IV (15). 5 and 6, cf. also V (10). 1-2).[2] Those who are not qualified to enter this world pass, we are told, into the world of the fathers and " after having remained in it as long as there is a residue (of their good works), then by that course by which they came they return again to be born in the world of men and animals according to their conduct (V (10). 5-7). The Brahma-world to which the soul which has found ultimate release goes, is described very realistically in Kauṣitaki I. 3-7 as having rivers, trees, lake, mountains, nymphs with fruits and garlands, and a hall where Brahma is seated on a throne. The soul is catechised as to who he is, and is required to say that he is Brahma Himself. Thereupon Brahma confers on him whatever belongs to His world. Similarly in Chānd. VIII. (1)-(5) it is declared that those who reach the Brahma-world come into possession of unlimited freedom,[3] obtain

[1] In Vedic times, the good soul was believed to dwell in bliss in heaven, and the bad soul to suffer punishment in hell. See article, *Vedic Religion*, A. A. Macdonell in E.R.E.

[2] Cf. also Bṛ. VI (2). 15 and 16.

[3] Cf. also Chānd. VII (1)-(14), (25).

whatever they desire, and even meet departed loved ones, as in dream-life, which is here taken as a foretaste of the Brahma-world.

Prajāpati teaches that those who reach the Brahma-world become like the gods who exist in the Brahma-world with reverence for Brahman and by this means obtain all worlds and all desires (Chānd. VIII (12). 6). They appear in their own form, and enjoy perfect freedom (VIII (12). 2 and 3). The Taittirīya says that he who reaches the Brahma-world goes about " eating what he desires, assuming what form he desires " (III (10). 5). It is said that as long as Indra understood not this Self, so long the Asuras (demons) overcame him. When he understood, then, striking down and conquering the Asuras, he compassed the supremacy (*śraiṣṭhya*), independent sovereignty (*svārājya*), and overlordship (*ādhipatya*) of all gods and of all beings. Likewise also, he who knows this, striking of all evils (*pāpman*), compasses the supremacy, independent sovereignty, and overlordship of all beings " (Kauṣ. IV. 20). The Kena declares in verse 34, " He verily, who knows it thus, striking off evil (*pāpman*), becomes established in the most excellent (*jyeye*), endless, heavenly world—yea, he becomes established." From all this, it is clear that although some philosophers regarded Release as becoming Brahman in such a way that consciousness and individuality were entirely lost, others from the beginning held that Release is the enjoyment by the soul of perfect power, freedom and bliss in the Brahma-world.[1]

This view is also taught in later Upaniṣads such as the Kaṭha, Muṇḍaka, Śvetāśvatara and Maitri. In the Kaṭha it is said, " In the heavenly world is no fear whatsoever. Not there art thou (i.e., Yama or Death). Not from old age does one fear. Over both (i.e.,

[1] This seems to suggest that, although some of these philosophers spoke as though Brahman and the self in the body were one and the same, they meant only to teach that Brahman exists in the body and not that He is completely identical with the self in the body.

Death and old age) having crossed—hunger and thirst too—gone beyond sorrow, one rejoices in the heaven world" (I. 12). "Heaven-world people partake of immortality" (I. 13). Similarly it is asserted that, casting off the bonds of death, with sorrow over-passed, one rejoices in the heaven-world (I. 18). "Whatever one desires is his" (II. 16). "One becomes happy in the Brahma-world" (II. 17). It is spoken of as "the fearless farther shore" (III. 2), "the highest place of Viṣṇu" (III. 9). He who hears and declares the true doctrine is said to become "magnified in the Brahma-world" (IV. 16); the true knower is said to become immortal (VI. 2, 8, 9, 14, 15, 18), and it is related of Naciketas that by means of this knowledge he "attained Brahma and became free from passion, free from death" (VI. 18).

The Muṇḍaka teaches the doctrine of the two worlds—one to which those who rely on good works go, and from which they return to earthly life when their merit is exhausted, and the other to which the Brahma-knowers go, "to where is that Immortal Person (*Puruṣa*) even the imperishable Spirit (*Ātman*) (I (2). 10 and 11), and where is the highest repository of truth (III (1). 6). This Upaniṣad, however, possibly owing to religious influences, regards the soul which reaches the Brahma-world as attaining mystic union with Brahma; "as the flowing rivers in the ocean disappear, quitting name and form, so the knower, being liberated from name and form, goes unto the heavenly Person, higher than the high. He, verily . . . becomes very Brahma" (III (2). 8 and 9). And it is said of such a one that he becomes immortal —a characterisation which seems to imply that the released soul does not completely cease to exist in the state of unification with Brahman (III (2). 9).

The same doctrine of union, but with much greater emphasis on the distinctness of the released soul from Brahman, is taught by the Śvetāśvatara. It declares that "Brahma-knowers become merged in Brahma"

(I. 7), that with Him "the seers of Brahma and the divinities are joined in union" (IV. 15). "By meditation upon Him, by union with Him, and by entering into His being more and more, there is finally cessation from every illusion" (II. 10). But it is said that the final stage which the soul reaches on release is "even universal lordship; being absolute (*kevala*), his desire is satisfied" (I. 11), which certainly suggests the older view of the released soul as enjoying perfect freedom, power and happiness. It is repeatedly said that the released soul attains immortality (I. 6; III. 7, 8, 10, 13; IV. 17, 20; V. 6, etc.). The wise are said to have "eternal happiness" (VI. 12), to be "released from all fetters" (I. 8; II. 15; IV. 16; V. 13; VI. 13), to be freed from sorrow (II. 14; III. 20; IV. 7), to enjoy "peace for ever" (IV. 14).

The Maitri, in the section which teaches that the individual is distinct from Brahman, declares in answer to the question how one may achieve complete union (*sāyujya*) with Brahman, "He becomes one who goes beyond Brahman, even to the state of supreme divinity above the gods; he obtains a happiness undecaying, unmeasured, free from sickness" (IV. 4).

Thus it is obvious that the view that the soul continues to exist after it has won release, is not infrequent in the Upaniṣads. Of those who believed this, the earlier seem to have thought of the released soul as existing in a heavenly world enjoying unlimited freedom and bliss. The relation of the Supreme Being to the soul at this stage is not discussed. The later, although sharing the view that the soul on release does not cease to exist but passes on to immortality, and enjoys fulness of power and happiness, appear to regard it as attaining a union with Brahman, such as does not exist so long as it is in the body.

We may conclude, then, that the predominant thought of the Upaniṣads regarding the relation of the Supreme Being to the self, is that He exists in the embodied individual as its principle of consciousness.

Some of the Upaniṣadic thinkers are so impressed by this fact that they tend to identify Brahman completely with the individual, although even while so doing, many of them tacitly assume that the migrating soul is not in all respects the same as Brahman, but has still to become Him. In some of the later Upaniṣads the thought appears, which is fully developed only in the Śvetāśvatara, that Brahman and the finite self are two, that the Supreme Being pervades the finite self as something distinct from it, that He does not share in its imperfections and that He seeks by His grace to grant to the finite self that knowledge which it requires for obtaining Release.

CHAPTER II

CONCEPTION OF THE DEITY IN THE BHAGAVADGĪTĀ

1. *The Nature of the Deity*

WE have seen how the pure monism of early Upaniṣadic thinkers, according to whom the Supreme Being is an unknown all-pervading conscious principle, was gradually developed till in the later Upaniṣads, notably the Śvetāśvatara, the Supreme Being came to be thought of in moral and religious terms. The same process, whereby religion steps in to clothe the Absolute of the philosophers with flesh and blood, is observable, but to an immeasurably greater extent in the Bhagavadgītā. Here an intensely ardent religion, whose history we shall seek to trace briefly later,[1] seeks to attach itself to, and to find support in, the speculation of Upaniṣadic sages. The more ardent the religion, the greater would be, it would seem, the difficulty of reconciling it with the pure monism of some of the Upaniṣads. It is this almost impossible task which the Gītā attempts in its teaching regarding the Deity.

In speaking of the Supreme Being, the Gītā uses terms such as Brahman, the Imperishable, the Unmanifest, *Ātman* and *Puruṣa*—terms already familiar to us in the Upaniṣads. Its own distinctive name for the Deity is Vāsudeva Kṛṣṇa, and it is under this name[2] that we must look for ideas distinctive of the Gītā.

[1] Pages 86-92 below.

[2] Kṛṣṇa is spoken of as Viṣṇu in three passages in the Gītā. Once at X. 21 where Kṛṣṇa claims to be Viṣṇu among the Ādityas (i.e., chief of a class), and twice (XI. 24 and 30) he is called Viṣṇu by Arjuna, when apparently His brilliant form reminded Arjuna of the sun. The mace and disc which are

While terms such as Brahman, the Imperishable, the Unmanifest, *Ātman* and *Puruṣa*, seem, as usual in the Gītā to imply very little about the nature of the Supreme Being beyond the fact that He is the ultimate conscious principle which pervades all things, and which in its difference from anything known in experience must be declared to be indefinable, the name Vāsudeva Kṛṣṇa reveals Him, as we shall see, as a God undoubtedly personal in character.

The Gītā's unique contribution lies in the thought that the Supreme Being of the Upaniṣads, the all-pervading unknowable One whom the philosophers proclaimed has assumed the form of Kṛṣṇa, Arjuna's charioteer. The Unknown, the Incomprehensible, That which cannot be described except in negatives, That indeed appears in human form, speaks through human lips, is concerned about human affairs. Revolution in the thought of the Divine can hardly be more complete. This is the wonder of wonders, the " Royal Mystery," hidden from the great philosophers of old, but revealed to the unphilosophic Arjuna by one who appears as his human friend and comrade, but is in truth Very God of very gods.

What attributes the Deity as thus revealed is found to possess, we shall now enquire. Kṛṣṇa, it would appear, has all the attributes hitherto ascribed to the Supreme Being. Hence He is spoken of as Supreme

---

ornaments of Viṣṇu are mentioned among the ornaments worn by the Deity in the glorious form in which He appeared to Arjuna (XI.17). Kṛṣṇa at VIII. 4 calls Himself Adhiyajña—the Principle of Sacrifice—and with sacrifice, Viṣṇu was early identified (see e.g., Tait. Saṁ. I. 74).

Twice Saṁjaya refers to Kṛṣṇa as Hari (XI. 9; XVIII. 77), which is another name for Viṣṇu. But Kṛṣṇa does not anywhere in the Gītā make an explicit claim to be Viṣṇu in preference to any of the other gods. Nevertheless the identification of Kṛṣṇa with Viṣṇu—a fundamental tenet of all the Bhāgavata churches—appears to be in the background of the Gītā also.

The name, Nārāyaṇa, does not occur at all in the Gītā nor is there any reference to Kṛṣṇa as Cowherd. The name Govinda occurs at I. 32, but as Bhandarkar points out (*Vaiṣṇavism*, *Śaivism*, etc., IX) it may be explained either as in the Ādiparvan and the Śāntiparvan by reference to a legend of Kṛṣṇa's finding the earth (*go*), or more probably as a later form of *Govid*, which is a name used in the Ṛgveda of Indra in the sense of the " finder of the cows." Govinda might also be a Prakrit form for Sanskrit *Gopenda*, lord of Herdsmen.

Brahman (*paraṁbrahma*) (X. 12), Highest Person (*puruṣottama*) (X. 15; XI. 3); Great Lord (*maheśvara*) (IX. 11); the "Imperishable Being, Not-being, That Supreme"[1] (XI. 37); Great Self (*mahātman*) (XI. 12, 20, 37, 50). As Supreme Being, He is incomprehensible (XI. 17, 42), infinite of form, having no end, middle or beginning (XI. 16), boundless (X. 19), from everlasting (XI. 18), primal (XI. 31), unborn (X. 3), changeless (XI. 18) and immutable (IX. 13). He is all-marvellous (XI. 11), terrible (XI. 20), facing every way (XI. 11), possessed of boundless strength and infinite might (XI. 40), resplendent and filled with glory (XI. 17, 30).

Besides such transcendent qualities which compel fear, awe and reverence (XI. 20-31), He has also numerous perfections which render Him the object of man's highest aspiration and love. He is the light of lights (XIII. 17), the discernment of the discerning, the brilliance of the brilliant (VII. 10), the source of memory and knowledge (XV. 15), the dispeller of doubt (XV. 15), the maker of the Vedānta (XV. 15). omniscient and unrivalled in knowledge (VII. 26), the source of the seven Great Seers, the four Ancients and the Manus (X. 6), identifiable only with the prime and most significant of every species of existence (X. 20-38); the perfections of this universe are only a fraction of the perfections which belong to His nature (X. 41).

Not among the least of the Deity's attributes is His ethical perfection. At His sight the Great Seers and Perfect ones (*siddha*) in hosts praise Him with hymns of praise abounding (XI. 21), the monsters (*rākṣas*) fear and run to every quarter (XI. 36). He is without fault (V. 19), and is strictly impartial (IX. 29). To meditate on Him has the effect of freeing the soul from its passion (V. 21; VI. 25-27). He always sets the standard for men to follow (III. 23). He has instituted the eternal laws of duty (*śāśvatadharmam*)

[1] Quotations are taken throughout from Mr. Hill's translation.

(XIV. 27), and is their unchanging Guardian (XI. 18). His chief purpose with Arjuna is to urge him to do his duty, for duty must never be neglected (III. 19). So important it seems to the Deity that the laws of duty must not be violated that, as in the present case, He even incarnates Himself in order to establish righteousness. "Whenever right (*dharma*) declines, O Bhārata, and wrong uprises, then I create myself. To guard the good and to destroy the wicked and to confirm the right, I come into being in this age and that" (IV. 7 and 8).

The thought that Righteousness is so all-important that the Deity considers even His infinitude of little account when righteousness needs to be established is a remarkable contribution which the Gītā makes to the conception of the Divine. Instead of Thought or Consciousness, which was the chief attribute of the Supreme Being in the Upaniṣads, Righteousness seems here to become His essential attribute.[1] The author of the Gītā was evidently too much of an eclectic to set this view in opposition to the view of the Upaniṣads, and accordingly, the new thought of the Deity here implied does not gain the pointedness and clarity of expression[2] which it deserves. Nevertheless it is clearly a contribution of very great significance.

Besides righteousness, another attribute which the Gītā ascribes to the Deity is love. He is "the friend of every being" (V. 29). We noticed in some of the later Upaniṣads the thought that the Supreme Being in His grace leads men to salvation. That thought is further developed in the Gītā, as we shall soon see. As Kṛṣṇa the Deity appears as Arjuna's comrade

[1] Thus illustrating our view that as speculation advanced, the tendency was to move away from pure monism, and to make room for moral and religious ideas.

[2] Passages occur which appear to teach that the Deity is beyond good and evil. These will be considered in the sequel (see pp. 76-80 below). It would, of course, be easy to explain them as Upaniṣadic teaching retained inconsistently by the author of the Gītā. But such a method of interpretation should not, it seems to us, be adopted except when other ways of explaining them fail.

(XI. 41). Nay more, He even stoops to be Arjuna's charioteer. So intimate and human is the Deity Kṛṣṇa's friendship that Arjuna is afraid that in negligence or love, he has not shown the reverence that is due to Kṛṣṇa (XI. 41 and 42), and asks that Kṛṣṇa should bear with him "as father with his son, as comrade with his comrade, as lover with his beloved" (XI. 44). Kṛṣṇa in His turn declares that Arjuna is exceedingly beloved of Him (XVIII. 64), and because of His love, He reveals Himself to Arjuna in a form in which no eyes had ever seen Him (XI. 47); and when Arjuna is filled with terror and awe at this His glorious form, He assumes a shape more pleasant to Arjuna and consoles the latter (XI. 49 and 50). The unmanifest and the Incomprehensible reveals indeed a heart of love and compassion, and Arjuna bursts forth in adoration at this wonderful revelation (XI. 43-45).

The Deity which the Gītā discloses is one who, although in His universal and transcendent nature He is unknown and has powers which far exceed human thought and imagination, is yet possessed of knowledge as well as other perfections, chief among these being righteousness and love. So excellent are His attributes that Arjuna declares, "There is none equal unto Thee; how could there be a greater in the three-fold world?" (XI. 43). "It is meet that Thy praise should move the universe to joy and love" (XI. 36).

2. *The Relation of the Deity to the world.*

Assuming that the world is real,[1] the Gītā teaches like most of the Upaniṣads that it forms a part of the Supreme, being created, supported and dissolved by Him. "Of the whole universe am I the origin and dissolution too" (VII. 6). "I am the father of this universe, the mother, the creator, the grandsire"

[1] The word, *māyā* (illusion) occurs in the Gītā, not as applicable to the material world as such, but as a power which the Supreme Being has of employing matter (*prakṛti*) to produce illusion (cf. IV. 6; VII. 13-15).

(IX. 17). "That also which is the Soul of every being am I, O Arjuna; nor without me can any being exist that moves or does not move" (X. 39). "In water, I am savour; in moon and sun I am the light . . . pure scent in earth; in fire I am the brilliance; life in all beings am I. . . ." (VII. 8 and 9). While thus accepting the general position of the Upaniṣads that the world constitutes a part of the Supreme Being, who is its creator, sustainer and dissolver, in short, the very life-principle or Soul on which it entirely depends the Gītā goes further than the Upaniṣads in the direction of describing the process of creation and dissolution, and enumerating the various elements involved.

The process of creation and dissolution is explained as taking place thus. "All beings . . . come to my Nature (*prakṛti*) when a Period ends; when a Period begins, I send them forth again. Resorting to Nature, which is my own, I send forth again and again this whole company of beings, powerless, by the power of Nature" (IX. 7 and 8). *Prakṛti*, then, is a principle with which the material world is always connected. It is that from which the world springs and that into which it returns. It is accordingly eternal, for while the world evolves from it and dissolves into it in periodic cycles, it remains as the material basis of the world through all time. It is accordingly said to be "without beginning" (XIII. 19). It is a principle which the Supreme Being employs in creation. It is the womb in which He lays the germ (XIV. 3). He is therefore always the ultimate cause of creation, although *prakṛti* is also always involved. *Prakṛti*, however, is not an independent principle which exists outside of, or side by side with, the Deity, for as the verse above cited clearly declares, it belongs to the Supreme Being. It is His own. In what sense it belongs to Him we are told in the 7th Adhyāya "Earth, Water, Fire, Wind, Ether, Mind (*manas*), and Reason (*buddhi*), and Individuation (*ahaṁkāra*)—thus eightfold is my

Nature (*prakṛti*) divided. This is the lower; but know my higher Nature to be other than this—Very Life (*jīvabhūta*), by which . . . this universe is upheld" (VII. 4 and 5). Brahman, then, in relation to the world is found to display a double nature. In one of His natures, He is *prakṛti*; in the other, He is the all pervading life-principle, i.e., on the one hand He is the material cause of the world, and on the other its instrumental cause. When therefore He creates out of *prakṛti*, He is really only creating out of Himself.

The Supreme Being, however, is not to be identified with merely these two aspects which are concerned with the universe, for His nature is said to transcend what is involved in the existence of the universe. While the universe constitutes the "Perishable," and the life-principle which pervades it is the "Imperishable," He Himself as the Supreme Person transcends both. "There are these two Persons (*puruṣa*) in the world, the Perishable (*kṣara*) and the Imperishable (*akṣara*). . . . But there is another, a Highest Person; He is called the Supreme Self. . . . Because I transcend the Perishable, and am also higher than the Imperishable, therefore am I known in the world and in the Veda as the Person Supreme" (XV. 16-18). The world, composed as it is, on the one hand, of *prakṛti*, and, on the other, of the world-soul or all pervading life-principle (*jīvabhūta*), constitutes then only one portion of His unconditioned Self. He is the Absolute, not to be equated with the universe, which exists in Him, even as the wind dwells in space (IX. 6).

Not only in this way does the Gītā seek to preserve the infinitude and absoluteness of the Supreme Being, but also by pointing out that the active relationship in which He stands to the universe as its creator, sustainer and dissolver does not indicate any limitation or lack on His part. Activity or work, it seems to suggest, is a sign of finitude and imperfection only when it is carried on out of a desire for personal profit, but the Supreme Being in relation to the universe is active without any motive of self-interest (III. 22), and hence His activity is not one which contradicts His absoluteness and infinitude. On the other hand, the ceaseless activity of the Deity in relation to the universe should, the Gītā argues, be understood as the standard which the Supreme Being sets for all beings to follow, of wholly disinterested activity. " For me, O son of Pṛthā, is no work at all in the three worlds, that I must do ; nor aught ungained that I must gain ; yet I abide in work. For if I were not, tireless, to abide ever in work—my path men follow altogether, son of Pṛthā—Did I not work my work, these worlds would fall in ruin, and I should be the worker of confusion, and should destroy these creatures. Just as, to work attached, the ignorant work, O Bhārata, so too, but unattached, should the wise work, wishing to effect the guidance of the world " (III. 22-25). In this way, the Gītā does not hesitate to regard the Supreme Being as actively related to His universe.

Creation of the universe proceeds, according to the Gītā, much as in Sāṁkhyan philosophy, except that *prakṛti* is regarded by the Gītā as a part of the Deity, as already described, and as controlled by Him in all its developments. *Prakṛti* or *avyakta* (unmanifest) at the time of creation, divides into numerous elements. These as enumerated in Sāṁkhyan philosophy are *buddhi* (consciousness) *ahaṁkāra* (egoism), *manas* (mind), the five *buddhīndriya* (organs of sensation), the five *karmendriya* (organs of action), and corresponding with these, five *tanmātra* (subtle elements) and five *mahābhūta* (gross elements). The Gītā, obviously uninterested in such cosmological questions, does not trouble to mention each of these elements individually, nor does it observe any consistent order in enumerating them. Much less does it seek to trace them step by step through the evolutionary process. The list at XIII. 5 mentions the *mahābhūta* (the five gross elements), *ahaṁkāra* (egoism) *buddhi* (consciousness), *avyakta* (the unmanifest), the ten *indriya* (five organs of sensation and five of action), and the onc (*manas* or mind) and the five *indriyagocara* (the five subtle elements). The list at VII. 4 mentions Earth, Water, Fire, Wind and Ether (which may stand for both the subtle and gross elements mentioned above), *manas* (mind—which may have been intended here to stand also for the ten *indriya*), *buddhi* (consciousness) and *ahaṁkāra* (egoism).

While the Sāṁkhyan doctrine of these principles is thus very inadequately dealt with by the Gītā, the doctrine of the three *guṇas*[1]—*sattva*, *rajas* and *tamas* —or the three ultimate constituents of *prakṛti*, in their bearing on conduct is very fully developed by it, as we shall see in the next section. Regarding them, it is declared that although they ultimately exist, as everything must exist, in the Deity, He does not partake of their nature. "Know thou that those states of Purity (*sattva*), of Energy (*rajas*), and of Darkness (*tamas*) are from me alone; but I am not in them; they are in me" (VII. 12).[2] In this way the Deity is sharply distinguished from *prakṛti* and its *guṇas*, but not, it must be noted, to the point of destroying the reality of *prakṛti* and dismissing it as illusion, on the one hand; or to the point of splitting up reality into an unbridgeable dualism between Spirit and Matter, on the other. *Prakṛti* with its *guṇas* forms an eternal part of the Divine Being. It

[1] In Sāṁkhyan philosophy, evolution is accounted for as due to the activity of the three *guṇas*. The *puruṣas* in the Sāṁkyyan system are each distinct and naturally are inactive, but when they come near to *prakṛti* the *guṇas* of which *prakṛti* is composed lose their equilibrium, and becoming active in various proportions account for the diversity of the evolved universe. This cosmic side of the doctrine of *guṇas* is not found in the Gītā, which fixes mainly on the psychological and ethical implications of the doctrine (cf. XVII. I-XVIII. 41).

[2] In all other relevant passages, the Gītā teaches that the *guṇas* spring from *prakṛti* (III. 5, XIII. 19, XIV. 5, XV. 2, XVIII. 40) and that the Supreme Being is without *guṇas* (XIII. 14, 31). The *guṇas* may, however, as in the passage quoted above, be said to be from the Supreme Being in the sense that He is the ultimate ground of *prakṛti* from which they spring.

is hence real, and at the same time entirely dependent on Him. Nevertheless the Deity does not share in its nature nor, as its pervading principle, is He "polluted" by contact with it. "Immutable is this Highest Self; for He has no beginning, and no strands (*guṇas*). . . . As ether everywhere present is not polluted, so subtle it is, even so Self abiding everywhere is not polluted in the body" (XIII. 31 and 32). The nature of the Supreme Being is so different from that of the material constituents of the world that he who fails to go beyond the material world to discover the Deity who is higher than it is, the Gītā declares, befooled, and under delusion (VII. 13 and 14).

The world, then, we may conclude, is according to the Gītā, a conditioned aspect of the Divine Being. He is both its material and its operative cause, for *prakṛti*, the material basis of the universe, forms one part of Him, while by another aspect of Himself He pervades it. He repeatedly brings it into existence, sustains it and dissolves it into Himself. But this active relationship which He bears to the world does not negate His infinitude, for His activity is not prompted by a desire to overcome any lack or imperfection in His nature. He Himself is "higher" than the world and transcends it, for although the latter is a part of Him and is pervaded by Him, its characteristics derived from Matter are not to be found in Him.[1]

3. *The Relation of the Deity to the finite self.*

The topic of the relation of the Supreme Being to the individual self is not dealt with in the Gītā in a manner free from ambiguity. When the author is thinking in terms of concepts borrowed from philo-

[1] Saṁkarṣana, Pradyumna, and Aniruddha, who with Vāsudeva, are in Pāñcarātra philosophy (see pp. 99-102, below) four *vyūhas* or emanations from the Supreme Being, as He evolves the universe out of Himself, are not mentioned in the Gītā. Nor is the doctrine of Śrī or Lakṣmī as the Śakti or creative aspect of the Supreme Being to be found in it.

sophical schools, the selfhood of the individual as distinct from the Universal Self does not gain recognition; but when his thought is guided by religious experience, he appears to recognise a self in the body different from the Supreme Self. Thus in II. 11-30, where the self is described in Upaniṣadic language,[1] it seems to be taught that the permanent and essential element in all individuals is the one Universal Self. "Know verily that cannot be destroyed whereby all this is pervaded; of this immutable none can work destruction. They have an end, 'tis said, these bodies of the embodied soul; but permanent is he and indestructible, incomprehensible" (II. 17 and 18). The self in the body is declared to be "all-pervading (*sarvagata*), stable, unmoved, from everlasting" (II. 24), and employing the imagery of the Field (*kṣetra*) and the Knower of the Field (*kṣetrajña*), the Field representing the body, and the Knower of the Field representing the self, Kṛṣṇa declares without hesitation that He is Himself the knower in all fields. "This body, O son of Kuntī, is called the Field, Him who knows it knowers of these call Knower of the Field. Know also me to be in all Fields Knower of the Field" (XIII. 1 and 2). He is therefore the conscious being which inhabits all bodies. There is none other, and it is said in imitation of the Ṛgvedic idea of the Primal *Puruṣa* that the Self is that which "everywhere possessing hands and feet, and everywhere possessing eyes and heads and mouths, and everywhere possessing hearing, abides all-enveloping in the world" (XIII. 13).[2] Besides such a Universal Self which exists in all bodies as their principle of consciousness, no other self is spoken of in the thirteenth Adhyāya, which purports to discuss the Knower of the Field and the Field, or the self and the body. It would therefore seem that what we call individual

[1] Cf. verses 19 and 20 with Kaṭha I (2). 18 and 19; and verse 29 with Kaṭha I (2). 7.

[2] Cf. Ṛgveda X 90. 1; also Śvet. III. 11-21.

self is nothing but the Universal Self which has assumed a particular body (cf. XV. 7-10). It exists in all bodies alike, and therefore the distinction of one self from another, or the belief in a plurality of souls, is false. "Undivided yet in beings seeming to dwell divided . . . is That" (XIII. 16).

When it is believed that no self exists in the body beyond the One Universal Self, the experience of individuality, change, activity, pain and suffering, which seem to demand the existence of an individual self different from the permanent and changeless Supreme Self, is explained as due to the body. "Know that changes and Strands (*guṇas*) are born of Nature (*prakṛti*). In the production of effects and causes, Nature is said to be the cause. . . . The Supreme Person in this body is called the spectator" (XIII. 19, 20, 22). The Supreme Self therefore exists in the body as an inactive conscious principle, all activity being due to the body. "Who sees that it is by Nature (*prakṛti*) that works are altogether done, and that Self works not, he sees indeed" (XIII. 29). The Self, however, while in the body, becomes attached to the body, and hence passes from birth to birth, experiencing the good and evil consequences which inevitably follow the good and evil deeds of the body." In the experience of pleasure and pain, the Person (*puruṣa*) is said to be the cause. For the Person, abiding in Nature (*prakṛti*), experiences the Strands (*guṇas*) born of Nature; his attachment to the Strands is the cause of his birth in good and evil wombs" (XIII. 21). Since attachment to the body is what causes His birth in worldly existence (*saṁsāra*), what is necessary is for Him to realise His pure non-bodily nature as Universal Self, and to renounce all attachment to the body. Knowledge and control are therefore the prime means of winning release from the bonds of the body (II. 49-72). When this is done, the Self, knowing its own true Self, draws itself from its sense-organs even as a tortoise draws back its limbs and becomes the Supreme unconditioned Brahman (II. 58).

Such according to one tendency of thought in the Gītā would appear to be the relation of the Supreme Being to the existence which we call individual selves. *Saṁsāra* (worldly existence) with its various centres of experience is real, but it is the Supreme Being who has entered numerous bodies and exists as the Experiencer in them all. When He gives up attachment to the body which He at any one time inhabits and realises His own true nature, His birth in *saṁsāra* ceases, and He once more becomes the unconditioned Brahman.

But to state this view thus sharply is in itself to transcend it, and to pass to the other view which, we said, is also to be found in the Gītā, and which admits of the existence of an individual self distinct from the Universal. For if existence in *saṁsāra* is real, as the Gītā always assumes, then it would seem that the Universal Self in assuming various bodies has really become differentiated into numerous individual existences; for however much it may be emphasized that it is the same Self which exists in various bodies, still so long as it is declared that each embodied being has, as it were, to work out its own release, it is clear that each in some sense is assumed to have an individuality of its own, which prevents it from becoming Brahman when some other attains Brahman, and which makes it necessary for each individually by cultivation of knowledge and control to become the Supreme Self. Thus it is obvious that the Gītā, even while advocating the purely monistic view that the Universal Self exists in all beings as their Self, assumes that somehow finite conscious beings have a certain element of individuality in them. This assumption becomes quite explicit when our author is not speaking the language of Philosophy but that of Religion. Thus in the ninth Adhyāya, where the author expounds the "Royal Mystery," or the religious view of Kṛṣṇa as the Deity incarnate —a doctrine not taught in the philosophies which he has hitherto been expounding—the distinction of the Supreme Being from the individual existence whom He pervades is so forcibly expressed that were it not for the author's general position that the Universal Self pervades all existences, we should have to conclude that the author was a deist, and taught that the Deity was quite external to the finite self. "Behold my Power as Lord! Sustainer of all beings, yet not dwelling in beings, is my Self, that brings beings to existence" (IX. 5). This sharp distinction between the Supreme Being and individual existences is maintained throughout this Adhyāya, and it now appears that there is a plurality of beings, who are sent by the Deity into worldly existence, nay more, that it is the same individuals who are sent by Him from time to time. "All beings, O son of Kuntī, come to my Nature (*prakṛti*), when a Period ends; when a Period begins, I send them forth again. Resorting to Nature, which is my own, I send forth again and again this whole company of beings" (IX. 7 and 8).

That the distinctness of finite selves from the Deity and their plurality is not purely verbal, arising from the employment of the language of common experience, but that it represents the point of view here advocated, is seen from the fact that it is now asserted that the way to obtain release from *saṁsāra* (worldly existence) is not to realise that one is after all the Supreme Self, but to worship the Deity with undivided heart. "If one worship (*bhaj*) me with undivided devotion, even though he be of very evil life . . . quickly he becomes righteous and goes to everlasting peace" (IX. 30 and 31). "Whatever work thou doest, whatever thou dost eat, whatever thou dost sacrifice or give, whatever be thine austere practices, do all, O son of Kuntī, as an offering to me. Thus from the bonds of work, from fruits both good and ill shalt thou be released" (IX. 27 and 28). And such devotion not only seems to require the distinction in *saṁsāra* of the individual soul from the Supreme, but also to demand the continuance of that distinction even after release.[1] Accordingly it is asserted that just as those who worship the Lords of Heaven go to their world (*svargaloka*) and "taste the heavenly joys of Heaven's Lords" (IX. 20, 25), so those who worship Kṛṣṇa will come to Him (IX. 25), and find everlasting peace (IX. 31). They do not perish (IX. 31).

If finite selves are thus distinct from the Deity, being sent into worldly existence, sustained and finally withdrawn by Him at the end of each world-cycle (IX. 5-11), it is necessary to enquire what attitude He bears to them. It would appear that primarily the attitude of the Deity to finite selves is one of love. He is jealous of any other besides Himself occupying their affection, and consequently wishes all to worship Him wholeheartedly, without allegiance to any other god (IX. 23 and 24). The body and senses produce attachment to the finite and the sensual, and are to be held in control (XIV. 21-7, II. 55-71). Whatever work is done—and work must be done—is to be done as unto Him, without attachment to anything besides Himself (XVIII. 2-6; IX. 27; III. 17-19). One's thought, one's remembrance, one's meditation are to be centred on Him, and on no other (III. 39-43; VI. 7; 14-27). Thus every method of directing oneself to the Deity, whether it be through devotion, control, work or knowledge, or all of these together, is advocated by the Gītā. "On me thy mind, to me be thy devotion, for me thy sacrifice, to me do reverence; thus holding thyself in control, and making me thine aim, even to me shalt thou come" (IX. 34). This new ethic taught by Kṛṣṇa to Arjuna discloses the new view which is now to be taken regarding the Deity's attitude to individuals. He is not the impersonal Absolute, for whom the individual counts for little. He is a personal

[1] This topic will be dealt with more fully later. See pp. 83-84 below.

God who loves the individual and wishes to possess him completely.

Since He thus loves, He plays an active part in redeeming the soul from *saṁsāra* (worldly existence). The soul is not left to work out its own salvation, by knowledge, control, work and devotion, but may obtain release by the grace of the Deity. Thus in the last Adhyāya, in declaring how the soul may obtain release, all the conditions previously formulated are enumerated, viz., control of sense and body, work, devotion and calm meditation leading to knowledge, and it is declared that when this culminating knowledge is reached, the soul enters into final union with the Deity (XVIII. 55). But immediately, in the very next stanza, it is added, that however unworthy a soul may be, still if it rely on the Deity, it also will obtain release. "Though he do every work at every time, yet if he rely on me, he by my grace wins to the realm eternal and immutable" (XVIII. 56). It is not asserted, however, that the soul has no part to play in salvation, everything being done by grace, for it is said, "Cast off in thought all works on me; make me thy goal; turn to the practice of discernment (*buddhiyoga*); fix thy thought ever on me. Fixing thy thought on me, thou shalt by my grace surmount all difficulties" (57 and 58). And yet it would appear that the loving Deity is not unwilling to extend His grace to the most undeserving, even apart from all qualifying conditions, if the latter comes to Him for refuge. Accordingly Kṛṣṇa declares, "Abandoning every duty (*dharma*) come to me alone for refuge. I will release thee from all sins, sorrow not" (66). But fearing that this doctrine of totally unmerited grace may lead to misunderstanding and a life of sin, Kṛṣṇa adds at once, "Never should this, thus taught to thee, be told to one whose life is not austere, to one without devotion, to one who does no service, nor yet to one who murmurs against me" (67). God is loving, it would appear; but He is also righteous, and does not wish His all-forgiving love to lead to unrighteousness.[1] That leads us to the question of the relation of the Deity to the evil which characterises the finite self.

The Deity, whether regarded as the self of the individual or as distinct from him, is always said to be not responsible for the evil of the individual. Thus we noticed that when He is regarded as the Self in all bodies, it is proclaimed that He exists in them merely as Spectator, and not as worker (XIII. 22, 29, 31), i.e., whatever evil the embodied being does or suffers is not due to the indwelling Divine principle. Similarly when the finite self is regarded as distinct from the Deity, we noticed that the tendency is to separate it so much from the Divine that it is declared that the Deity creates and sustains it, but does not dwell within it. Under both assumptions, then, the Deity is freed from responsibility for the evil of souls.

If then it is asked, from where this evil arises, the answer seems to be that evil is due primarily to the *guṇas* of the body. It is the *guṇas* which incite the embodied self to activity, and it is therefore they that are chiefly responsible for the good and evil deeds which bind the soul to *saṁsāra*. "Purity (*sattva*) Energy (*rajas*), Darkness (*tamas*)—these are the Strands (*guṇas*) that spring from Nature (*prakṛti*); they bind . . . in the body the embodied soul immutable. Of these Purity is luminous and knows not sickness, for it is stainless; it binds with the attachment of pleasure and with the attachment of knowledge (*jñāna*).[2] . . . Energy, know thou, is passionate, sprung from thirst, and attachment; it binds the embodied soul . . . with the attachment of work. Darkness, know thou, is born of ignorance, and deludes all embodied souls; it binds with heedlessness and indolence and sleep" (XIV. 5-8). Further,

[1] The relation of God's grace to the law of *karma* is not discussed. It is assumed throughout that grace can wipe out all past sin and its effects.

[2] *jñāna* is here a faculty of *buddhi*, part of *prakṛti* (Hill)

it is declared that the *guṇas* of the body determine one's nature (XIV. 5-13), one's life hereafter (14-20), the kind of faith one has (XVII. 2), one's worship (4), one's diet (8-10), one's sacrifice (11-13), the nature of one's austerities (14-19), one's acts of charity (20-22), one's renunciation (XVIII. 7-9), one's character as agent (26-28), one's moral perception (30-32), one's steadiness of purpose (33-35), one's pleasures (37-39), and one's duty in society (41-44). And it is not surprising that in Sāṁkhyan fashion, the Gītā declares that the self is inactive, all work being done by the body (XIII. 29).

Though the Gītā seems thus to accept the view that the self is entirely powerless, while the body determines all its acts, its assumption throughout is that the self has the power of controlling the body. It is noteworthy that not one chapter is to be found in the whole of the Gītā—except, of course, the first, which is merely a preface to the rest—in which Kṛṣṇa does not either command Arjuna to control sense and desire, or extol the virtue of control. Thus it would seem that the Gītā tacity assumes the power and the freedom of the self to control and overcome the body. In this connection we cannot pass unnoticed the text which says that if Arjuna decides not to fight, vain is his resolve, for even against his will Nature (*prakṛti*), will constrain him to do what he himself does not desire (XVIII. 59 and 60). Here we seem definitely to be told that the individual has no power over the *prakṛti*-constituted body, which will have its way whether he will or no. But when we regard these words in the light of their context, it appears that Kṛṣṇa is seeking, by this exaggerated emphasis on the powerlessness of human will, to urge Arjuna not to use his freedom to oppose the will of the Divine. Verses 58 and 61 declare that if through thought of "I" Arjuna hearkens not, he will perish, and the Deity will have His way. He will employ *prakṛti*, it would seem, to constrain Arjuna to do what He wishes done. Futile, therefore, it is to oppose the will of the Divine. But that at the same time the individual does have a will of his own appears in verse 63, where Kṛṣṇa concludes—This have I taught thee; "Fully consider this; then, as thou wilt, so act." In this way, the freedom of the self seems to be assumed,[1] although on the one hand, it is declared that the body is all-determining, and on the other, that the Deity is all-supreme. If this be so, then it would seem that ultimately the responsibility for evil is to be traced to the free agency of the moral individual. At any rate, it is certain that the Deity is clearly freed from any touch of evil. Evil is to be traced either to the *guṇas* of the body or to the self, but not to the Deity. Stated positively, the Deity is altogether good.

If He is essentially good and free from evil, then it would appear that the soul who would please Him and ultimately win release, may do so only by pursuing the good and fleeing from evil. Several virtues are accordingly mentioned as leading to the "Divine Estate," and likewise several vices which lead to the "Devilish Estate." "Fearlessness, purity of heart, steadfastness in devotion to knowledge, liberality, self-restraint, sacrifice, sacred study, austerity, uprightness, harmlessness, truth, an even temper, abandonment, quietude, an unmalicious tongue, tenderness towards beings, a soul unruffled by desire, gentleness, modesty, constancy, ardour, long-suffering, fortitude, cleanness, freedom from hatred and arrogance—these are his born to Divine Estate, O Bhārata. Hypocrisy, pride, and self-conceit, wrath, insolence and ignorance —these are his . . . who is born to Devilish estate. The Divine estate is deemed to lead to release, the Devilish to bondage" (XVI. 1-5).[2] And throughout the Gītā Kṛṣṇa urges upon Arjuna the necessity to

[1] The problem of the freedom of the will or individuality is not faced by the Gītā. Hence the unsatisfactory way in which it is left. We have sought merely to bring together the salient points.

[2] Cf. also the rest of this Adhyāya.

control sense and desire, and to do one's duty as unto God.[1]

Unfortunately, however, the author of the Gītā, in seeking to express himself in the language of the philosophers, uses words which imply that the Deity is beyond good and evil; and since on the basis of these it is possible to maintain a view quite opposed to the one which we have expounded, it is necessary to consider them in some detail, and to show that in spite of them the main position of the Gītā is to uphold the ethical nature of the Deity.[2] Kṛṣṇa declares, "Now that man whose delight is but in Self, whose pleasure is in Self, whose satisfaction is in Self alone, has no work that he must do. For him there is no purpose here in work done or left undone" (III. 17 and 18). This seems to teach that he who is devoted to the Deity has no concern with duty. He transcends both good and evil. Similarly it is said, "He who hopes for nothing . . . abandoning every enterprise—that man is dear to me. . . . He who does not rejoice, nor hate, nor grieve, nor crave, abandoning good and ill—that man is dear to me, my worshipper devout. He who regards alike both foe and friend, honour and dishonour . . . blame and praise . . . that man is dear to me, my worshipper devout" (XII. 16-19). "Excellent is he whose judgement holds as equal the lover . . . the enemy . . . the hateful . . . the good too and the sinful" (VI. 9). In these passages it seems to be taught that he who has definitely abandoned good and ill, and has lost all sense of value such as that of friend and foe, honour and dishonour, praise and blame, the good and the sinful, is dear to the Deity. Further Kṛṣṇa declares,

[1] Cf. II. 55-71; III. 7-9; IV. 17-24; V. 7-10; VI. 1, 26-32, etc.

[2] It would, of course, be easy to dismiss the problem by saying that the author of the Gītā was such an inconsistent thinker that he retained side by side teaching utterly contradictory of each other. It may be he was; but it is clearly not legitimate to prejudge the issue, for it may also be that in seeking to placate philosophical schools of thought he used their language, but gave it a meaning of his own, which is to be gathered from the context in which they appear, and in general from his own distinctive position.

"do all . . . as an offering to me. Thus from the bonds of work, from fruits both good and ill, shalt thou be released" (IX. 27 and 28). It is not only from evil that the devotee is redeemed, but also, it would appear, from good. Then again passages are not lacking which seem to imply that it is knowledge alone which is necessary for release, and knowledge cancels all good and evil works. "Though thou art of all sinners the most sinful by the boat of knowledge, alone shalt thou pass over all crookedness. Just as a burning fire makes ashes of its fuel, Arjuna, so does the fire of knowledge make ashes of all works" (IV. 36 and 37). All these passages appear to teach that ultimately good and evil are transcended by the individual and that the one who reaches Brahman has no further use for ethical distinctions. In this way, indirectly, it seems to be implied that the Deity Himself is non-ethical. Not only is this implied, but it appears definitely to be taught in a passage which seems to mean that for the Deity the good and evil deeds of men have no meaning, for He neither approves of them, nor rejects them. "He takes not to Himself, that all-pervading Lord, sin or good deed of any man" (V. 15). That the good man and the bad are both alike to the Deity seems to be taught by Kṛṣṇa in the following words: "All beings I regard alike, not one is hateful to me or beloved" (IX. 29).

Although these passages when torn from their context can be interpreted as we have done above, when regarded in the light of their context they appear to necessitate a very different interpretation. Taking them in order, the passage which declares that he whose satisfaction is in the Self has no work which he must do or must not do, appears in a chapter which, far from teaching that duty need not be performed, urges Arjuna to do his duty (cf. III. 4-9), and it is only necessary to refer to the verse immediately following the one in question, to be convinced that the Gītā without doubt teaches that one's duties must be performed. The verse runs thus: "Therefore without attachment ever perform the work that thou must do: for if without attachment a man works, he gains the Highest" (III. 19). What the passage means therefore seems to be that ultimately the soul's sole duty is attachment to the Deity, and that the various duties incumbent on the embodied soul, being determined as they are by impermanent bodily relationships (e.g., by the *guṇas*, XVIII. 41-44), are binding on the soul only while in the body. These must be done without attachment to bodily relationships, remembering that ultimately the only duty permanently binding on the soul is attachment to the Deity. The soul, then, in release, need not be understood as altogether transcending the Good. What it transcends would appear to be the impermanent form of the Good which is binding on it in its embodied life. Similarly, the passage which declares that the one who abandons good and evil is dear to the Deity, occurs in a chapter which is concerned with pointing out the merits of whole-hearted devotion to the Deity—a devotion which, abandoning all other things, finds its sole happiness in the Deity, abandoning even what men usually consider to be good. Everything pales into insignificance for the devotee who has found the pearl of great price, and the verses which follow and declare that he who is dear to the Deity regards alike both friend and foe, honour and dishonour, praise and blame, are, it would seem, to be interpreted in this light. Nothing is to stand as a rival to the Deity in the affections of His devotee. But that by this the Gītā does not intend to teach that the individual who is attached to the Deity should be entirely indifferent to the world, cold and deprived of all sense of value, appears from a preceding verse which declares, "He who hates not any being, he who is friendly and compassionate, without a thought of mine or I . . . with mind and reason dedicated to me—that man is dear to me" (XII. 13). The verse above cited, which teaches that he is excellent who holds as equal the lover, the enemy, the hateful, the good and the sinful, appears in its context to bear the same meaning as the above (cf. verses 4-8), together with the additional meaning which is developed in the succeeding verses (cf. especially verses 29-32) that for the sage all beings are in the end alike, since the Deity pervades them all. This is not, it would seem, to be understood, in the sense that the sage loses all sense of value, but that he is impartial. He does not attach himself to some and despise others. "The man whose spirit is controlled, who looks on all impartially, sees Self abiding in all beings, and all beings in Self. Who sees me everywhere and everything in me, I am not lost to him nor is he lost to me" (VI. 29 and 30). The devotee is to be impartial even as the Deity is impartial (V. 18 and 19). Regarding the passage in which Kṛṣṇa declares that the soul which is devoted to Him will be released from fruits both good and evil, it need only be remarked that "fruits both good and evil" refers to the reaping of the consequences of one's deeds in *saṁsāra* (worldly existence), and not to good and evil in general, for the verse obviously aims to teach that he who has devotion to the Deity finds release from birth in this world. If further evidence were necessary, it need only be pointed out that the chapter in which it occurs is concerned with expounding the "Royal Mystery" by means of which release from *saṁsāra* may be obtained (cf. 1-3; 20 f.). It would seem, then, that these passages, which appear to teach that ultimately the individual transcends the Good, have a very different meaning in the light of their context.

With regard to knowledge as the way of salvation, the Gītā, as though fearing that knowledge may be interpreted to exclude moral practice, adds immediately after the two verses which we have quoted above, "here is naught that purifies like knowledge; he that is perfected in control himself in due time finds that in his self. The single-hearted man of faith, with senses held in check, gains knowledge" (IV. 38 and 39). The knowledge that cancels all one's works, and redeems the soul from *saṁsāra*, is not one, then, which excludes morality, but one which is the ripe fruit of morality. It is the man who is "perfected in control," the one who has his senses in check, that gains this redeeming knowledge.

It is thus possible not only to uphold the view that in spite of the passages above cited the Gītā does not regard the individual as transcending ethical distinctions, but also to maintain that the two passages which seem to teach that good and evil have no meaning for the Deity have as a matter of fact a very different meaning. The one, for example, which declares that although all-pervading He takes not to Himself sin or good deed of any man, may be taken as either signifying that although the Deity pervades the individual self, He is not responsible for the latter's good or evil deeds—in which case, it cannot be used to prove that the Deity has no use for good or evil; or as not referring to the Deity at all, but to the individual self, which has been the topic of discussion in the chapter so far, in which case again it cannot be used to prove that the Deity has no use for good and evil. The other passage which we cited and which declares that the Deity regards all beings alike, none being either hateful to Him or beloved, appears to teach nothing more than that He is impartial (cf. V. 19). That it does not imply that the Deity does not appreciate the love of those who worship Him in spirit and in truth is evident in the second part of the verse which we cited, and which reads, "those who with devotion worship me abide in me, and I also in them" (IX. 29), implying that though the Deity abides in all beings alike, He becomes united in a special sense with His devotee. Thus it would appear that in spite of passages which seem to imply the contrary, the Gītā's main position is that the Deity is an ethical

Being, and that the individual who would realise Him must therefore also be ethical.

The earnest desire of the Deity that righteousness should prevail was, as we saw, the chief motive given by the Gītā for His incarnating Himself from time to time. We have already noted the general significance of this idea. A few points of particular interest with regard to the Gītā's theory of incarnation must here be mentioned. Firstly, Kṛṣṇa being identified with Viṣṇu it would follow that he is an incarnation of the latter. Besides, he regards himself as an incarnation of the Supreme Being (cf. IV. 6; XV. 17-19). Secondly, it is asserted that the Deity incarnates Himself repeatedly, and that He has already appeared several times in incarnate form (IV. 5). but no details are given, as in the Nārāyaṇīya and other Vaiṣṇava literature (see pp. 110 and 111 below), as to what exactly these forms are in which He appeared. Thirdly, the work which the Deity achieves in His incarnate form is said in the Gītā generally to be "to guard the good and to destroy the wicked and to confirm the right" (IV. 8); also, it would appear, to teach the true doctrine (IV. 1 and 3). Specific works, crude and mythological are ascribed to the Deity in His incarnate forms in other Vaiṣṇava writings (see p. 111 below). Of these the Gītā knows nothing or if it knows them it completely ignores them. Fourthly, the relation in which Kṛṣṇa stands to the Supreme Being is not considered in the Gītā. Kṛṣṇa undoubtedly identifies Himself with the Supreme Being when He declares that all beings dwell within Him and that He sends them out into bodied existence from time to time (IX. 4-10), and also when He declares that those who win Release, even those who win it by contemplating the imperishable and unmanifest Brahman, come ultimately to Him (XII. 1 f.). But at times, even after He has disclosed His supreme nature to Arjuna, Kṛṣṇa speaks of the Supreme Being in the third person, as though He were not entirely identical with, but only a partial manifestation of, the Supreme One (cf. V. 19-26; VIII. 8, 10, 22; XVIII. 61 and 62). The later Vaiṣṇava view, as expressed in the Bhāgavata Purāṇa (I. 3, p. 9), is that unlike other incarnations which are partial manifestations of the Supreme Being, the Kṛṣṇa incarnation is a complete manifestation of the Deity. Such problems as these do not exist for the Gītā, which in all these ways shows itself to reflect an early stage in the theory of incarnation among the Vaiṣṇavas.

One more topic remains to be dealt with, and that is, the relation of the Deity to the soul which has departed from this life. We have seen thus far that generally in regard to the soul the Deity is taught by the Gītā to be loving and gracious as well as righteous and good. Such being His Nature, He decrees one of two ends for the soul as it passes from this life. His righteousness demands that good deeds should be rewarded, and evil deeds punished. Accordingly the soul which has given itself to such deeds is reborn to reap their fruits. This may be either in a temporary heaven, where it dwells till the results of its good deeds have been enjoyed, and then returns to earth, or directly, on this earth, in the world of men or of sub-human beings according to its deserts; the reason for such rebirth being that the soul may thus be gradually led to perfection.[1] "He that has fallen from control attains the worlds of those that do deeds of merit, and after dwelling there for endless years is born again in the house of the pure and the wealthy. There he obtains that union with discernment which he had in the former body; and thence . . . he strives once more for perfection" (VI. 41 and 43). "If when purity (*sattva*) has increased, the body-bearing soul comes to dissolution, then he proceeds to the spotless

[1] Although the eschatological ideas here expressed are, in essentials, the same as what we found in the Chāndogya and Bṛhadāraṇyaka, they are, it must be noted, given special significance in the Gītā, by its doctrine that re-birth is for the perfecting of the soul. (Cf. especially VIII, 23-26 with Chānd. XV (15). 5 f.; Bṛ. VI (2). 15 f.)

worlds of the most wise. If when energy (*rajas*) has increased, he goes to dissolution, he is born among men attached to work; and if dissolved when darkness (*tamas*) has increased, he is born in the wombs of the witless" (XIV. 14 and 15).

But the love of the Deity leads Him, it would appear, to wish to be united with the soul, and accordingly, as already noticed, He seeks by His grace to wean the soul away from attachment to the finite, till when it has succeeded in directing its entire mind, will and devotion to Him, He does not send it once more into rebirth, but takes it to Himself, never again to be separated from it by *saṁsāra*. "With thought controlled by constant practice, and seeking no other resort, one goes to the Supreme Celestial Person." "To that ascetic, ceaselessly controlled, who ever ceaselessly with individual thought remembers me, easy am I of access, son of Pṛthā. When they have come to me, great souls win not rebirth, abode of pain, unduring; to highest perfection have they gone. The worlds, even to the realm of Brahmā are subject to return, O Arjuna; but for him who comes to me . . . there is no rebirth" (VIII. 4; 14-16).

In what relation the soul which has reached its final goal stands to the Deity, we are told in scattered references. The desire of the Gītā to placate philosophical thought of the advaitic type, and possibly also the difficulty of describing a state which is beyond present experience, appear to prevent it from giving us very definite teaching. But considering all relevant passages, one is inclined to think that the view which the Gītā generally favours is that the released soul enters into the being of the Deity[1] (IV. 10; XIV. 19; XVIII. 55), the eternal and immutable abode (VIII. 28; XV. 5; XVIII. 56, 62), which is beyond death (II. 15; XIII. 12, 25; XIV. 18, 27), and where no sickness is (II. 51). Though it thus enters into the Deity, it does

[1] Possibly, a metaphorical way of saying that it becomes closely united with the Deity.

not become merged in Him, losing its individuality completely; for it abides in Him (V. 19, 20), enjoying contact with Him (VI. 28), filled with calm and peace (II. 72; IV. 39; V. 12, 24-26; VI. 15, etc.), having attained highest bliss (V. 2; VI. 28), highest perfection (VIII. 15; XIV. 1), and a nature similar *sādharmya*) to that of the Deity (XIV. 2). At a creation it does not come into birth, nor at a dissolution is it disturbed (XIV. 2). In this way the Gītā teaches that in Release the soul becomes closely united with the Deity, enjoying communion with Him and sharing in His peace, bliss and perfection.

Although, then, as already noticed, the Gītā often speaks as though the Supreme Being were one without difference with the individual self, its own distinctive position, as indicated by its predominantly moral and religious character, is that the Supreme Being is distinct from the individual whom He pervades and controls.

In conclusion, we may say that the Deity as revealed in the Gītā appears to be one who, though in His transcendent aspect He is essentially unknown, is revealed in His relation to the universe as Supreme Self or Person, possessed of wonderful powers and excellences. All that exists, matter and souls, form a part of Him; and He in one aspect of Himself brings them into existence, pervades, governs and withdraws them into Himself. Though containing, supporting and pervading all things, He does not share in their evil nature, nor is He polluted by His relationship to them. He is the principle of Consciousness which exists in all individuals, but He is not responsible for their actions. He is characterised by righteousness and incarnates Himself from time to time to establish it. He institutes the rule that righteousness should be rewarded and evil punished, whether in this birth or in others. He is also characterised by grace. He loves all beings alike, whether good, bad or indifferent but more especially His devotees, whom He wishes to possess completely. Nothing therefore delights Him so much as their whole-hearted devotion. He is pleased with those who with mind centred on Him seek to gain Him by strenuous discipline, unselfish work, knowledge or simple devotion. He gives of His grace to even the most undeserving, so that they may come to Him quickly, and freeing them from sin, He finally takes them to Himself, to eternal peace, bliss and perfection, never again to return to the weary cycle of births and deaths.

CHAPTER III

CONCEPTION OF THE DEITY IN PĀNCARĀTRA AND PURĀṆIC LITERATURE[1]

Historical Introduction.

Vaiṣṇavism appears to have had a long history, going back to very remote times. Its origin and early history are not known with any great degree of certainty. For our purpose it must suffice barely to note certain main stages in its historical development.

Vaiṣṇavism, as its name suggests, is a religion centering round the worship of Viṣṇu. The deity of this cult bears also the sectarian names, Vāsudeva-Kṛṣṇa, Nārāyaṇa and Kṛṣṇa Gopāla. These names indicate the four main streams which mingled into one through a period of several centuries to form the religion which Rāmānuja inherited. We shall briefly lay down what seem to us to have been its probable development, although from the evidence so far available, it must be admitted that no certainty can be claimed for our conclusions.

As a sectarian movement, it would seem that the cult must be traced to Vāsudeva Kṛṣṇa, a Kṣatriya warrior who fought at Kurukṣetra. He belonged to the Vṛṣṇi or Sātvata clan.

His father's name was Vasudeva, his mother's Devakī. He had an elder brother, Balarāma or Saṁkarṣaṇa. He lived at a time when, as in the period of the Brāhmaṇas, religion became lost in meaningless ritual. His religious instructor, however, sought to preserve the theism of an older day.[2] Ghora

[1] Under this general heading we propose to deal with works which we enumerate on p. 92 below.

[2] As is evidenced by his closing his discourse with verses from the Ṛg Veda.

Aṇgirasa was the teacher's name. He was a worshipper of a deity manifested in the form of the Sun, and presumably identical with Viṣṇu in his post-Vedic character, and instructed Kṛṣṇa (*a*) that one's whole life must be regarded as a continual sacrifice; (*b*) that virtues such as austerity, almsgiving, uprightness, harmlessness, and truthfulness, are as effective as one's gifts to the priests; (*c*) that at the hour of death one should turn one's thoughts to the Imperishable, the Unfailing and the very Essence of Life; and (*d*) that the highest goal is to attain Sūrya (the Sun), the God of gods (Chānd. III (17). 6). What is noteworthy in this teaching is the heretic belittling of Brahminic ritualism and the implied throwing of the way to God to all, the emphasis on the practice of certain virtues, and on the directing of one's mind to the Deity. It is easy to see how this doctrine of catholicity, of living one's life as an offering to God, of the practice of virtue, and of having one's devotion fixed on the Deity, is to be heard now loudly, now dimly in the chequered history of Vaiṣṇavism. How much of this teaching Kṛṣṇa accepted, or how much he added to it, we cannot say. But it seems to be fairly well preserved in the Bhagavadgītā, which (*a*) teaches that everything is to be done as a sacrifice to the Deity (IX. 27); (*b*) mentions the virtues[1] taught by Ghora, along with others (XVI. 1-3); (*c*) emphasizes the importance of last thoughts (VIII. 5, 10), and generally, as we have seen, teaches that one's mind should be fixed on the Deity; and (*d*) also associates its doctrine with the Sun-god, here called Vivasvān (IV. 1 f.). Consequently, we may believe that doctrines similar to what he learnt from Ghora, were what Kṛṣṇa also taught. His teaching was singularly successful, for he became the centre of a theistic movement, which in the course of time began to worship him along with his friend Arjuna. Reference

[1] Of these, it must be noted, one is "harmlessness," a characteristically Vaiṣṇava virtue.

to this fact is found in Pāṇini's (400 B.C.)[1] grammar (IV. 3 98). His being coupled with Arjuna would seem to indicate that Kṛṣṇa was at this time revered only as a demi-god. We have definite evidence, however, of his having attained the rank of Supreme God in the Besnagar inscription[2] (180 B.C.), which records the erection of a Garuḍa column to Vāsudeva, the God of gods (*devadeva*). This inscription is also significant for the fact that Garuḍa, a bird sacred to Viṣṇu, is here associated with Vāsudeva, and the inscription adds that " three immortal steps . . . when practised lead to heaven . . . self-control, charity and diligence "[3]—which seems very much like an effort to moralise the three strides associated with Viṣṇu, even as Ghora moralised every state of a man's life. At any rate, this inscription clearly shows that by about 200 B.C., Vāsudeva-Kṛṣṇa was fully identified with Viṣṇu. This brings us to the second current which flowed into the making of Vaiṣṇavism. Of it we must now seek to give a brief account.

Viṣṇu is a Vedic god, and therefore much more ancient than Vāsudeva-Kṛṣṇa. Although in the Ṛg-Veda the powerful personality of Indra seems to put Viṣṇu rather in the shade, he gradually rises to importance, till in the Brāhmaṇas[4] he is spoken of as the highest god. Once having attained supremacy, Viṣṇu would in the course of time be thought by the worshippers of Vāsudeva-Kṛṣṇa to be the same as their " God of gods," especially because of some winsome qualities in Viṣṇu's character. He is, for example, in the Ṛg-Veda, predominantly the friend and helper of Indra. This quality of helpfulness undoubtedly impressed the early worshippers, who began, it would seem, to think of Viṣṇu not only as a helper of Indra, but also as a helper of mankind. He is

[1] E. W. Hopkins, *Great Epic of India* p. 391. A. A. Macdonell, *Hist. of Sanskrit Literature*, p. 17.
[2] *Epigraphia Indica* Vol. X, inscription No. 669.
[3] Dr. Barnett's translation, *Hindu Gods and Heroes*, p. 88.
[4] Cf. Ait. Br. I. 1 ; Śat. Br. XIV. (1). 1.

accordingly said to have thrice traversed the earthly spaces for man in distress (R.V. VI. 49. 13), and in order to bestow it on man for a dwelling (R.V. VII. 100. 4; VI. 69. 5 and 6). He is spoken of as a protector of embryos (R.V. VII. 36. 9). In the Brāhmaṇas, he is said to have assumed the form of a Dwarf in order to gain dominion over the earth for the gods (Śat. Br. I. 2. 5), and in the Mahābhārata numerous stories are told of Viṣṇu's acts of grace and helpfulness, his assuming various incarnations in order to aid gods and men in distress.[1] It is not surprising that this god of helpfulness was gradually appropriated by the followers of Vāsudeva Kṛṣṇa, who according to the Bhagavadgītā also taught a God of grace, who repeatedly incarnates Himself.

Further, Viṣṇu was, if not earlier, certainly in the period of the Brāhmaṇas,[2] regarded by some as the Spirit of the Sun, and he has that characteristic in the Bhagavadgītā (cf. X. 21; XI. 30). When Viṣṇu was regarded as the Sun, it would be natural for the spiritual descendants of Ghora Āṅgirasa, a priest of the Sun, to worship him as their god. Indeed, it is possible that Ghora was himself a worshipper of Viṣṇu as the Sun, and consequently that the Vāsudeva-Kṛṣṇa cult was a sect which grew up within Viṣṇu-worship, and when it deified its leader Vāsudeva Kṛṣṇa identified him with the god whom he had preached.

In the period of the Brāhmaṇas, Viṣṇu was very definitely identified with the Sacrifice (Śat. Br. XIV. 1. 1, 1 ff., also I. 2. 5, 1 ff.). In the Bhagavadgītā, Kṛṣṇa identifies himself with the Principle of Sacrifice (*adhiyajña*) (VIII. 4), thus again showing the close affinity between the Viṣṇu-cult and the Vāsudeva-cult. If they were two, it is not surprising therefore that before long they became one. In the Anugītā, which

[1] E.g., Mah. Bh. III, 102, 8756 ff.

[2] Cf. the story about Āditya (sun) being Viṣṇu's head, Śat. Br. XIV (1). 1, 10. Viṣṇu is mentioned along with the Ādityas in A.V. XI (6). 2 but never in the Ṛgveda. See Bohtlingk Roth's Lexicon under *Āditya*.

claims to repeat[1] the message delivered by Kṛṣṇa to Arjuna in the Bhagavadgītā, and is hence later than the Bhagavadgītā, the identification, which we noted as first mentioned in the Bhagavadgītā, of Vāsudeva with Viṣṇu is complete, for the name most often used in the Anugītā for the Deity is Viṣṇu.

The third element which contributed to the development of Vaiṣṇavism was, it would appear, the worship of Nārāyaṇa. Nārāyaṇa with Nara is mentioned in some passages of the Mahābhārata[2] as an ascetic saint, and tradition alleges[3] that a certain sage, Nārāyaṇa, composed the famous Puruṣa Sūkta of Ṛg-Veda X. 90. Puruṣa Nārāyaṇa is said in Śatapatha Brāhmaṇa XII. 3. 4 to have sacrificed himself and become the whole world. Here it would seem that the followers of the sage Nārāyana had begun to deify him and to identify him with the Universal Puruṣa, from whose body he had taught that the universe sprang. Nārāyaṇa thus became the Universal Spirit,[4] and when the old stories of his great attachment to Nara were remembered and narrated, the parallelism of the friendship of Kṛṣṇa for Arjuna was striking, and it is repeatedly declared in the Mahābhārata that the Universal Spirit Nārāyaṇa is the same as the Supreme Being Vāsudeva Kṛṣṇa, and his comrade Nara is the same as Arjuna.[5]

Once this identification of Vāsudeva with Nārāyaṇa was made, ideas peculiar to the Nārāyaṇa cult would influence the further development of the Vāsudeva sect. And this is what we find. Puruṣa Nārāyaṇa is said in Śatapatha Brāhmaṇa XIII. 61 to have planned a Pāñcarātra Sattra or continued sacrifice for five days, and it is quite possible, as Dr. Schrader suggests,[6] that the central dogma of one section of the

[1] Cf. Aśvamedha Parva XVI. vs. 2-13, which are an introduction to the Anugītā.

[2] Cf. Mah. Bh. I. 230, 18; III. 12, 45; 47, 10; V. 48, 15, etc.

[3] Bhandarkar—*Vaiṣṇanism, Śaivism*, etc. p. 31.

[4] Cf. also Taitt. Ār. X. II.

[5] Cf., e.g., VI (23). 818; VI (66). 3004; (68). 3053, etc., etc.

[6] *Introduction to the Pāñcarātra*, etc., p. 25.

Vāsudeva cult, that God manifests Himself in a five-fold form, viz., in His *para* (supreme) *vyūha* (emanation), *vibhava* (incarnation), *antaryāmin* (inner self) and *arcā* (idol) forms, arose out of an effort to interpret philosophically the Pāñcarātra Sattra of Nārayaṇa; and that when this doctrine had been established those who upheld it came to be known as the Pāñcarātrins. It shows how the identification of Vāsudeva with Nārāyaṇa was the means of producing quite a distinctive theology within one section of the community.

Regarding the date when Vāsudeva was identified with Nārāyana and Viṣṇu, if we may judge from the passage in Taitt. Ār. X. 1. 6, in which hymns are addressed to Viṣṇu, Nārāyaṇa and Vāsudeva as three phases of one God, it would seem that such identification was being made about the third century B.C., which is regarded as the probable date of the passage.[1]

While ideas connected with Viṣṇu, Vāsudeva and Nārāyaṇa thus mingle together to form the religion of the Vaiṣṇavas up to about the opening of the Christian era, soon after the beginning of this era[2] an entirely new element is observable, which speaks of Kṛṣṇa as a cowherd, and dwells with great devotion on his birth, childhood, youth, amorous dalliances and feats of strength. It is possible that, as Bhandarkar thinks,[2] as Vaiṣṇavism spread, it came into contact with a pastoral tribe, the Ābhīras, who worshipped a cow-herd deity, whom now they identified with Vāsudeva-Kṛṣṇa. Stories connected with this deity accordingly flowed in and played a great part in the future development of Vaiṣṇavism, expressing itself in Purāṇic literature, and in an intensely emotional religion[3] which dwells on incidents connected with

[1] Berriedale Keith, J.R.A.S. 1915, p. 840; also Garbe, *Indien und das Christentum*, pp. 213, 265.

[2] Bhandarkar, *Vaiṣṇavism, Śaivism*, etc., pp. 35-38.

[3] Such, e.g., as the religion of the Āḷvārs, of whom we shall give an account later, and who were not characterised by the eroticism of some of the later sects.

the life of the cowherd, Kṛṣṇa Gopāla, and is at times led into eroticism by dwelling on his sport with the herdswomen.

Having thus traced briefly the main elements which during the centuries contributed to the distinctive features of Vaiṣṇavism, we may proceed to examine some typical Vaiṣṇava literature prior to Rāmānuja in order to elicit from it some characteristic views which it developed regarding the Deity. We shall confine ourselves to the Nārāyaṇīya and the Anugītā[1] sections of the Mahābhārata, the early Pāñcarātra Saṁhitās, and the Viṣṇu and Bhāgavata Purāṇas. Their theology is developed in the light of the prevalent philosophies of the day, and these are, in the main, the advaitism of some Upaniṣads and the Sāṁkhya-Yoga. Our aim will be to focus on ideas distinctive of this literature rather than to give an exhaustive account which would not only involve repeating ideas already mentioned in connection with the Upaniṣads and the Bhagavadgītā, but would clearly also carry us too far afield.

1. *The Nature of the Deity.*

The qualities which are predicated of the Divine Being in these writings are essentially the same as those mentioned in the Bhagavadgītā ; this is only to be expected, for these writings are the work of men who belonged to the same religious cult as the author of the Gītā, and like him were seeking to express their view of the Deity in the language of the then prevailing philosophical schools.

Like the Gītā, they regard the Supreme Being as having a transcendent nature which must be declared to be incomprehensible and past human understanding.

[1] Nārāyaṇīya and Anugītā probably belong to a period between 200 B.C. and A.D. 200, according to Farquhar (O.R.L.I., p. 45). The older Saṁhitās, according to Dr. Schrader, must have been earlier than the 8th cent. A.D. (*Introd. to the Pāñcarātra* p. 19) ; Farquhar assigns them to A.D. 600-800 (O.R.L.I., p. 182). The Viṣṇu Purāṇa is dated by Farquhar as not later than A.D. 400, and the Bhāgavata Purāṇa as not later than A.D. 900 (O.R.L.I., p. 143 and p. 232).

The Nārāyaṇīya says of Him that He is one whose motions are infinite, whose bodies are infinite, who is without end and without beginning, and without middle, whose middle is unmanifest, whose end is unmanifest . . . who is beyond the ken of logic or argument, who is unknowable" (339. 4).[1] He is described at times in terms which recall the language of the Upaniṣads: "He that cannot be seen with the eye, touched with the sense of touch, smelt with the sense of scent, and that is beyond the ken of the sense of taste" (340. 21). Similarly the Anugītā declares that "He is without symbols and qualities" (34. 5),[2] and that it is only those who lack proper understanding who "regard that entity, through their own ignorance, as invested with the properties of knowledge and others" (34. 6). The Saṁhitās, likewise, recognise the transcendent aspect of the Deity, but just because it is transcendent and unknowable, they quite consistently make little effort to describe it, but deal only, and, in general, very fully, as we shall see, with the Supreme Being as He stands in relation to the universe—His transcendent nature remaining always in the background. The Viṣṇu and Bhāgavata Purāṇas also are not lacking in passages which describe the Deity as beyond human thought.[3]

While recognising thus the transcendent and unknowable aspect of the Deity, emphasized so much by philosophers, their own distinctive view seems to be that the Deity may be known by his devotees. Thus most of the passages above cited occur in contexts which reveal a great deal of knowledge of the nature of the Deity—this fuller knowledge being regarded in

[1] Quotations from the Nārāyaṇīya are taken throughout from P. C. Ray's translation of the Mahābhārata Vol. 12 *Śānti Parva*.

[2] Quotations from the Anugītā are also taken from the same author's translation, Vol. 14 *Aśvamedha Parva*.

[3] Viṣṇu Purāṇa I. 2; I. 9, p. 40; I. 14, pp. 71 and 72; I.20, p. 101; Bhāg. P IV. 9, p. 44; 11. p. 54; IV. 24, pp. 108, 111, etc. Quotations which follow are taken from M. N. Dutt's translation of these two Purāṇas in the *Wealth of India*, Volumes I, II and III, and the pages cited refer to pages in this work.

these writings as directly bequeathed to the devotee by the Supreme Being Himself. It is true that He may not be known by the natural processes of sense and understanding as the passages above cited declare; but what is hidden from the cold reasonings of philosophers is revealed, it would appear, to devout worshippers. This truth that the Deity reveals Himself to those who are devoted to Him is taught by means of many illustrative instances in the Nārāyaṇīya. The Deity "incapable of being seen by anyone else . . . showed Himself to His worshipper," king Uparichara (337. 12);[1] but He was invisible to the priest Bṛhaspati; who performed the great Aśvamedha Sacrifice. On the priest becoming indignant at this, he was told that "He (God) is incapable of being seen either by ourselves or by thee, O Bṛhaspati'! Only he can see Him to whom He becomes gracious" (337. 19). Ekata, Dvita and Trita practised austerities for four thousand years: but were sent away without a vision of the Deity, with the message: "That Great Deity is incapable of ever being seen by one that is destitute of devotion. (He) can be seen only by those persons that . . . succeed in devoting themselves wholly and solely to Him" (337. 52 and 53). The Deity, then, though transcendent, is not past human grasp.

These writers, however, are so eager to identify their Deity with the Supreme One of the philosophers, that the Deity when He reveals Himself is made to say, "I am known as Puruṣa. Without acts, I am the Twenty-fifth. Transcending attributes, I am entire and indivisible. I am above all pairs of attributes and freed from all attachments" (340. 42 ff.). They are eager to identify Him with everything which symbolises greatness and perfection; for example, with the Lords of creation with the four-headed

[1] This is a reference to the Nārāyaṇīya which forms sections 336 ff. of the *Śānti Parva* of the Mahābhārata. In what follows, references to the Nārāyaṇīya, will not be indicated by name, but may be recognised by the fact that the number of its sections always falls between 336 and 360.

Brahman, with the Sun, with the Emperor or the king, with Indra and Varuṇa, with the sacrifices and Vedic studies, with the Sāṁkhya-Yoga, with the syllable Om, with Yogic perfections and such like (339).[1] But merely to regard the Deity as thus identical with what is high and significant does not throw light on the individual perfections which constitute His nature. It is these that we shall now seek to discover.

Besides what we might call "natural" perfections such as infinitude, eternity, unchangeability, omnipotence, and omnipresence, which the Deity may be expected to have as the Supreme Being of the philosophers, He has also, it would seem, "spiritual" perfections which may be classified as knowledge, beauty and goodness.

That Brahman is Thought or the principle of Intelligence was, as we saw, one of the main doctrines of Upaniṣadic philosophy. That is always retained. He is spoken of as "only mind," as "Lord of Speech," as "the embodiment of correctness of judgment or reasoning," as identifiable with the wisdom of the Sāṁkhya-Yoga (339. 4), as "the Preceptor of the universe" (340. 43),[2] "the highest Intelligence" (Anugītā 52. 12). In the Saṁhitās, *jñāna* or wisdom is spoken of as not merely an attribute of the Supreme Being, but as constituting His very essence,[3] and the Nārāyaṇīya, declares that when all things have perished, knowledge remains as the sole companion of the Deity (340. 69).

The beauty of the Deity is indescribable and can be suggested only by means of inadequate analogies. "He resembled in some respects the feathers of a parrot, and in some a mass of pure crystal. He resembled in some respects a hill of antimony and in some a mass of pure gold. His complexion somewhat

[1] Cf. also Anugītā 54 (7). 10; Viṣṇu Purāṇa I. 8. pp. 35 and 36; 9. p. 42 Bhāgavata Purāṇa II. 5. p. 17; XI. 16. pp. 62 and 63.

[2] Cf. also Bhāgavata Purāṇa VIII. 7. p. 26.

[3] Schrader *Introduction to the Pāñcarātra*. p. 33; cf. also Viṣṇu Purāṇa I. 20. p. 101.

resembled the coral when first formed. In some respects it resembled the hue of the blue *lapis lazuli* and in some that of sapphire. In some respects it resembled the hue of the peacock's neck, and in some that of a string of pearls. He had a thousand eyes and was possessed of great beauty" (340. 3-6). The Anugītā declares, "The stainless lunar light is thy smile. O thou of eyes like the (petals of the) lotus" (52. 11 and 14), and adds that the beauty of creatures is really the beauty of the Deity Himself (52. 13). The Purāṇas abound in passages which describe the incomparable beauty of the Lord.[1]

The ethical perfection of the Deity is proclaimed in no less mistakable terms. If earthly morality consists in performance of vows and ceremonies and in Yogic restraint, the Deity is perfect in these for He "has completed all the vows and ceremonies mentioned in the Vedas" (339. 4). He practises the "severe and flawless vow of Brahmacārya" (Bhāgavata Purāṇa I. 3, p. 7). He is "the embodiment of one who has not fallen away from Yoga" (339. 4). *Dharma* is His "eldest born offspring" (Anugītā 54. 11). He establishes laws, and in order to set the standard for men, conforms to them Himself. "The ordinances I set are followed by all the worlds. Those ordinances should always be adored, and it is therefore, that I adore them" (342. 25). The Anugītā declares, "*Puruṣa* is dependent on goodness . . . the wise believe in the identity of *Puruṣa* and goodness. There is no doubt in this" (48. 7 and 9.[2] Even the very names of the Deity have a sanctifying and cleansing power (342. 2). The Deity Himself declares, "I have never uttered anything base or anything that is obscene. The divine Sarasvati who is Truth's self, and is otherwise called by the name of Ṛta, represents my speech and always dwells in my tongue"

[1] Cf. Viṣṇu P. VI p. 457; Bhāgavata P. III. 8, pp. 38 and 39; 15. pp. 78 and 79; III. 28 pp. 134-136, etc.

[2] Cf. also Bhāgavata P. IV. 3, p. 12; Viṣṇu P. III. 7, p. 189; 8, pp. 191-3.

(343. 73). "I have never swerved from the attribute of Sattva (goodness)" (343. 75). "I always hear words that are pure and holy, O Dhanaṁjaya, and never catch anything that is sinful. Hence I am called by the name of Śuciśravas" (343. 89). The discourse of the Deity being ended the narrator exclaims, "there is nothing holier on earth or in heaven, and nothing higher than Nārāyaṇa. Having listened to this discourse, we feel that we have been cleansed of all our sins and sanctified entirely" (344. 16 and 17).[1]

The perfection of the Deity consists, it would appear, not merely in such Righteousness which expresses itself in moral laws and institutions, and is strongly opposed to sin, but in Love which shows infinite tenderness and grace to the sinner. The quality of friendly helpfulness was, as we saw, the characteristic of Viṣṇu, even in Ṛg Vedic times, where he appears as a friend of Indra, helping him in his battles. So also in the Mahābhārata, as we noted, as Kṛṣṇa he appears as the special friend of Arjuna, and as Nārāyaṇa, the special friend of Nara. This quality of the Deity as a friend and companion, helping whom He will, becomes ever more prominent in the writings of the Vaiṣṇavas, till, as we shall see, it forms the one theme on which the Āḻvārs love to dwell. In the Nārāyaṇīya and in the Purāṇas the grace and protecting care of the Deity are the theme of many a passage. "Through Nārāyaṇa's grace" king Vasu ascended to heaven, "to a spot that is even higher than the region of Brahman himself" (337. 61, 62), and by His grace the king was rescued when cast from heaven by a curse of the Ṛṣis (339). The Deity is the "grantor of every wish" (339. 4).[2] His "troops go everywhere for protecting His worshippers" (339. 4).[3] He is "kind to all His worshippers," "fond

[1] Cf. also Bhāgavata P. I. 16, p. 69; Viṣṇu P. III. 7, pp. 188 and 189.
[2] Cf. also Viṣṇu P. I. 12, p. 61.
[3] Bhāg. P. II. 9, p. 38; Viṣṇu P. I. 22, p. 107.

of them," "ever affectionate towards them" (339. 4; 344. 53 and 54).[1] He is "the greatest friend" (339. 4),[2] and "the one sole Refuge of all men" (342. 39).[3] "He dispels the fears of all persons" (347. 17). From Him "springs the attribute of forgiveness" (345. 6).[4] He removes the misery of the humble (Viṣṇu P. I. 9, p. 39). He is "the abode of wonderful grace" (Viṣṇu P. I. 9, p. 43). He is "running over with mercy" (Bhāg. VIII. 3, p. 9).[5]

The Deity that is disclosed in these writings, if one pierces behind the veil of philosophical language which is used to describe His nature, is an Infinite and transcendent Being who is characterised by knowledge, and even more especially, by beauty, goodness and love.

2. *The Relation of the Deity to the world.*

In the writings with which we are here concerned the universe, with all the celestial and terrestrial beings of which it consists, is not regarded as an illusion arising from ignorance, as the Advaitins hold, but as a real something which needs to be explained in relation to the Divine Being.[6] Consequently numerous theories are put forward to show how the universe came from the Deity. We shall not attempt to deal with them all for most of them either adopt the Sāṁkhyan cosmology,[7] to which we have already referred in connection with the Bhagavadgītā, and

[1] Cf. Bhāg. P. III. 9, p. 43.
[2] Bhāg. P. I. 2, p. 5.
[3] Viṣṇu P. I. 22, p. 111.
[4] Bhāg. P. VI. 3, p. 15.
[5] Viṣṇu P. I. 20, p. 102.
[6] No effort is made in these writings either to assert or refute the doctrine of *Māyā* (illusion), but throughout a realistic attitude to the universe is maintained. Regarding the Saṁhitās, Dr. Schrader remarks that "illusionism (*māyā-vāda*) is altogether absent from them." (*Introduction to the Pāñcarātra*, p. 93.) In the Bhāgavata Purāṇa the Universe is regarded as a manifestation of the illusory power of the Supreme Being, but not as itself an illusion. The Deity is said sportively to assume the diverse shapes of the universe by virtue of His illusory power. (See II. 5; 10; III. 5; IV. 17, etc.)
[7] For Sāṁkhyan accounts, see Nārāyaṇīya 340. 24. 32; Anugītā. 18. 24-27; 35. 19-23; 40; 42. 2; 50. 34-56. Viṣṇu P. I. 2.; Bhāg P. II. 5; III. 5; 26 and 27; XI. 24.

regard the universe as emanating principle by principle as in the Sāṁkhya, from *Prakṛti*, which, however, they regard as contained in the Supreme Being and controlled by Him; or they adopt fanciful mythological accounts of creation.[1] To gain some idea of the cosmology distinctive of this cult, we must turn to the Pāñcarātra section of the Vaiṣṇavas. Its doctrines are found in germ in the theory of *Vyūhas* (emanations) mentioned in the Nārāyaṇīya, and come to be very fully elaborated in the Pāñcarātra Saṁhitās.

In the Nārāyaṇīya (340. 33-41) we are told that the Supreme Being exists as Vāsudeva, and in creating the Universe enters into union with earth, wind, space, water, and light, the five primal elements, and in combination with these appears as Jīva (embodied soul) and is called Śeṣa or Saṁkarṣaṇa. By Saṁkarṣaṇa's spontaneous act, there evolves from him Pradyumna, who is the Mind of all creatures and into whom all creatures merge at a dissolution. From Him again arises Aniruddha, who is consciousness. He is the creator who creates all things in the universe. Thus the Supreme Being does not Himself create, but goes through a series of emanations till Aniruddha the creator appears. Aniruddha creates but the Supreme Being underlies the whole process (340. 41).[2]

The doctrine of the Saṁhitās is much more elaborate. Here[3] Nārāyaṇa is regarded as dwelling for timeless

[1] For mythological accounts, see Nārāyaṇīya 341. 72-101; 350. 16-61. Viṣṇu P. I. 4; I. 5-7. Bhāgavata P. II. 10; III. 12.

[2] It must be noted that the four forms here enumerated, Vāsudeva, Saṁkarṣaṇa Pradyumna and Aniruddha, were not always recognised in this cult. The Nārāyaṇīya itself says so (349. 57), and this is attested also by inscriptions. Thus the Ghosundi inscription (about 150 B.C. *Epigraphia Indica* XVI p. 25) and the Nānāghat inscription (about 100 B.C., *Archaeological Survey of Western India*, pp. 60 f.) mention only two forms, Vāsudeva and Saṁkarṣaṇa. This fact suggests that originally only Vāsudeva (Kṛṣṇa) and Saṁkarṣaṇa (Baladeva, Kṛṣṇa's brother) were recognised, and afterwards when, as Dr. Schrader suggests, "this original, non-Brahmanic Pāñcarātra was to be brought into agreement with the Veda and the famous saying of the Puruṣa Sūkta (fourth stanza) about the four quarters of God, one of which only had become the world, two more members of the family of Kṛṣṇa, namely his son and grandson were deified, that is, made aspects of God," and we thus obtain the four *vyūhas*. *Introd. to Pāñcarātra*, pp. 144 and 145.

[3] I give a summary of the very able account given by Dr. Schrader in his *Introduction to the Pāñcarātra*.

ages in His transcendent form, till the creative aspect of Himself, His Śakti, spoken of figuratively as His consort Lakṣmī, awakens, as it were by His command, and with an infinitely small part of herself appears in her dual aspect of *kriyā* (acting) and *bhūti* becoming), that is, as formal and material cause. At this stage, Nārāyaṇa passes from His transcendent and undifferentiated form and comes to be characterised by six *guṇas* or attributes, which are necessary for creation. These attributes are *jñāna* (knowledge), *aiśvarya* (lordship), *śakti* (ability), *bala* (strength), *vīrya* (virility), and *tejas* (splendour). As possessed of these attributes and as distinct from His Śakti, the Supreme Being is called Vāsudeva. This may be called the first *Vyūha* or emanation from the Supreme Being.

From Vāsudeva, characterised thus by six attributes, emanates Saṁkarṣaṇa. Two only of the six attributes are manifest at this stage, although the Supreme Being Himself is present with His six attributes in this as in all the other stages of evolution. The two attributes which are manifest in this stage are *jñāna* and *bala*, and "non-pure"[1] creation becomes dimly manifest in an embryonic condition. From Saṁkarṣaṇa comes Pradyumna, where the duality of *Puruṣa* and *Prakṛti* makes its appearance, i.e., the Group-Soul called *Kūṭastha Puruṣa*, which is the primordial form of all finite souls in the mass, and *Māyā Śakti* or Primordial matter. The two attributes that function at this stage are *aiśvarya* and *vīrya*. The *Kūṭastha Puruṣa* begins now to have within itself the sources of the four orders of man (i.e., the four castes), and *Māyā Śakti* now manifests itself in two forms, the *Guṇa*-body (usually recognised as *Prakṛti* in Sāṁkhya philosophy), consisting of the three *guṇas*, *sattva*, *rajas* and *tamas*, and the Time-body, consisting of

[1] Non-pure creation is the creation of the universe as we know it. Pure creation consists of Vāsudeva and His Śakti, the Vyūhas, the Avatāras (incarnations) and Vaikuṇṭha (Heaven with all the heavenly beings and objects).

Kāla (Time) and its subtle cause, *Niyati* (Restriction). These, viz., the *Kūṭastha Puruṣa* and the threefold *Māyā Śakti*, are now transferred by Pradyumna to the last *Vyūha*, Aniruddha. The two attributes which appertain to Aniruddha are *vīrya* and *tejas*. At this stage the *Kūṭastha Puruṣa* enters into the material elements, one by one, as they emerge from Aniruddha in succession; first *Māyā Śakti*, from *Māyā Śakti Niyati*, from *Niyati Kāla*, from *Kāla Sattva*, from *Sattva Rajas*, and from *Rajas Tamas*. In the process of entering into each of these *Tattvas* (elements), the Manus, of which the *Kūṭastha Puruṣa* is composed, appropriate successively the individual faculty which each of these *Tattvas* is capable of bestowing. When the *Kūṭastha Puruṣa* has entered the last of the material principles, viz., *Tamas*, the three *guṇas* unite to form an undifferentiated mass called *Avyakta* (unmanifest) or *Mūlaprakṛti*; and after that, evolution proceeds much as in Sāṁkhyan philosophy by the mutual relation of *Puruṣa* and *Prakṛti*, with this difference, however, that in the Saṁhitās the process is regarded as being influenced by a third principle, viz., Time,[1] and only one *Puruṣa* is recognised at this stage. From *Avyakta* proceeds *Mahat*, and from *Mahat Ahaṁkāra*, which endows the Manus of which the *Kūṭastha Puruṣa* is composed with individuality (*ahaṁkāra*), mind (*manas*) and the ten organs (five of sense, and five of action), and corresponding with these the ten elements of the material universe. Once these various existences have come about, they are massed together into a Cosmic Egg; from which Brahmā the creator is born, and from him descend all things movable and stationary.

There are many divergences in detail in different Saṁhitās, but the main stages in the evolution of the universe from the Supreme Being seem to be as

[1] In the Viṣṇu and Bhāgavata Purāṇas also, Time always occurs as a third principle besides *Puruṣa* and *Prakṛti*; cf. Vis: P. I. 2; Bhāg. P. II. 5; III. 5; 26; 27; XI. 24.

described above, and serve to indicate how complicated the doctrine of the four *Vyūhas*,[1] mentioned in the Nārāyaṇīya, became in this section of the Vaiṣṇava community.

Full of suggestion and interest as are the details in this theory of the evolution of the universe from the Supreme Being, we must now pass on to consider what significance this and other theories of creation found in the writings with which we are here concerned, have for a view regarding the relationship in which the Deity stands to the Universe.

All our writings agree, we noticed, in regarding creation as an evolution or development from one stage to another, either according to the Sāṁkhyan enumeration of principles, or according to the Pāñcarātra doctrine of *Vyūhas*. The chief merit of this theory, and hence its primary significance, is that according to it creation is " a process which, while bringing the product into existence, leaves the source of the product unchanged."[2] The Deity is thus regarded as being quite unaffected by the changes which are necessary to bring about the universe. He is the unchanging One, who though unchanging is the explanation of all change. Further, the many stages which are postulated between God and the universe seem to make less difficult the transition from God to a universe, which is so different from Him in character. In this way, an effort is made to relate to the Deity a world which appears far removed from Him in nature, and we seem able to understand how " as the light and

[1] As already said, the doctrine of the *Vyūhas* does not occur in the Bhagavadgītā, nor in the Anugītā. In the Viṣṇu Purāṇa, the names of the four *Vyūhas* appear only as the names of Kṛṣṇa and members of his family (cf. Viṣ. P. V). They occur in the same way also in the Bhāgavata Purāṇa Book X. But often in this Purāṇa the Deity is greeted as having the four forms of Vāsudeva, Saṁkarṣaṇa, Pradyumna and Aniruddha; but what the Deity is or does under these forms is not elaborated (cf. I. 5, p. 18; VI. 16, p. 69; X. 40, p. 182; XI. 5, p. 20; XII. 11) except in one passage, IV. 24, p. 108, where Vāsudeva is equated with the trancendent, Saṁkarṣaṇa with the subtle, Pradyumna with the understanding and Aniruddha with mind.

[2] J. C. Chatterji—*Kashmir Śaivism*, p. 59.

heat are stronger or feebler proportionate to the distance of the spot, so the energy of Brahman is more or less manifest in beings as they are more or less remote from Him " (Viṣṇu Purāṇa I. 22, p. 110).

The same desire to preserve the purity and unchanged nature of the Supreme Being in relation to the changing universe gives rise to the view in the Saṁhitās that it is not the Supreme Being who is responsible for creation, sustenance and absorption of the universe, but His Śakti. Śakti thus, in the Saṁhitās, practically usurps the place of the Deity in relation to the universe, being in one aspect of Herself, as we saw, both the material (*bhūti*) as well as the instrumental (*kriyā*) cause of the universe. But she is prevented from becoming the Deity by the fact that she is always regarded as subordinate to the Supreme Being.[1] What exactly her relation to the Transcendent One is, is not very clear, for although she is personified as Śrī or Lakṣmī, the wife of Viṣṇu, she seems to be understood only as an aspect of the Supreme One, and not as a distinct person, for she is said to be related to the Deity as a quality (*dharma*) is to its subject (*dharmin*) or as sunshine is to sun, that is, as attribute to substance (cf. Ahirbudhnya Saṁhitā IV and Lakṣmi Tantra II. 2 ff.). And yet, in order to preserve the transcendent character of Viṣṇu, Laksmī is also regarded as a principle eternally distinct from the Deity. As Dr. Schrader remarks, " in spite of frequent assurances as to the real identity of Laksmī and Viṣṇu, the two are actually regarded as distinct : even in *Pralaya* they do not completely coalesce but become only ' as it were ' a single principle (Ahir. Saṁ. IV. 78), the Lakṣmi eventually emerging from the Great Night being the old Lakṣmī, not a new one." " Still," he concludes, " the dualism is, strictly speaking, a makeshift for preserving the transcendent character of Viṣṇu : Lakṣmī alone acts, but everything she does is the mere expression of the Lord's wishes "

[1] Cf. *Introduction to the Pāñcarātra*, pp. 29 and 30—Schrader.

(*Introd. to the Pāñcarātra*, p. 30). Thus it would seem that the Supreme Being is related to the universe through one aspect of Himself, viz., His Śakti, which, however, is so eternally distinct from His own Supreme nature that, though engaged in creating, sustaining and absorbing the universe, it leaves His essential nature unchanged.[1]

A similar desire to preserve the Divine transcendence and perfection which seem incompatible with His being an active agent in relation to the universe, gives rise to the mythological account, in the Nārāyaṇīya and in the Purāṇas, that the Deity Himself does not do this work, but commissions Brahmā, who spontaneously rises out of Him,[2] to create and superintend the universe. To preserve the supremacy of the Deity, Brahmā is regarded as obtaining from the Divine Being the intelligence necessary for his task,[3] as well as his great commission which is dramatically expressed in the Nārāyaṇīya thus: "Do thou, O Brahman, duly think of the courses of acts which creatures are to follow. Thou art the great ordainer of all created beings. Thou art the master and lord of the universe. Placing this burden on thee, I shall be free from anxiety" (Nārāy. 341. 89; Bhāg. P. 8, pp. 44-46). And we are told that "Having unveiled to the Creator of the cosmos the objects that had to be evolved, that Prime Person furnished with a lotus-navel vanished in His native form" (Bhāg. P. 8, p. 46), and adopted the course of actionless *Nivṛtti* (Nārāy. 340, 64 and 65), or Yogic sleep (348, 45 and 46).

[1] In the Viṣṇu Purāṇa, Śrī is invoked as "the Mother of all beings" and as "the bestower of the fruit of emancipation" (cf. I. 9, p. 46) which seem to suggest the Saṁhitā doctrine of Śrī as the creative principle, and also the later Vaiṣṇava doctrine of Śrī as an intermediary in the matter of salvation. But generally both in this Purāṇa as well as in the Bhāgavata Purāṇā, Śrī is not a philosophical principle, but only the consort of Viṣṇu. See Viṣ. P. I. 8 and 9, Bhāg. P. II. 2, p. 6; 9, p. 37; VIII. 8.

[2] Mythologically Brahmā is said to arise from a lotus which springs out of the navel of Viṣṇu as He reposes on a serpent on the primeval waters. Bhāg. P. III. 8, pp. 36 and 37; cf. also, Viṣṇu P. I. 2, p. 11.

[3] Cf. Nārāyaṇīya, 350. 16-27; Bhāg. P. III. 8, pp. 36 and 37, also II. 5 and 6.

However, this way of overcoming the difficulty, though seemingly satisfactory, is really no solution to the problem at all, for it is asserted that Brahmā, who creates and superintends the universe, is after all none other than the Supreme Being Himself. "The same transcendent Lord, assuming the three qualities of matter—purity, energy and dulness—wears for the purposes of creation, preservation and destruction, the different designations of Hari, Virinci (Brahman) and Hara" (Bhag. P. I. 2, p. 6), and Brahmā, speaking to an enquirer, declares, "Myself thyself . . . and all other creatures . . . are the manifestations of that *Puruṣa*. . . . As the sun illumines its own orbit as well as the outer world, so the universal form of the Great God manifests itself and exhibits all inner and outer objects" (Bhāg. P. II. 6, p. 21).

All these theories of evolution, of *Vyūhas*, of Śakti, and of the creator-Brahmā, are, it would seem, attempts made by these thinkers to relate the Supreme Being to the universe. In so far as the mediating principles were regarded as distinct from the Supreme Being, they served to bridge the gulf between God and the world; but when it was realised that they could not be regarded as really distinct for then the problem arose of explaining the relation of the Deity to them, they were immediately declared to be none other than the Deity Himself in one or other of His aspects. Their double nature was accordingly their chief merit. The elaboration of such principles shows how realistically the universe was conceived by these thinkers, and how they sought to relate it to the Deity, without thereby detracting from the transcendence and perfection of the Supreme Being.

3. *The Relation of the Deity to the finite self.*

Although these writings adopt, as we have seen, a realistic attitude towards the universe, they seem to be influenced a great deal by Advaitism in their view regarding the relation of the Deity to the finite self. At times they seem to teach that the Deity has Himself entered into numerous bodies, and exists in them as the finite self, there being no finite self in the body beyond Him. Thus completely identifying the individual self with the Supreme, the Anugītā describes death as a case of Brahman leaving the body: "Deserted by Brahman the person is said to be dead" (17. 24).[1] The Saṁhitās, although much less advaitic in tendency than the Anugītā, are, as Dr. Schrader points out,[2] not altogether free from advaitic passages. The Lakṣmī Tantra declares that "the *ātman* of the *Para* and the *Kṣetrajña* are one" (I. VI. 15).[3] "As the *ākāśa* in a pot moves when the pot is moved, truly there is no difference between the *Para* and the *Jīva*" (I. VI. 20).[3] Even the Purāṇas at times speak in a similar manner. Thus Prahlāda, persecuted for being a worshipper of Viṣṇu, triumphantly exclaims, "Salutation again and again unto Viṣṇu, in whom all things exist. . . . Salutation to Him who also am I. . . . I am all things and all things are from me who am eternal. I am undecaying, eternal, the Asylum of the Supreme Spirit. Brahma is my appelation, that is at the beginning and end of all things."[4]

While these thinkers tend thus at times to blur all distinction between the Deity and the individual

[1] Note also the manner in which the soul is regarded as attaining release viz., by suppressing all its qualities till it passes into the Brahman-state of being free from attributes (Anugītā 19. 11-14, 19-26; 42. 48-50; 51. 25-35). It would appear that the individual self is Brahman suffering births and deaths because of attachment to the body, and when this attachment is cut off, the individual becomes the Infinite Brahman that he always was (31. 8-14) "Merging themselves in their souls (men) succeed in attaining to Brahman" (27. 22). The released one declares as though he were himself Brahman, "By me is pervaded everything that exists in this universe" (33. 2), and he instructs his enquirer, "with thy heart intent upon the Real entity, it is my soul into which thou wilt come" (33. 8). In a similar vein it is asserted that "He that knows him (viz., the released person) knows the Veda" (51. 27).

[2] *Introd. to the Pāñcarātra*, p. 49, footnote 3; cf. also pp. 91 and 123; chapter 31 of Ahirbudhnya Saṁhitā.

[3] Quoted in P. T. Śrīnivāsa Aiyaṅgār's *Outlines of Indian Philosophy*, pp. 184 and 185.

[4] Viṣṇu Purāṇa, I. 19, p. 100; cf. also VI. 7, p. 458; Bhāg. P. IV. 22, p. 97; XI. 3, p. 9.

they seem on the whole, as will be evident from what follows, to distinguish between the Supreme and the individual self, and to indicate how the two are related to each other. We shall seek to describe the relation in which in these writings the Deity is conceived to stand to the finite self in the three forms of its existence, that is, prior to *saṁsāra*, in embodied form, and in Release.

The Nārāyaṇīya and the Anugītā say nothing about the existence of souls prior to *saṁsāra*. The Saṁhitās, on the other hand, incline to the view that souls exist eternally, and therefore prior to creation, in a subtle form within the Deity in one of His aspects. According to them, souls and the objects of the universe form an eternal part of Bhūti Śakti, which is one aspect of Lakṣmī, and Bhūti Śakti is said, by way of contrast with Kriyā Śakti which is "undivided" (*niṣkala*), to be divided in many ways (*nānābhedavatī*)[1]—which would seem to indicate that the plurality of the universe is retained in a subtle form in it. Consistently with this, Lakṣmī, to whom Bhūti Śakti belongs, declares that prior to creation, she exists as inseparably one with the Deity "with all the world taken into her lap,"[2] and adds, "All *jīvas* are established in me; all of them are in me." Similarly the *Kūṭastha Puruṣa*, which exists prior to gross creation as that from which souls come into embodied existence, and that into which *karma*-bound souls pass at the dissolution of the universe, is described in the Ahirbudhnya Saṁhitā as "an aggregate of souls, similar to a bee-hive, the pure-impure condition of Bhūti—such is the *Puruṣa* piled up by souls blunted by beginningless Germ-impressions (*vāsanā*)" (VI. 33-34).[3] The Bhāgavata and Viṣṇu Purāṇas also

[1] Ahirbudhnya Saṁhitā, Ch. XIV. 9; cf. V. 9-11; Schrader, *Introd. to Pāñcarātra*, p. 30, and footnote 5 on the same page; also p. 114.

[2] Cf. Lakṣmī Tantra, II. 12-35, XIII. 18-29, quoted in P. T. Śrīnivāsa Aiyaṅgār, *Outlines of Indian Philosophy*; also Schrader, *Introd. to Pāñcarātra*, p. 86.

[3] Dr. Schrader's translation in the *Introd. to the Pāñcarātra*, p. 69; cf. also Lakṣmī Tantra, VII. 11-12.

assert that the Deity contains all souls within Himself in a subtle form prior to creation. "When this universe was under waters at the time of dissolution, the Deity alone reposed on His mighty serpent couch; His eyes were closed though He did not do away with the power of understanding. . . . And although He had placed within His person all incorporeal bodies, He sent the energy of Time to arouse Him again at the time of creation. . . . Sleeping for four *yūgas*, and thousands of years with His own created energy He espied within His person all those creatures."[1] According to this view, then, the soul exists even prior to creation, as something eternally distinct, although it exists only in the Supreme Being and is completely dependent on Him.

In the second stage of existence above distinguished, viz., as embodied creature, it would appear that the individual self is pervaded by the Supreme Being as its soul or principle of consciousness. So much is the Deity regarded as the soul of embodied individuals, that, as already indicated, He seems at times to usurp the place of the individual self. Nevertheless the fact that the embodied self suffers from many evils seems to have prevented them from completely identifying the individual with the Supreme Self. Thus the Anugītā, which, as we have noticed, is often advaitic in tone, speaks in the language of the Svetāśvatara of a triad, when it is faced with the unintelligent and sinful nature of the embodied creature. "There are the two birds which are immutable, which are friends, and which should be known as unintelligent. That other which is different from these two is called the Intelligent. When the inner self which is destitute of knowledge of Nature, which is unintelligent, becomes conversant with that which is above Nature, then understanding that *Kṣetra* and endued with an intelligence which transcends all

[1] Bhāg. P. III. 8, pp. 36 and 37; cf. also Viṣṇu P. I. 12, p. 59.

qualities and apprehends everything, (it) becomes released from all sins" (47. 16 and 17).

In the Saṁhitās, the difference of the embodied self from the Supreme Being is so clearly preceived that, as we have seen, the individual in his embodied form is regarded as derivable from the Supreme Being only after a long series of emanations, during which he acquires step by step the properties of matter, and thus becomes further and further removed from the nature of the Supreme Self. How different from the Deity the individual thus becomes is seen from the three "taints" with which he is now afflicted, with regard to his form, power and knowledge: (1) atomicity as compared with the omnipresence of the Deity, (2) impotence as compared with Divine omnipotence, and (3) ignorance as compared with His perfect knowledge.[1] Besides, the individual is subject to passions arising from the *Guṇas*, of which the Deity is characteristically free; hence a special "descent" of the Supreme Being into the embodied individual becomes necessary, and we are told that the Deity by a special incarnation descends into the lotus of the heart and takes His abode there as *Antaryāmin* or Inner Ruler.[2]

Not only the Saṁhitās and the Anugītā, but also the other writings[3] with which we are here concerned regard the embodied individual as suffering from imperfections; and the problem has therefore to be faced in what relation the Deity stands to these imperfections if He exists within the individual as his Soul. As usual in Indian thought, the imperfections of the embodied being are declared to be not in any way due to the Deity who resides within it, and in seeking to understand how the Divine principle may exist in the individual without being responsible for

[1] Cf. Ahirbudhunya Saṁhitā XIV. Schrader, *Introd. to the Pāñcarātra*, p. 115.

[2] Schrader, *Introd. to the Pāñcarātra*, p. 49.

[3] Cf., e.g., Nārāyaṇīya, 349. 76-8; Viṣṇu P. VI. 5, pp. 440-4; Bhāg. P. III. 9, p. 41; 27, pp. 29-32.

these imperfections, recourse is had to the Sāṁkkyan conception of the *Puruṣa*, who is Spectator or Witness merely and not Agent. "The one *Puruṣa* . . . transcends all *puruṣas* and is invisible. The many *puruṣas* that exist in the universe constitute the basis upon which that one *Puruṣa* stands. Though divested of body, He dwells in every body. Though dwelling again in bodies, He is never touched by the acts accomplished by those bodies. He is my inner Soul. He is thy inner Soul. He is the all-seeing Witness dwelling within all embodied creatures and engaged in marking their acts.[1]

The Saṁhitās also free the Supreme Soul from all responsibility for the evil that characterises the life of the individual. In their view disease and other evils suffered by the embodied individual are always due to sins committed by him in former lives,[2] not to the Deity. In this manner those thinkers maintain that though the Supreme Being exists within the individual, He does not share in its evil nature nor is He responsible for it.

While then in relation to the evil which characterises embodied souls, the Deity exists merely as Spectator, His relation to embodied souls themselves is not one of passivity or indifference, but one[3] of intense active interest and love. Accordingly He lays aside His Supreme form when necessary and assuming finite form enters the world for their benefit. The doctrine of incarnation is very fully elaborated in these writings.[3] While the Bhagavadgītā, and following it, the Anugītā, merely lay down the doctrine of repeated incarnation, the other writings enumerate in detail all the incarnations of the Deity in the past, as well as any still to come, and also narrate the circumstances and purpose

[1] Nārāyaṇīya 351. 25; 352-6; cf. 352. 14. 15; also Viṣṇu P. I. 19, p. 100; Bhāg. P. IV. p. 54.

[2] Ahirbudhnya Saṁhitā, Ch. 38; Schrader, *Introd. to the Pāñcarātra*, p. 129; cf. also Bhāg. P. VI. 1, p. 5; 15, p. 67.

[3] Nārāyaṇīya 340. 74-102; 341. 89-90, etc.; Anugītā 54. 12-22; for Saṁhitās see Schrader, *Introduction to the Pāñcarātra*, pp. 42-49; Viṣṇu. P. I. 4; III. 2. p. 177, etc.; Bhāg. P. I. 3, etc.

of each incarnation. In the Nārāyaṇīya, the Deity is said to assume the form of a boar to bring back the Earth from the waters "for the good of all creatures" (340. 74); as a man-lion to slay Hiraṇyakaśipu for the benefit of the deities (76); as Āditya to defeat the *asura* who appropriates the sovereignity of the universe from the deities (79); as Rāma of the race of Bhṛgu to exterminate the Kṣatriyas who become proud (81); as Rāma, son of Daśaratha, to slay the Lord of the Rākṣasas, that "thorn of all the worlds" (85); as Kṛṣṇa to slay Kaṁsa, and the innumerable Dānavas who will be as "thorns in the sides of the deities," and all such as have done some form of injury or other to others (86 and 87). He with Arjuna will consume a large number of Kṣatriyas "for doing good to the world," and in these various ways will lighten the burden of the earth (97 and 98).

It is to be noticed how the interest is fixed in all this on the Deity's desire to do good to those whom He loves. While in the Bhagavadgīta, Righteousness was emphasized as the chief motive of incarnation, Love occupies the chief place here.

The Purāṇas add to the list of incarnations given in the Nārāyaṇīya; the Bhāgavata Purāṇa mentions as many as twenty-two, and adds that the incarnations of the Lord are "numberless" (I. 3). The Saṁhitās generally enumerate thirty-nine incarnations.[1]

The Viṣṇu and Bhāgavata Purāṇas distinguish themselves in their elaboration of the Kṛṣṇa-incarnation among the cow-herds of Mathura (Viṣṇu P. V; Bhāg. P. X). The tenth book of the Bhāgavata Purāṇa—the longest and most popular section of that work—is devoted entirely to the birth, life, amours and miraculous deeds of Kṛṣṇa among the herdsmen and herdswomen of Mathura.

What, we may ask, is the significance of this theory of incarnation, which plays so great a part in our

[1] Cf. Schrader, *Introduction to the Pāñcarātra*, p. 42.

writings? The belief in non-human forms, such as that of boar, fish, tortoise and such-like, which the Deity is said to assume, probably indicates the function which the theory of incarnation originally performed, viz., that of relating the Deity to the primitive worship of an earlier day, or to contemporary worship among some classes of the people. By this means, it would appear, peace was made between worshippers of different gods. He who worshipped the Deity in the form of a Boar was a worshipper of Viṣṇu no less than he who worshipped the high-souled Kṛṣṇa. All were in the end worshippers of the same Deity, and accordingly there was little need for sectarian animosity. This is indeed the function which the theory consistently performs in later Hindu thought, when heroes such as Rāma and Kṛṣṇa or philosophers of great renown, such as Buddha and Kapila, are raised to incarnations of Viṣṇu (cf. Bhāgavata Purāṇa I. 3), and thus their followers are reconciled with the devotees of Viṣṇu.

Besides this, the theory of incarnation, as developed in the writings with which we are dealing, seems to have had also a more particular significance, arising from the peculiar moral and religious fervour of the followers of this cult. The only Supreme Being that the philosophers knew anything about was the Transcendent One, who, though immanent in the universe, was still so far removed from it in character that He not only was incapable of being described in terms of anything known in experience, but was also incapable of being regarded as actively related to it. It was necessary therefore that the Supreme Being should assume finite form for the sake of His worshipper, who, however full of devotion, found it hard to worship the Unmanifest. Accordingly in the Saṁhitās, it is declared that the primary purpose for the finite manifestations of the Deity is that He may become the object of the devotee's worship and meditation.[1]

[1] Schrader, *Introd. to the Pāñcarātra*, p. 49.

For this purpose, He is even said to enter inanimate objects and become incarnate in idols.[1] The function which the theory of incarnation performs seems accordingly to be, in addition to the general one mentioned above, to bring the Supreme One of the philosophers into living and loving touch with the moral and religious life of His devotees.

The Saṁhitās distinguish between primary and secondary incarnations, the primary being the Supreme Being appearing in a body which is non-material (*aprākṛta*), while the secondary are the Deity entering into and possessing the body of an ordinary finite being in order to carry out some particular purpose.[2]

It is generally believed that the incarnate being is a portion of, or emanation from, the Supreme Being. Thus the Viṣṇu Purāṇa declares, " He who is the soul of all . . . descends for the preservation of the earth in a small portion of His essence to establish righteousness below " (V. 1, p. 319), and speaking of the incarnation of the Deity as Kṛṣṇa and his brother, Saṁkarṣaṇa, declares, " the Supreme Being plucked off two hairs, one white and one black, and said to the celestials : 'These my hairs shall go down upon earth and shall relieve her of the burden of her distress ' " (V. 1, p. 321), which indicates that the incarnate beings are a small portion of the Supreme Being. This is generally conceded by the Bhāgavata Purāṇa also, which, after enumerating the twenty-two incarnations of the Deity, declares, " All these are either portions or emanations from the Person," although making an exception in the case of the Kṛṣṇa-incarnation, it adds, " but Kṛṣṇa is the Lord Himself " (I. 3, p. 9).

The Saṁhitās, however, with their elaborate cos-

[1] Five forms of the Deity are recognised generally in Pāñcarātra literature : (1) *Para* (or Supreme form), (2) *Vyūha* (emanation), (3) *Vibhava* (incarnations), (4) *Antaryāmin* (Inner Ruler), and (5) *Arcā Avatāra* (incarnation in idols). See Schrader, *Introd. to the Pāñcarātra*, pp. 25 and 49.

[2] See Schrader, *Introd. to the Pāñcarātra*, p. 47.

mology and an entirely transcendent Supreme Being, regard the incarnations as either all springing from Aniruddha,[1] or some only from Aniruddha and the rest from the other three *Vyūhas*.[2] But since the *Vyūhas* are themselves only manifestations of the Supreme Being, the incarnations may ultimately also be regarded as manifestations of the same.

The love of the Deity, according to our sources, not only leads Him to assume finite forms for the sake of His worshippers, but also actively to concern Himself in seeking to free them from *saṁsāra*. This work is, in the Saṁhitās, allotted to the Sudarśana portion of Lakṣmī, the Supreme Being being too transcendent to be engaged in such matters.[3] It functions as Grace, leading the soul in numerous ways to Release. It "awakens" the soul. "That person upon whom Nārāyaṇa looks with compassion succeeds in becoming awakened. No one, O king, can become awakened through his own wishes" (Nārāyaṇīya, 349. 75 and 76). "(It) causes the soul to discern its goal (Liberation) and to strive after it."[4] It sometimes deprives a man of wealth and friends in order to wean him from attachment to the finite (Bhāg. Purāṇa. X. 88, p. 398). It leads the Deity to reveal Himself, His attributes and His purpose to the devotee, as already seen, in order "to set a keener edge" on the eagerness of the devotee, and to arouse in him "a holy yearning" after the Deity (Bhāg. Purāṇa I. 6, p. 21). It makes the past *karma* of the individual null and void, for with regard to a soul seized by the grace of God, they are as powerless, and consequently as indifferent, as robbers towards a traveller guarded by a strong retinue."[5] It preserves the faith of the devotes so that it may never flinch (Bhāg. Purāṇa I. 6, p. 21).

[1] Viṣvaksena Saṁhitā and Lakṣmī Tantra II. 55. See Schrader, *Introd. to the Pāñacātra*, p. 48.
[2] Padma Tantra I. 2, 81. ff. See Schrader, *Introd. to the Pāñcarātra*, p. 48.
[3] Ahirbudhnya Saṁhitā, Ch. XIV. Schrader, *Introd. to the Pāñcarātra*, pp. 114-6.
[4] Schrader, *Introd. to the Pāñcarātra*, p. 116.
[5] Schrader, *Introd. to the Pāñcarātra*, p. 116.

Although the Deity thus works for the salvation of the individual, the individual has his part to play, for " Hari never casts a kind eye upon the person subject to birth (and death), that is endued with such a mixed nature " as that which partakes of *rajas* and *tamas* (349. 76 and 77). Salvation, therefore, though entirely dependent on Nārāyaṇa " (349. 70), is conditioned by the soul renouncing the evil qualities of *rajas* and *tamas*, and pursuing the good qualities of *sattva*, for " emancipation is regarded as made up of the attribute of *sattva* " (349. 70). " The grace of God is the crown and consummation of religious duties piously practised " (Bhāg. Purāṇa I. 2, p. 5).[1] Other qualities such as knowledge[2] and Yogic practice[2] are also mentioned as required before the Deity can grant release, but above all is demanded the devotion of one's whole soul[3] to Nārāyaṇa, for it has as much merit as the knowledge or yoga advocated by the Sāṁkhyas (349. 74). Indeed in one passage, the Nārāyaṇīya casts off all fears of opposition from the recognised schools of philosophy and asserts, " Without doubt, the religion of devotion seems to be superior (to that of knowledge) and is very dear to Nārāyaṇa. The end that is attained by Brāhmaṇas, who attending to due observances, study the Vedas with the Upaniṣads . . . and by those that adopt the religion of Yatis (ascetics), is inferior, I think, to that attained by persons devoted to Hari with their whole souls " (349. 4 and 5). With greater force and certainty, the Bhāgavata Purāṇa declares, " Neither the fact of being a twice-born one, a celestial or an anchorite, nor character nor experience, nor charity nor religious austerity, nor sacrifice, nor purity, nor observance of vows, is capable of bringing about the satisfaction of Mukunda. Hari is pleased only by means of unalloyed

[1] Cf. also Viṣṇu P. III. 7, p. 189.

[2] Cf. Nārāyaṇīya, 349-72; Viṣṇu P. I. 22, p. 109; Bhāg. P. VII. 11, pp. 64 and 65; VIII. 3, p. 10.

[3] Cf. Nārāyaṇīya, 349. 74; Viṣṇu P. I. 20, p. 102; Bhāg. P. VII. 7, p. 38.

devotion. Shorn of devotion, the other things recited are mere mockeries" (VII. 7, p. 38).[1]

While thus the soul has its part to play in securing Release, it is aided in all its efforts, as we have seen, by the grace of the Deity. Whether in its efforts to rescue man from *saṁsāra* grace encroaches upon the freedom of the soul and becomes irresistible, is not considered. Nevertheless the conditions mentioned above, which are regarded as necessary for the soul to fulfil, would seem to indicate that grace functions only along with, and not in spite of, the individual.

Besides *anugraha* or the work of furthering the soul on its way to release, the Deity (spoken of in His active aspect as Sudarśana) is said in the Ahirbudhnya Saṁhitā[2] to have also *nigraha* or the power of obstructing the soul "at the beginning" by contracting its form, power and knowledge, and making it atomic, impotent and ignorant, thus bringing about the imperfections which bind it to *saṁsāra*. Such a view suggests the doctrine of Predestination,[3] according to which the Deity predetermines souls to salvation or condemnation; but it is in conflict with the view usually advocated that the evils which the soul suffers

[1] It is to be noted that the heretic and catholic element in Ghora's teaching asserts itself even at the time of the Bhāgavata Purāṇa, and this in spite of efforts of the followers of this cult, right through its history, to make terms with the orthodox.

It must be remarked that Devotion, as inculated in the Bhāgavata Purāṇa, tends to become highly emotional and ecstatic. It is said that under the influence of devotion, a man's "heart melts away; he then like a maniac, having no control over himself, sometimes laughs aloud, weeps, cries, sings and dances" (XI. 2 p. 7). In the Viṣṇu Purāṇa, on the other hand, devotion is restrained and contemplative and consists of calm meditation on the Supreme Being. See VI. 7, pp. 452-4, also I. 11, p. 54.

The Bhāgavata Purāṇa distinguishes itself also by teaching that the preceptor (*guru*) is to be regarded as the Deity (XI. 3, p. 10) and worshipped (X. 86, p. 387), a doctrine not found in our other sources. It further advocates uttering the name of the Deity (III. 9, p. 42), singing and hearing His praise, and reciting His deeds, as ways of winning His grace (I. 2, p. 5; I. 5, pp. 16 and 17; III. 5, pp. 21 and 22). In all these respects, it seems to reflect the religion of the Āḷvārs, of whom we shall give an account later.

[2] Chapter XIV. See Schrader, *Introduction to the Pāñcarātra*, pp. 114 and 115.

[3] Cf. Schrader, *Introd. to the Pāñcarātra*, p. 88.

are always due to its own past deeds.[1] All that is meant therefore is probably that prior to each creation the Deity determines the soul to adopt the "contracted" form which it has merited by past deeds.

If Release is then what the Deity in his love for embodied souls seeks to bring about, we may next consider what relation the Deity bears to the soul, when it has attained Release. The teaching on this point is not free from ambiguity. In consonance with the advaitic attitude already described—according to which the individual soul is nothing but Brahman Himself in finite form—it is sometimes asserted that Release is the return of Brahman into His own true nature. "He who sees his soul devoid of the attributes of the five elements, though enjoying them, becomes emancipated. Abandoning with the aid of the understanding all purposes relating to body and mind, one gradually attains to cessation of separate existence, like a fire unified with fuel" (Anugītā 19. 11 and 12). Likewise it is stated in the Nārāyaṇīya that "The cessation of separate conscious existence by identification with Supreme Brahman is the highest attribute or condition for a living agent to attain" (343. 79). To enter into Brahman and become merged in Him is more to be desired than all other ends (335. 42 and 43).

And yet what exactly such entering and merging, which are often declared in the Nārāyaṇīya[2] to be the goal of men, involve, it does not seem easy to determine conclusively. The elements involved in this process are thus described. "The path that is theirs . . . that are stainless . . . is fraught with auspiciousness and felicity. Sūrya (Sun), who is the dispeller of the darkness of all the worlds, is said to be the door (through which the emancipate must pass). Entering Sūrya, the bodies of such persons become consumed

[1] Ahir. Saṁ., Ch. XXXVIII. See Schrader, op. cit., p. 129. The Purāṇas do not explicitly assert that *karma* is beginningless, but they assume it to be so. Cf. Bhāg. P. VI. 1, p. 5; XI. 3, p. 9; Viṣ. P. I. 3, p. 25.

[2] 337. 27; 340. 25, 42, 48, 125; 341. 8; 344. 15; 345. 19; cf. 349. 66, 75; 352. 12; 363. 16; 365. 8.

by his fire. They then become invisible for after that they cannot be seen by anybody at any time. Reduced into invisible atoms, they then enter into Nārāyaṇa (who resides in the centre of Sūrya). Passing out from him also, they enter into the form of Aniruddha. Losing all physical attributes altogether and transformed into Mind alone they then enter into Pradyumna. Passing out of Pradyumna, those foremost of regenerate persons . . . then enter into Saṁkarṣaṇa, who is otherwise called Jiva. After this, divested of the three primal attributes of *sattva, rajas* and *tamas,* those foremost of regenerate beings quickly enter the Supreme Soul otherwise called Ksetrajña, and which itself transcends the three primal attributes. Know that Vāsudeva is He called Ksetrajña. Verily shouldst thou know that Vāsudeva is the abode or original refuge of all things in the universe" (345. 13-18). The stages of Aniruddha, Pradyumna, and Saṁkarṣaṇa, through which the soul passes before it enters Vāsudeva, the Supreme Being, are readily recognised as the same as those gone through in the evolution of the individual soul and the material universe from the Supreme Being, the order being reversed because the process now described is the return of the soul to the Deity. In this process, we are told that the individual loses gradually all his material qualities till finally he is completely free of anything material and enters the Supreme Soul.

Side by side with this, the description of the emancipated beings,[1] found in the White Island suggests that, though souls released from *saṁsāra* are very similar to the Deity in their effulgence, glory and freedom from material qualities, they are quite distinct from Him, and are engaged in devout worship and adoration of Him. "We beheld a number of men of auspicious features. All of them were white and looked like the moon, and possessed every mark of blessedness. Their hands were always joined in prayer. They were

[1] That they are "emancipate" is declared by the Deity Himself (340. 19).

engaged in silently thinking on Brahman." "The effulgence that was emitted by each of these men resembled the splendours which Sūrya assumes when the time comes for the dissolution of the universe" (337. 32, 33 and 35). "They are divested of senses. They do not subsist on any kind of food" (337. 28. "Worshippers of that foremost of all beings, they are devoted to Him with their whole souls. They all enter that eternal and illustrious Deity of a thousand rays" (337. 27). The fact that such "emancipated ones" are said as in this passage to "enter," or, as in other passages,[1] to be "competent to enter," the Supreme Being, shows that although emancipation was not regarded as the same as entering into the Deity, still it was assumed to lead to such a consummation.

What the relation of the soul to the Deity is, in this ultimate end, is never carefully considered, nor perhaps could it be. At times, the oneness which the soul attains with the Deity is emphasized to such an extent that it is explicitly said to involve "cessation of existence"[2] for the soul. At other times this extreme view seems somewhat modified. Thus a pictorial representation of a soul entering the Deity is given in 363. 11-18, where it is said that the soul, "piercing through the firmament, entered into Sūrya's disc. Mingling then with Sūrya's energy, he seemed to be transformed into Sūrya's self. When the two energies thus met together, we were so confounded that we could not any longer distinguish which was which" (363. 16 and 17). The assumption underlying this description seems to be that, though the soul becomes practically identical with the Deity, making it impossible for us to distinguish it from the Deity, it is not entirely identical with Him. This general impression is confirmed by the earlier part of this section, which reads, "The divine Sūrya is the refuge or home of innumerable wonders. Innumerable *munis*

[1] 340. 20, 125; 341. 8

[2] 341. 8, 11; 343. 79.

(saints), crowned with ascetic success, together with all the deities, reside in the rays of Sūrya like birds perching on the branches of trees" (363. 2 and 3).

The same difficulty in understanding how exactly the liberated soul was conceived as related to the Deity is pointed out by Dr. Schrader[1] with regard to the Saṁhitās. He remarks that the relation between the individual and highest soul is described in several Saṁhitās in language which is "thoroughly advaitic."[2] He believes, however, that such passages represent merely a "formal" borrowing from advaitic sources, for "the general trend of the Pāñcarātra is clearly non-advaitic." Besides the non-advaitic passages which he cites in evidence, his reason for thinking so is that "all Pāñcarātra Saṁhitās recognise the existence of the Nityas or 'ever-free' beings (' Viṣvaksena, etc.) and cannot, therefore, admit that a previously bound soul should become more inseparably united with the Lord than these are."[3]

It is interesting to note that the Nārāyaṇīya, which is the spiritual predecessor of the Saṁhitās, raises this problem in the form that, since the deities and the denizens of heaven continue in existence, they seem to be ignorant of the way of securing an annihilation of conscious existence," which is here assumed to be the highest end (341. 11), for turning away from the religion of emancipation, which is absorption into the Deity, they have adopted the religion of *Pravṛtti*, "which leads to conscious existence that is measured by time" (341.12). The problem is said to relate to a "deep mystery" (341.16), and it is solved by saying that these eternally free beings are created by the Deity for certain functions that they have to perform (e.g., Brahmā to create and govern the universe) (341. 54-76).[4] They therefore continue in existence to perform them, while the released soul attains the highest end of cessa-

[1] *Introduction to the Pāñcarātra*, pp. 91-93.
[2] P. 91.
[3] P. 92.
[4] Cf. also Schrader, *Introd. to the Pāñcarātra*, pp. 56 and 57.

tion of conscious existence. It seems thus to be definitely admitted that a previously bound soul does attain to a greater union with the Deity than the denizens of heaven, who have never suffered *saṁsāra*, so that it does not seem necessarily to follow that, since the Saṁhitās assume the existence of eternally free beings, they must also believe in the continued separate existence of released souls. And yet it is likely that this problem and solution arose from the need of reconciling the belief in a heaven inhabited by freed souls—which, being more naïve, no doubt represents an earlier view—with the advaitic tendency of later times. But even so, it seems doubtful, if we may judge from the Nārāyaṇīya, whether the borrowing from advaitism was merely formal, for, as we have tried to show, the Nārāyaṇīya seems consistently to hold that the soul does attain to a closer unity with the Deity (even perhaps complete adsorption into Him), than a life in heaven implies. Nor is the idea of attaining unity with, and becoming lost in, Him so entirely foreign to the fervent mystic temperament[1] of the followers of this cult, who regarded complete devotion to God as man's chief duty, as to necessitate the conclusion that advaitic passages regarding the ultimate goal of the released soul must always be regarded as merely cases of borrowing. It seems, therefore, that if we are to do justice to both advaitic and non-advaitic passages, which occur so frequently together, we must think that these philosophers regarded the soul in Release as attaining very close union with the Deity, although it also maintains some form of distinction from Him, not capable of being defined, or consciously grasped. Thus in the Padma Tantra[2] it is asked, "What is the difference, O Highest Spirit, between Thee and the liberated soul?" and it is replied, "They (the liberated) become I; there is no difference whatever"; but this

[1] As illustrated, for example, in the case of the Āḻvārs. See pp. 137-139 below.

[2] I. 4, 14-15, quoted in *Introd. to the Pāñcarātra*, by Dr. Schrader, p. 91.

plain advaitic teaching is modified by the assertion which is now added, "as I live (*viharāmi*) just so live the liberated souls," which may mean either that the liberated souls continue to live, as Dr. Schrader interprets it,[1] or that they live only in so far as the Deity lives, that is, only in His living and not with any distinct existence of their own. This same ambiguity characterises other passages as well,[2] and indicates that the relation of the Deity to the soul in Release was not clearly grasped by these men. They certainly teach that the released soul becomes much more one with the Deity than the soul in *saṁsāra*, for, as already pointed out, they regard the highest end as "becoming" Brahman or "entering into Him; but whether they believed that in this process the soul completely lost its individuality, it is not easy to say. It is possible, however, that they believed generally that the soul in Release becomes closely united with the Deity, without completely losing its distinctness —much more closely united, it would seem, than existence with other free spirits in a heavenly abode implies, but also somehow distinct. "Just as gold in the midst of fire, shines separately, as though it were not in contact (with the fire) even so he who is clinging to Brahman (*brahmaṇi lagna*) is seen to exist in the form of a gem (*maṇi*)" (Viṣṇutalaka II. 100).[3] "He who has become attached to the Jewel of gems (*maṇi-ratna*) is said to have attained identity (with the Lord)" (Viṣṇutilaka II. 54).[4] Or even more explicitly, "Just as by means of gates of various kinds, people go forth from a town, even so the souls go forth from Brahman—this is called creation; and as,

[1] *Introd. to the Pāñcarātra*, p. 91.

[2] Cf., e.g., Padma Tantra I. VI. 15 f., which Dr. Schrader uses (*Introd. to Pāñcarātra*, pp. 92 and 93) to prove non-advaitism as the teaching of the Saṁhitās, and which Mr. P. T. Śrīnivāsa Aiyaṅgar uses (*Outlines of Indian Philosophy*, pp. 184 and 185) to establish advaitism as the view towards which the Saṁhitās incline.

[3] Translated and quoted by Dr. Schrader in his *Introd. to the Pāñcarātra*, p. 92.

[4] Translated and quoted by Dr. Schrader in his *Introd. to the Pāñcarātra*, p 52

through those gates, the inhabitants of that town enter it again, just so (the souls) go (back) to that Brahman—this is called Withdrawal" (Viṣṇutilaka II. 95).[1]

In the Viṣṇu and Bhāgavata Purāṇas a similar doctrine regarding the relation of the released soul to the Deity is to be found. In line with what probably was popular belief, they speak of a heaven, where the soul lives in bliss with the Deity and all his celestial host.[2] But they do not seem to regard this as the final state of Release, for it is said that souls who have become free from sin dwell here till the end of a Kalpa,[3] and then proceed through other states till finally they become "immersed in the great Soul."[4] Accordingly the Viṣṇu Purāṇa teaches that, as the state of the gods is a thousand times superior to that of pious men, so the state of liberated souls is a thousand times superior to that of the gods in heaven.[5] Dwelling as the gods in heaven is only a stage[6] in obtaining final emancipation, which he who remembers Hari obtains at once without the necessity of going through the intermediate stages. "He obtains final emancipation considering even heaven as impediment. He considers, O Maitreya, even the dignity of Indra as an obstacle to final liberation."[7] Similarly in the Bhāgavata Purāṇa Siva declares that the devotee reaches directly the state of Viṣṇu, which he and other deities finally attain,[8] thus again making it clear that the final state of Release is different from dwelling with the deities or free souls in heaven.

What exactly this highest state of release is, which is superior even to the state of the deities, we are not told precisely, but it is described, as in our other

[1] Translated and quoted by Dr. Schrader in his *Introd. to the Pāñcarātra*, p. 93. It must be remarked that this passage is not of direct value, for it speaks, not of souls in release, but of bound souls at the period of dissolution, when the universe is withdrawn.

[2] Cf. Viṣṇu P. II. 8, p. 144; II. 2, p. 119; Bhāg. P. II. 2, p. 8; 9, p. 36; III. 15.

[3] Cf. Viṣṇu P. II. 8, p. 144; Bhāg. P. II. 2, p. 8.

[4] Bhāg. P. II. 2, pp. 8 and 9.

[5] Viṣṇu P. II. 6, p. 132

[6] See references 2 and 3 above.

[7] Viṣṇu P. II. 6, p. 133.

[8] Bhāg. P. IV. 24, p. 107

sources, as a merging into the Deity, when the creature-soul becomes one with the All-Soul.[1]

What this merging implies is left as ambiguous as in the other writings, for at times it is said to involve an extinction of sense as in sleep (Bhāg. P. III. 7, p. 32), the cessation of the idea of ego, and with it the disappearance of all distinction between subject and object, seer and seen,[2] in short, the rejection of the idea of duality,[3] and of all differences between the individual and Universal Soul.[4] At other times, some kind of a distinction between the soul and the Deity is assumed as in the account of Prahlāda attaining unity with the Supreme Being, when we are told that "He forgot his individuality and was not conscious of anything. And he thought that he himself was the endless undecaying Supreme Soul. And on account of this efficient notion of identity the undecaying Viṣṇu . . . appeared in his mind which was wholly purified from sin" (Viṣṇu Purāṇa I. 20, pp. 100 and 101). According to this account it would appear that the soul, in its beatific experience of union with the Deity, forgets itself or loses consciousness of itself, not that it ceases to exist. This impression, gained on the human side from the experience of the soul which had attained unity with the Divine, is confirmed also on the Divine side by the words of the Deity Himself. "I do not love my (own) soul or the extremely beloved Lakṣmī (so much as I love) those devoted to me, and (are) good, to whom I am salvation. How can I abandon those who, having renounced wife, house, children, relations (their own) souls and wealth, have become devoted to me, who am thus absolute? The virtuous whose hearts are fastened unto me (and who are) indifferent (to pleasure and pain) have enthralled me, as a good wife (binds and enthrals) a

[1] Viṣṇu P. I. 22, pp. 109 and 110; II. 14, p. 164; VI. 7, pp. 453-9; Bhāg. P. I. 3, p. 10; III. 7, p. 32; VII. 12, p. 72; IV. 22, pp. 98 and 99.

[2] Viṣṇu P. II. 14, p. 164; VI. p. 458. Bhāg. P. IV. 22, p. 98.

[3] Viṣṇu P. I. 22, p. 109; Bhāg. P. VII. 12, p. 72.

[4] Viṣṇu P. VI. 7, p. 458.

good husband. The virtuous are my heart and I am the heart of the virtuous. The virtuous do not know anything beside me (nor) do I know a particle apart from them" (Bhāg. Purāṇa, IX. 4, p. 17).

The view, therefore, towards which these writers tend on the whole seems to be that in Release the soul becomes intimately but not completely one with the Deity. The love of the Deity would seem to require both the continued existence of the individual as well as an intimate and inseparable union with him.

The soul, then, in all the stages of its existence, viz., in the period prior to worldly existence, in the state of embodied existence, and in the state of Release, though much more closely related to the Deity than the material universe, is not, it would seem, entirely identical with Him. He, in one aspect of Himself sends it into worldly existence and dwells within it as its inner Soul. Filled with love for it, He incarnates Himself from time to time, assuming finite forms for its benefit and for purposes of its meditation and worship. By His grace He seeks to rescue it from *saṁsāra* into which it has fallen by its evil deeds, and when the necessary knowledge and goodness, and more especially whole-hearted devotion to the Deity, are attained by it, He rescues it by His grace and entering into intimate and inseperable union with it, makes it practically a part of His own being.

In conclusion, we cannot do better than summarise the conception of Deity revealed in these writings in the following words of the Viṣṇu Purāna. "He dwelleth internally in all beings and all things dwell in Him; and thence the Lord Vāsudeva is the creator and preserver of the world. He though identical with all beings is beyond and separate from material nature, from its products, from properties and from imperfections. He is beyond investing substance. He is Universal Soul; all the interstices of the universe are filled up by Him. He is one with all good qualities, and all created things are endowed with a small portion of His individuality. Assuming various shapes He bestows benefits on the whole world, which is His work. Glory, might, dominion, wisdom, energy, power and other attributes are collected in Him. Supreme of the supreme, in whom no imperfections abide, Lord over finite and infinite, God in individuals and universals, visible, and invisible, omnipotent, omnipresent, omniscient, almighty" (VI. 5, p. 446).

CHAPTER IV

FROM THE ĀḺVĀRS TO RĀMĀNUJA

1. *The Religion of the Āḻvārs*

THE Āḻvārs, of whom twelve are mentioned, are Tamil Vaiṣṇava saints, who lived before the time of Rāmānuja. One of them, Tirumaṅgai, whom tradition regards as the last of the Āḻvārs, is believed to have lived in the first half of the eighth century.[1] Their intense religious experience is reflected in the Nālāyira Prabandham, a collection of 4,000 verses attributed to them, and used in Vaiṣṇava worship even at the present day. These verses are valuable not for any new philosophical conception of the Deity that they have to disclose, but for the fact that they reveal the depth of religious feeling to which the view of the Deity as incarnating Himself out of love for His creatures and desiring their whole-hearted devotion gave rise. One of the Āḻvārs, Āṇḍāḷ, was a woman, and some of them were of low birth. Thus Nammāḻvār, the greatest of the Āḻvārs, was a Śūdra;[2] Tirumaṅgai, also one of the more celebrated of them, belonged to the thief caste, and Tiruppāṇ was an outcaste.[3] One of them, Madhurakavi, taught and practised the worship of the *guru* (religious teacher).[4]

Of all the Āḻvārs, Nammāḻvār appears to have been the most philosophic. At any rate, it is in his hymns that we find expressed anything like a philosophic

[1] British Museum Catalogue of Tamil Books, p. vi; Madras Government Epigraphist's Report for 1908, p. 69; *Epigraphia Indica*, Vol. 8, p. 294.
[2] S. Kṛṣvasvāmi Aiyaṅgār, *Some contributions of South India*, etc., p. 266.
[3] A. Govindācārya, *Holy Lives of the Āzhvārs*, p. 146 and p. 136 resp.
[4] A. Govindācārya, *Holy Lives of the Āzhvārs*, p. 225.

conception of the Deity, the other Āḻvārs directing their attention almost exclusively to His characteristics in one or other of His *avatārs*. Nammāḻvār declares of the Deity, " It is impossible to say that He has this, not that. He cannot be reached by any thought either on earth or in the heavens. He has a form ; He has no form. He is closely connected with the objective world yet He is apart from it (Tiruvāymoḻi c. 1. 1. 3)[1]. " He is the material cause of substantial visible expanse, air, heat, water and earth. He is pervading them all. He, in the form of life, is pervading all bodies and in all places. At times He swallows all these up " (c. 1. 1. 7). " He destroys the world in the form of Hara. He recreates it in the form of Brahma " (c. 1. 1. 8).

Though " it is impossible even for gods to know His real nature," and " He is beyond the beyond " (c. 1. 1. 8), Nammāḻvār declares triumphantly " yet He is to me of a definite nature " (c. 1. 1. 6). " He is very easily accessible to His devotees. His ways are very mysterious to others " (c. 1. 2. 1). What He reveals Himself to be is as follows. " He is the highest goal of virtue and is higher than the highest " (c. 1. 2. 3). " In Him, Wisdom, Strength, Power, Lordship, Prowess and energetic Splendour,[2] attain their perfection. He has neither beginning nor end," and has " innumerable good qualities " (c. 1. 2. 5). The Lord's nature is very deep. It is very wide and very high, and it is very sweet and it is above material existence " (c. 1. 2. 6). " He is perfect goodness. . . . His nature is to give wisdom and to be blissful " (c. 1. 2. 2). But more than all these qualities what the Āḻvār most appreciates is that the Deity is loving and gracious, not spurning even the most degraded. " To be condescend-

[1] This and other passages of the Tiruvāymoḻi cited below are taken from N. Kūrattālvār Aiyaṅgār's *Free Translation of Tiruvāymoḻi of Śathakopā*. The abbreviation c. 1. 1. 3, stands for " first centum, first tenth, third stanza," each centum being divided into ten Tens, and each Ten into ten or fewer stanzas.

[2] The six qualities which play an important part, as we have seen, in Pāñcarātra philosophy.

ing is His nature" (c. 1. 2. 2). "My Lord is of such a nature that any man of any knowledge can understand that my Lord is very condescending" (c. 1. 2. 3). "He is the Lord who does not cast out the undeserving nor does He take up only the deserving" (c. 1. 6. 3 and 5). The thought that the Deity in His love does not reject the undeserving fills the soul of the Āḷvār with ecstasy and he declares, "My tongue sings to me divine songs. My body dances as if it is possessed by a deity, worships the Lord and reverts to Him. The angels and the gods discuss about His nature and reel as if their brains were deranged. He does not take a few deserving only. He does not leave off the undeserving. He is not vexed with sinners nor does He love the good only. He is unseconded nectar to those that join and love him" (c. 1. 6. 3-5).

It is this love and 'condescending nature' of the Deity that chiefly appeal to the Āḷvārs, and consequently it is on the Deity in His incarnate forms that they delight to dwell for the most part. So completely do they do this that in meditating on incidents connected with His earthly life as the cowherd Kṛṣṇa, they identify themselves with individuals who are said to have borne special love for Kṛṣṇa and address the Deity accordingly. Thus Nammāḷvār regards himself as a *gopi*-lover of Kṛṣṇa and is concerned lest the Deity should come to grief at the hands of the *asuras* (demons). "O! My Lord! Go not Thou to tend the cows. Many *asuras* set up by Kaṁsa take alluring forms and wander about in Thy meadows and entice Thee. If they succeed many evils will come upon Thee. I implore you to listen to me" (c. 10. 3. 9). He also longs like a *gopi* (herdswoman) to be embraced by Kṛṣṇa and cries, "Thy soothing words burn my soul as I brood over them. Thou wentest to graze the cows in the daytime. O Kṛṣṇa, the night came with the cool wind. . . . Thou embracest us so closely that the jasmine wreath and glittering gem Kaustubha on thy breast are pressed upon me, and perfume my bosom. Thou givest the ambrosia of Thy mouth and placest Thy hand upon the heads of us Thy poor maids. Thou placest Thy fair feet on our heads; we are Thy poor maids. O beautiful Kṛṣṇa, on Thy way there are many better maids to hold Thy feet and serve Thee in the resting places. Let that be. Our women's nature yields to Thee. Our lovely eyes will not cease shedding tears. Our minds will have no rest. Therefore Thy going away to tend the cattle is unbearable to us. Our souls burn like wax in the fire" (c. 10. 3. 5 and 6). Likewise in the Tiruviruttam, a poem consisting of a hundred stanzas, Nammāḻvār represents himself as a maiden disconsolate and pining for Kṛṣṇa, her absent lover. Similarly Āṇḍāḷ in her Tiruppāvai imagines herself a *gopi,* who rising in the morning wakes up other herdswomen (cf. verse 16) and goes with them to arouse the sleeping Kṛṣṇa. The picture is evidently one of Aṇḍaḷ assembling her friends at dawn to worship at the shrine of Śrī Raṅgam, where the image is of the god in a lying posture; and throughout the poem there is no trace of sensual love, Kṛṣṇa's character as the supreme Deity Viṣṇu not being forgotten[1] in the thought of Him as a herdsman.

In their love for the Deity in His incarnate form as Kṛṣṇa, they not only identify themselves with *gopis,* but also with Yaśodā, Kṛṣṇa's foster-mother. Thus Periyāḻvār calls the moon to come to his infant Kṛṣṇa, who wishes to play with it. "My little one, precious to me as nectar, my blessing, is calling thee, pointing, pointing with his little hands! O Big Moon, if thou wishest to play with this little black one, hide not thyself in the clouds, but come rejoicing." "He calls thee in his baby speech, prattle unformed, sweetened with nectar from his pretty mouth. O big Moon, if thou heedest him not, whose name is Śrīdharan, who is so friendly to all, when he calls and calls, 'twere well for thee if thou wert deaf" (Tirumoḻi 1. 4. 2 and 5).[2]

[1] Cf., e.g., verses 17, 20 and 21 of the Tiruppāvai.
[2] Mr. J. S. M. Hooper's translation in *Hymns of the Āḻvārs,* p. 37 and 38.

They dwell with love not only on the Deity as incarnate in individuals like Kṛṣṇa or Rāma,[1] but also as incarnate in images. They gaze at the image, and with hearts filled with emotion they shed tears of joy.

> " O dewy tears of joy, why screen my gaze
> When hungry eyes of mine are feasting on
> The matchless charms of Him, the lotus-eyed
> And carmine-mouthed so tempting sweet, reclined
> On Ananta great . . . ? "
>
> (Tirumaṇgai-Tirumālai, v. 18.)[2]

Like Āṇḍāḷ they love to go to the shrine, even before the temple-doors are opened, to wake the Deity[3] and to greet Him with flowers.

> " pray awake, O Lord,
> That sleep'st the sacred Kav'ri midst,
> And haste to bless this worm, my puny self,
> Who waits Thy doors with loads of Tulsi wreaths."
>
> (Toṇḍaraḍippoḍi-Tirupaḷḷi Yeḷuchi, 10.)[4]

They call upon all to sing His praise.

> " Oh, join the devotees who hymn Nārāyan's name,
> Oh, haste, till town and country with your song resounds."

> " And hail his thousand names ; oh, come, his feet adore ! "
>
> (Periyāḻvār-Tiruppallāṇḍu, 4 and 5.)[5]

So dearly do they love the temple in which the image is enshrined that Kulaśēkhara Āḻvār, who was a king in Travancore,[6] declares that rather than be a king in this world or in heaven, he would fain be a crane or a fish in the temple-tank, a tree in the temple-garden, a road upon the temple-hill, a step at the threshold of the temple, or anything whatsoever so long as he is in the vicinity of the shrine (cf. Perumāḷ Tirumoḻi c. 4).

[1] Cf. for Rāma *avatāra*, Tirmaṅgai-Periya Tirumoḻi I. 2, 2 ; V. 8, 1 and 2; Āṇḍāḷ—Tiruppāvai 12 ; Nammāḻvār-Tiruviruttam 36, etc. Tiruvāymoḻi c. ii, 4, 10 ; Toṇḍaraḍippoḍi-Tirumālai 7, 11 ; Tirupaḷḷi Yeḷuchi 4.

[2] From the translation in the Viśiṣṭadvaitin, Vol. I, Nos. 10 and 11.

[3] The image being in a sleeping posture.

[4] Translation—Viśiṣṭādvaitin, Vol. I, Nos. 12, 13, 14.

[5] Hooper, *Hymns of the Ālvārs*, p. 35.

[6] T. Rājagopālācāriar-*Vaiṣṇavite Reformers*, p. 139.

Besides incarnations such as Rāma and Kṛṣṇa, and images at Vaiṣṇava shrines, stories connected with Viṣṇu and his great acts of helpfulness are dwelt upon with great devotion.[1]

Thus referring to the rescue by Viṣṇu of the elephant from the crocodile, Tirumaṅgai sings:

"The elephant by mighty crocodile
Was seized, so that its end was nigh:
He thought upon the shelter of thy feet . . .
Knowing the mighty wrath thou hadst,
Such that the life of that beast, cruel-mouthed,
Was shaken. I, too, come to thee,
Thy slave, the refuge of thy feet, I seize."

(Periya Tirumoḻi V. 8, 3—Hooper.)

Similarly he sings of the snake Sumukha being rescued from the kite Garuḍa, and of Mārkaṇḍeya being delivered from the power of Yama, the god of death (V. 8, 4 and 5), and he exclaims that just as they received help from the Deity by crying to Him in their trouble, so he also would fly to God for refuge. Frequent allusions are made to other deeds of Viṣṇu undertaken in the interests of men and gods against demons, e.g., his delivering Prahlāda from the demon Hiraṇyakaśipu,[2] his securing the earth for the gods by taking three strides,[3] his swallowing the seven worlds to preserve them at the time of the Flood,[4] his churning the ocean,[5] his rescuing the earth in the form of a boar,[6] and from all this it is concluded that he is the mighty All-powerful one who helps those who flee to Him[7] however unworthy they may be.

[1] Cf., e.g., Nammāḻvār-Tiruvāymoḻi, c. 1. 8; c. 1. 9; c. 2. 6.

[2] Tirumaṅgai-Periya Tirumoḻi 1, 2, 4; Periyāḻvār-Tirupallāṇḍu 6; Nammāḻvār-Tiruviruttam 46; Tiruvāymoḻi II. 6. 6.

[3] Tirumaṅgai-Periya Tirumoḻi 1. 4. 8; Āṇḍāḷ-Tiruppāvai 17; Nammāḻvar-Tiruviruttam 38, 58, 61; Tiruvāymoḻi I. 8, 6 and 10.

[4] Nammāḻvār-Tiruviruttam 20, 56; Tiruvāymoḻi I. 8. 7.

[5] Nammāḻvār-Tiruviruttam 51; Tiruvāymoḻi 10. 10. 7.

[6] Tirumaṅgai-Periya Tirumoḻi 1. 1. 4; Nammāḻvār-Tiruvāymoḻi I. 8. 8.

[7] Toṇḍaraḍippoḍi-Tirumālai 9-12, as well as references cited above, especially those from Nammāḻvār.

"What mercy in Thee pray, who when of yore,
Through æons and æons, Brahma, the lotus-born,
And Rudra of the Ganges-dwelling crest,
Fiery penance made to seek Thy feet,
Relentless yet to them; while shamed they stood,
An El'phant's cry to heed, in fev'rish haste
Thou plunged wroth adown, while angels stared!"

(Toṇḍaraḍippoḍi-Tirumālai, 44. Viśiṣṭādvaitin, Vol. 1, Nos. 10 and 11.)

It is then the personal qualities of His *avatārs*, the visible manifestation of the Deity in His image, and His acts of grace that chiefly evoke the devotion of the Āḻvārs and determine their conception of the Deity, although, as already noted in the case of Nammāḻvār, the transcendent character of the Deity is not overlooked, and remains in the background.

If there is anything which may be fixed on as the predominant characteristic of the religion of the Āḻvārs, it is their passionate devotion to the Deity. Like a lover pining for his beloved, the Āḻvār steals into the darkness of the night, when all the world is asleep, and seeing a heron flit by he asks if it too like him is unable to sleep because of its great love for the Lord. Similarly he addresses the andril bird 'whose tunes are thick with sorrow,' the sea which mourns and is restless, the gentle breeze which untiringly searches hill and dale, sea and sky, the dark rain-bearing cloud which weeps, the languishing moon which has lost its brilliance, the thick darkness which covers the earth, and the flickering light which is at pains to keep alive its feeble flame of love. All these speak to him of a soul-consuming passion which is restless till it finds its rest in God (Nammāḻvār-Tiruvāymoḻi II. 1).

The devotion of the Āḻvārs is so all-absorbing that everything beside the Deity seems to them utterly worthless.

"No kinship with this world have I—
Which takes for true the life that is not true.
'For thee alone my passion burns,' I cry,
'Raṅgam, my Lord!'"

(Kulaśēkharan-Perumāḷ Tirumoḻi, C. 3. 1—Hooper.)

"Where shall I go and live?
Save for thy feet, like a great bird am I
Which goes around and sees no shore and comes at last
Back o'er the tossing sea and perches on ship's mast!"
(Kulaśēkharan-Perumāḷ Tirumoḻi, C. 5. 5—Hooper.)

Such single-minded devotion expresses itself, as already noticed, in worshipping at the shrine, offering flowers to the Deity, singing His praise, joining with others in uttering His names, gazing at His image, reciting His great and glorious deeds of grace, meditating on His incarnations till finally the soul is filled with ecstatic joy.[1]

But it must not be imagined that this was all that was required of the devotee. Moral qualities are necessary, and without them no man can be a true worshipper of the Deity. "To leave off wicked deeds and the blackest sin, and to be engaged in good deeds and to rise, is to go to the grove where God resides" (Nammāḻvār Tiruvāymoḻi C. II. 10. 4).[2] He must be rid of all self-interest—"Go to the Lord, rooting out all ideas of you and yours completely" (Nammāḻvār-Tiruvāymoḻi C. I. 2. 3).[2] He must not be a sensualist, eager to gratify his appetite.[3] He must be without flaw.[4] He must spread the name of Nārāyaṇa by means of his good conduct.[5] Āṇḍāḷ mentions austerities which lead to control of appetite, and the abandoning of self-love and vain-glory as necessary as well as good deeds and charity.

"Hearken, ye happy dwellers in the world,
The deeds that we must do to keep our vow,

[1] Cf. Periyāḻvār-Tiruppallāṇḍu; Nammaāḻvār-Tiruvāymoḻi c. II. 6. 3, 4 and 6; X. 1; X. 2.

[2] Translation by N. Kūruttāḻvār Aiyaṅgār; cf. also Periyāḻvār-Tiruppallāṇḍu, 3 and 4.

[3] Kūḻātpattu nindṟirkaḷai yeṅgaḷ kuḷuvinir pukataloṭṭom (Tiruppallāṇḍu, verse 3).

[4] Paḷipilō (Tiuppallāṇḍu, verse 3)

[5] Nalvakaiyāl namo nārāyaṇavendṟu nāmam palaparavi (Tiruppallāṇḍu, verse 11).

I have taken the texts 2, 3, 4 given above from the Nityānusandhānam Series edited by Śrīnivāsa Aiyaṅgār, and have translated them as above to bring out their full significance. In transcribing I have followed the system indicated by Mr. Hooper in the *Hymns of the Ā.vārs.*

Singing the feet of him, the Lord supreme.
. . . Bathing at break of day,
Nor ghi nor milk we'll eat; we will not paint
Our eyes with black; flowers shall not deck our hair;
No deeds unfit we'll do; no evil words
We'll speak, but give kind alms, and muse with joy
Upon this way."

(Tiruppāvai 2—Hooper.)

Toṇḍaraḍippoḍi finds that so long as he is steeped in sin, he has no communion with the Deity (Tirumālai, vs. 16 and 17; 23-35). Tirumaṅgai likewise contrasts throughout the first ten stanzas of his Periya Tirumoḻi his previous state of utter moral depravity when he knew not God, and his present one when by the grace of God he is transformed and feels fit for heaven. Similarly Nammāḻvār sings joyously of the victory which he has obtained over sin, for it enables him to enter the service of the Lord (Tiruvāymoḻi C. II. 6. 5).

Although it is necessary thus to obtain mastery over sin, to discipline oneself, to root out self-love and sensuality, and to practise goodness, the sinner who knows no virtue, and is despised and rejected of men need not fear that he will be rejected by God.

" Ye hardened souls, judge ye our Lord by this,
Fierce Kṣatrabandh, the fellest sinner in
This world, from all his teeming evils hard
Was freed but utt'ring His three-letter'd name.
Sweet Govinda! Most loving Raṅga Lord,
Whose yearning heart, e'en darkest sinners saves!"

(Toṇḍaraḍippoḍi-Tirumālai 4. Viśiṣt, Vol. 1, Nos. 10 and 11.)

Though a man who is steeped in sin is thus accepted by the Deity, he is required when he has become a devotee to flee from sin, as already pointed out, and to practise righteousness. Indeed the inevitable result of worshipping the Deity in truth is to shun evil and choose the good, for the very thought of the Lord suffices to make one renounce evil.[1]

[1] Cf. also Nammāḻvār-Tiruvāymoḻi c. i. 7. 1.

"... horrid murderers and fierce,
Who terror-shrouded, burn and kill
And make universal havoc—even they
If they but would firm concentrate Thee in
Their hearts—how e'en their rankest sinnings flee!"
(Toṇḍaraḍippoḍi-Tirumālai 40. Viśiṣt, Vol. 1, Nos. 10 and 11.)

Moral purity then is a quality which necessarily characterises him who cherishes the Deity in his heart.[1]

[1] As against all this, it is true that there is the story of Tirumaṅgai and his several acts of unscrupulousness, even after conversion (See A. Govindācarya, *Holy Lives*, etc. pp. 173-186). But it must be remembered that if he was unscrupulous after his conversion it was because of his overpowering zeal to carry out what he believed to be God's will, such, e.g., as the repairing and rebuilding of the temple at Śrī Raṅgam, for which work he felt himself divinely commissioned (p. 173). The end seemed to him to justify the means. But this does not mean, as Mr. Hooper thinks, that Tirumaṅgai's *bhakti* left his character "entirely unaffected" (*Hymns of the Ālvārs*, p. 29), for whereas before his conversion the Āḷvār is said to have lived entirely for himself and the pleasures of the body (*Holy Lives*, pp. 147-58), after his conversion he is said to have gone north and south visiting shrines, composing hymns and preaching his Lord (pp. 169-72). It is true that the ethics he practised, of the end justifying the means—an ethics not by any means outgrown even at the present day, e.g., with regard to war—does not appear to us to be the highest, but it is hardly fair to condemn the conduct of a man who lived a thousand years ago as unethical because it fails to conform to the requirements of what some of us to-day believe to be ethical. The question is whether his *bhakti* led him to live up to what he regarded as the best, and to that the answer must, it seems to us, be clearly in the affirmative, for all his action is prompted by a desire to do what he conceived to be God's will (cf. pp. 173-186). If that be so surely the Āḷvār's *bhakti* is more than a "fervent glow of emotion" to which Mr. Hooper in the end reduces it (*Hymns of the Ālvārs*, p. 30), for it appears to have transformed the whole centre of the Āḷvār's life, and to have led him to attempt great things for his Lord.

That Viṣṇu is not regarded as correcting the Āḷvār as Mr. Hooper complains (p. 29) is only to say that the Āḷvār knew no better, for rightly or wrongly man regards the dictates of his own moral perception as the voice of God. That the Āḷvār's later followers also do not criticise him (p. 29) may prove only that also they did not rise above the ethics of the Āḷvār. It need not prove that their *bhakti* had no necessary connection with character.

That the stories which grew up around the Āḷvārs suggest that apparently "the power of a *mantra*, the repetition of the sacred name, or even the use of the right ceremonial, are as effective as right living and true thinking," may only reveal the total failure of those of a later day to understand the deep devotion, of which these acts were for the Āḷvārs only external expressions. That the Āḷvārs themselves sang hymns of praise, uttered the sacred names of the Deity, and called upon others to do the same, as an expression of their devotion, we have seen. But the mere heartless repetition of a *mantra* or mechanical performance of ritual is so antagonistic to the sincere devotion which finds expression in their hymns that it seems impossible to ascribe such teaching to them.

That they regarded Kṛṣṇa's improprieties with the *gopis* as so many signs of his infinite condescension, regarding which Mr. Hooper writes that "if God can so condescend, morality is indifferent to Him" (p. 29), appears to

Worldly existence or life in *saṁsāra* is regarded by the Āḻvārs with great horror and hatred.

> "Like sailors caught in midst of storm I timid am
> Lest in the pit of birth again I plungéd am."
>
> Like sharing bed with serpent mate I timid am
> Lest into doleful births again I plungéd am."
> (Tirumaṅgai-Periya Tirumoḻi XI. 8, 2. 3—Hooper.)

The reason for wishing to flee from *saṁsāra* is not merely that it is itself evil,[1] but also because it separates the soul from the Deity, while the Āḻvār longs to be with the Lord or to be merged in Him. Thus Nammāḻvār impatiently cries, "I do not know when I shall be able to join the company of his servants" (Tiruvāymoḻi C. II. 3. 10); and imagining himselt a love-sick maiden, weeping day and night, and wasting away for her lover, he expresses the yearning of his heart to be united with the Lord (cf. Tiruvāymoḻi

---

reveal their essentially moral attitude towards God, which attitude leads them to make this ingenious attempt to find a moral motive for what otherwise they could not morally approve.

That in the partial incarnations of Viṣṇu "There is no recognition of morality as a requisite" (p. 29) does not reflect so much the religion of the Āḻvārs as the conceptions which they inherited from an earlier day, and which again they moralised by dwelling, as we saw on His helpfulness and condescension in these *avatārs*.

Mr. Hooper's contention that "in the symbols at the great Śrī Raṅgam temple as at other temples, there is much of what anywhere else would have to be called indecency; but there is no suggestion that this is repugnant to Viṣṇu" is an argument from silence. Besides, it is a debatable point whether the figures in the temple at Śrī Raṅgam or any of the other temples at which the Āḻvārs worshipped are indecent. Even if they are, it is probable that these indecencies like the stories about Kṛṣṇa with the *gopis* were given a spiritual signification and were understood by the Āḻvārs only in a spiritual sense, in which case it is not surprising if they did not evoke the same disapproval as they do in one to whom the symbols have no meaning beyond what appears to the eye.

That "deliverance from sin, after all, is not what is chiefly desired; sin is not the problem, but life itself" (p. 29), need not prove that deliverance from sin was not recognised as a condition to be fulfilled for Release. Indeed we shall see that it was believed that no soul can be released from *saṁsāra* and be united with the Deity till all its sins were consumed. One reason at any rate that life itself is their problem rather than sin is, as we shall now see, that their heart was set on the Deity, with whom they found that perfect communion was not possible in this life. They longed for the Deity himself, and not merely for morality, which may be regarded as only one aspect of Him.

[1] Cf., e.g., Tirumaṅgai cited above; Nammāḻvār-Tiruviruttam 1 Toṇḍaraḍippoḍi-Tirumālai 3, 12 and 13.

C. II. 4). Tirumaṅgai, whose words expressive of dread of worldly existence we cited above, prays that He may never leave the Deity:

> "That the great grace Thou further purposed him
> —Never to leave Thy sacred feet—
> May also come to me, Thy feet I seize."
>
> (Tirumaṅgai-Periya Tirumoḻi V. 8. 6—Hooper.)

And the hope expressed at the close of the Tiruppallāṇḍu is that souls will gather around God, and there 'Namonārāyaṇa' unceasing cry. Kulaśēkhara Āḻvār will not rest content with anything short of entering into the Deity.

> "With gathered waters all the streams ashine
> Must spread abroad and run
> And enter the deep sea
> And cannot stand outside. So refuge mine,
> Save in the bliss of entering Thee, is none,
> Vitruvakōdu's Lord, thick cloud-hued, virtuous one!"
>
> (Kulaśēkharan-Perumāḷ Tirumoḻi C. V. 8—Hooper.)

And the stories connected with some of the Āḻvārs[1] relate that they merged in this fashion into the Deity. Thus it is said of Āṇḍāḷ that in the presence of all assembled she, "ascending the soft Śeṣa bed of the Lord, more and more pressed on to His side; and lo, where was she? She had passed into Him. Her distinct person was no more cognizable to mortal ken. Glory merged in glory."[2] And yet it is not as though in this process of merging, the soul becomes extinct, for, as it is said of the union obtained by the Śaiva saint Māṇikka Vāśakar, it seems to be assumed that "the soul retains its personal identity, since the union is the union of love, not of identification or annihilation."[3] It is then either to live eternally in the presence of the Divine Beloved, unceasingly singing

[1] Periyāḻvār, Āṇḍāḷ and Tiruppāṇ. See A. Govindācārya, *Holy Lives*, pp. 39, 54 and 144 respectively.
[2] A. Govindācārya, *Holy Lives*, p. 54.
[3] Siddh. Dīp., p. 90, Vol. V, quoted in A. Govindācārya's *Holy Lives*, p. 144, footnote 2.

His praise, or to become intimately united with Him, that the Āḻvārs passionately desire; and since worldly existence comes in the way of their achieving this end, they long to be rid of it. A day in *saṁsāra* seems to them accordingly like the dark and joyless night, a thousand ages long, for it separates them from their Loved One for whom they become pale and languish.

> " Like days, months, years, and ages—crowding nights
> Have come, to make me pale for tulasi
> —Sweet garland on the head of heaven's Lord
> With the curved discus! Now to destroy me quite
> Comes this one night, a thousand ages long!"
>
> (Nammāḻvār-Tiruviruttam 70—Hooper.)

For reaching this goal they believe, as already suggested, that neither asceticism nor ceremonial, neither knowledge nor high birth is required. Tirumaṅgai, who belonged to the thief caste and could not claim any of these distinctions—not even the distinction of a virtuous life—is loudest in proclaiming God's mercy which stoops to accept the simple devotion of even the most degraded. Thus, e.g., in Periya Tirumoḻi V. 8 he dwells with great feeling on God's grace shown at sundry times to those of low estate, and regarding himself he says:

> " Ācārya sought I none, the Veds to con;
> On matters needing senses five
> Their use alone, I bent my mind. Hence wretch
> I am, failed to be alive
> T' the wisdom real. Intent but how to wreck
> Fell pains on all my fellow-men
> That dwell this world, I roamed. Yet grace hath come
> And stainless shine I now. So then
> To mokṣ attain, I've caught that matchless name
> Nārāyaṇa the universes claim."
>
> (Periya Tirumoḻi I. 1. 8—Viśist., Vol. I. No. 9.)

In similar vein, Toṇḍaraḍippoḍi declares that even the lowest of the low, if they have devotion, are dearer to the Deity than men of high caste, deep in learning.

" O Thou, whose crown fresh tulsi fillets wreathe!
Pretentious birth, but vain I ween to gain
Thy bliss, if *bhakti* weds it not. For Lord!
Dost not esteem Thou more those blessed souls
Who though human'ty's lowest ranks inborn
Yet in rapturous affection sweet thy feet
Close-set adore, than those the high-born priests
Who though well-versed the Vedic lore the four,
Yet hearts set not on service high of Thee!"

(Tirumālai 39, Viśist., Vol. 1, Nos. 10 and 11.)

When, then, such simple devotion is found, it would appear that the Deity in His infinite mercy destroys all sin and takes the soul to Himself. " First He cuts off the two kinds of sin in me. Then wipes off the residue. Then leads the mind towards Him by degrees. Then gets the heaven decorated and takes me there" (Nammāḻvār-Tiruvāymoli C. I. 5. 10—Kūrattāḻvār Aiyaṅgār). Āṇḍāḷ likewise declares:

" When thus all pure we come, strewing fair flowers,
Adoring, and with songs upon our lips,
And meditating in our hearts on Him—
. . . faults past and faults to come
Cease like to cotton that within the fire
Flames into dust."

(Tiruppāvai 5—Hooper.)

Whether in redeeming man from sin grace operates in such a way as to make man's efforts in that direction superfluous, is not considered. The Āḻvārs, conscious as they are of their own weakness and unworthiness, are apt to ascribe all the transforming work to the Deity's grace. Thus Toṇḍaraḍippoḍi who was lost in a life of sin till, as tradition has it,[1] the Deity Himself intervened and redeemed him from it, speaks of grace as operating on him in spite of himself.

" O gracious Lord! my days would ne'er I spend
In decking sweet Thy golden feet with blooms;
Nor flute in pure and holy tunes Thy fame.
And rites apart, have I Thee e'er with love
Impassioned loved? Oh. no. Nothing I own,
O Raṅga bright! Yet e'en Thou triest draw
Me to Thy holy feet against my will."

(Tirumālai 26, Viśist., Vol. 1, Nos. 10 and 11.)

[1] A. Govindācārya, Holy Lives, pp. 4-15.

His heart's devotion, he declares, was forced out of him.

> " Is not Raṅgam the glorious shrine of Him
> . . . Who gracious oped my darkened heart and there
> Enthroned, forced the current of my love
> To Him . . . ? "
>
> (Tirumālai 16, Viśiṣṭ., Vol. 1, Nos. 10 and 11.)

Nevertheless in living the life of a true devotee great effort was also necessary on the Āḷvār's part, as is shown by his earnest prayer for grace against besetting sins.

> " O truth have I forsworn ! caught in the snares
> Of wily dames of flowing locks, come I
> An erring soul, Refuge for all the sins
> That teem the world. O gracious Sire, Raṅga !
> 'Tis but my certain hope Thy grace will save
> Which bold me makes to walk to Thee and wait."
>
> (*Opus cit.*, verse 33).

Repeatedly [1] he prays thus for grace—he who only a few stanzas earlier declared that grace drew him even against his will.

Nammāḷvār declares that the Deity takes the initial step in the work of salvation. " It is not on my request He comes and resides in my mind. He took abode there of His own accord. . . . First He infused His spirit into my flesh, then into my life, and became one with my soul " (Tiruvāymoḷi C. I. 7. 7—Kūrattāḷvār Aiyangār). Residing in the soul, " He will not allow the five senses of His refugees to go in their own way. He takes up all souls of all places to the higher and higher state of goodness gradually " (C. I. 7. 2). He destroys " all the cruel sins in the period of a moment " (C. I. 6. 9) and drives away the ignorance of the devotee (C. I. 7. 4). He produces the love which He requires of the worshipper. " Thou keptst me, Thy servant, in Thy service, creating in me love of it even when I was ignorant and planted (rooted) in matter ; what a great wonder is this ! " (C. II. 3. 3). Although the Deity seeks in all these ways actively to redeem

[1] Cf. verses 29, 30, 32, 33, 35, etc.

the soul, it would appear that His grace is not irresistible, for "He leaves him who goes away desiring other things" (C. I. 7. 10), so much so that the Āḻvār declares that "it is difficult to enter into Him" (C. I. 7. 10).

From all this we may conclude that though the Āḻvārs regarded the work of salvation as being done by the Deity, and some of them even declared that it is done in spite of themselves, they generally assumed that the soul's efforts were also necessary.

Such in outline appear to be the ideas which find expression in the religion of the Āḻvārs. The Deity is above all gracious, and though in His transcendent form He is beyond human conception, He has manifested Himself in incarnate form, e.g., as Rāma and more especially as the heart-entrancing herdsman, Kṛṣṇa. In times past, as Viṣṇu, He came in diverse finite forms to help those who cried to Him in trouble. In His infinite mercy He exists in images, delighting the hearts of men and receiving their worship. What He desires from His devotees is their entire devotion, expressing itself in loving worship at the shrine, uttering His name, meditating on His acts of grace, and joining with others in singing His praise, till they lose themselves in ecstasy of unbounded love. He Himself aids them in this by His grace, however ignorant, morally depraved, down-trodden or unworthy they may be, and entering into their hearts He wipes out their sin and ignorance, and making them morally pure, He takes them to Himself.

Note.—The relation of the Deity to evil is not considered in the hymns we have examined. Judging from scattered references in the utterances of Nammāḻvār, the most philosophic of all the Āḻvārs, it would seem that the doctrine of *karma*, that evil results inevitably follow the evil deeds of the soul (cf. Nammāḻvār-Tiruvāymoḻi c. i. 4. 2), and further the view that *karma* is beginningless (c. i. 3. 8), are assumed. With regard to matter (*prakṛti*) it is declared that the Deity transcends it, and is not touched by its evil qualities (c. I. 2. 6; I. 3. 7; X. 10. 10). In these respects, the Āḻvārs assume the general philosophical beliefs expounded in the previous sections, with this difference, that the elaborate cosmology of the Saṁhitās with their account of the *Vyūhas* is apparently unknown to the Āḻvārs. Cosmology has no interest for them, for their one all-absorbing passion is the Deity in relation to themselves.

2. *Transition to Rāmānuja*

The Ācāryas.[1] The intense religious experience of the Āḻvārs received intellectual championship in the hands of their successors, the Ācāryas (teachers), among whom Rāmānuja was chief. Unlike the Āḻvārs, who compased in Tamil, the Ācāryas were learned men who were well-versed in Sanskrit.

Nāthamuni (? died A.D. 920)[2] was the earliest of them on record and it is to him that we owe the gathering together of the various hymns of the Āḻvārs extant in his day into the Nālāyira Prabandham. He is also said to have set them to music and introduced the system of their regular recitation in Vaiṣṇava temples. His philosophical works—the Nyāya Tattva and the Yoga Rahasya—do not appear to be extant.

His successor was his grandson *Yāmuna* (? died A.D. 1040),[2] otherwise called Āḷavandār. Yāmuna appears to have been a worthy predecessor of Rāmānuja, who as tradition has it, regarded it his mission merely to propagate Yāmuna's teaching. Rāmānuja was not mistaken in the choice of his spiritual leader, for Yāmuna was a great religious teacher and philosopher, who appears to have combined within himself the fervent religious experience of the Āḻvārs with a deep knowledge of classical philosophical literature, such as the Upaniṣads, the Bhagavadgītā, and the Vedānta-sūtras, as well as of commentaries and works, both advaitic and viśiṣṭādvaitic, on the Vedānta sūtras. In his Siddhi Traya, he seeks to establish the existence of the individual soul as distinct from the Supreme Soul, and refutes the advaitic doctrine which regards the individual soul as the mere product of illusion. In the Āgamaprāmāṇya, he aims to establish the

[1] I follow in the main the account given by Mr. T. Rājagopālācāriār in *Vaiṣṇavite Reformers*, etc., pp. 1-49.

[2] T. Rājagopālācāriār—*Vaiṣṇavite Reformers of India*, pp. 1 and 49 respectively. The dates are uncertain. Mr. Rājagopālācāriār will not own any responsibility for them for he gives them merely as "what is said." We may believe, however, that the Ācāryas lived after the Āḻvārs and before Rāmānuja.

orthodoxy of the Bhāgavata or Pāñcarātra sect as against the advaitin, who classifies it as a heretical school condemned by the Vedānta-sūtras. In his Gītārthasaṁgraha he seeks, as the name indicates, to give a summary of the teaching of the Bhagavadgītā, and we may believe that Rāmānuja obtained much help from these works.

Besides these, Yāmuna also composed a devotional hymn, the Stotra Ratna, which shows how deeply he drank of the religion of the Āḻvārs. He longs, as did the Āḻvārs, for the Deity. "When shall I see with my eyes Thy lotus-feet, my soul-treasure, which playfully strode over the worlds of both the high and the low, and which took pains to cure the pains of those that bowed in submission" (V. 30).[1] "As Thou Thyself out of compassion has roused in me this knowledge of being eternally Thine, so too, O Lord, grant me that love which is of the nature of enjoying no other than Thee" (V. 54). "Down with me who am unclean, insolent, ruthless and shameless. Such a notorious person like me, O Lord, desires the status of Thy servant. O Saviour, out of sheer mercy make me thine own" (vs. 47 and 48).

It is this religion of passionate devotion, as well as its philosophical formulation in the light of concepts derived from classical philosophical literature, that Rāmānuja inherited from his immediate predecessor.

[1] This and other citations which follow are taken from the translation of the Stotra Ratna in the Brahmavādin, Vol. IV, pp. 696-705.

PART TWO

RĀMĀNUJA'S CONCEPTION OF THE DEITY

INTRODUCTION

1. *Life of Rāmānuja*

Rāmānuja was born probably in the first half of the eleventh century.[1] At an early age, he was placed under the tuition of Yādavaprakāśa, who belonged to the Advaitic School of Śaṁkara. His characteristic independence of judgment soon brought him into conflict with his teacher, with whom he could not agree in the interpretation of sacred texts. He thereupon placed himself under the influence of certain Vaiṣṇava teachers who were the pupils of Yāmunācārya, the great philosopher of Vaiṣṇava religion and head of the temple at Śrīraṅgam. His attitude towards caste was so broad that it could not be tolerated by his orthodox wife, from whom on this account, it is said, he separated and became a *Sannyāsī*. On the death of Yāmunācārya, Rāmānuja, though still a young man, was appointed to fill the vacancy thus caused. This made him at once the religious as well as the intellectual leader of the Vaiṣṇava community at Śrīraṅgam. While here, he learnt all that was possible of the doctrines of his predecessor, taught, discussed and made many converts to the Vaiṣṇava religion. In his zeal for the faith, it is said that he undertook an extensive tour which took him as far north as Kashmir. He sought by these means not merely to disseminate his beliefs, but to gather from various seats of Vaiṣṇava

[1] Tradition gives the date of his birth as 939 Saka (i.e., A.D. 1017), cf. S. Kṛṣṇasvāmi Aiyaṅgār—Viśiṣṭādvaitin, Vol. 1, No. 8, p. 180. But since he is said to have died in 1137, i.e., 120 years after his birth, it seems unlikely that the traditional date of his birth is to be relied upon. It seems certain, however, that many of his activities fell in the last quarter of the 11th century. Cf. S. Kṛṣṇasvāmi Aiyaṅgār, *loc. cit.*, Dr. Berriedale Keiths's article on Rāmānuja in E.R.E. I rely for information regarding the main events in Rāmānuja's life on books referred to in the Bibliography.

learning as much knowledge as he could of the works of earlier Vaiṣṇava philosophers and commentators. Most of his days were spent at Śrīraṅgam in teaching, preaching and carrying on his religious activities. During the latter part of his life, he was forced to flee from there, owing to persecution by the Chola King, Kulottunga, who was a staunch adherent of Śaivism. He moved to the dominions of the Hoysala princes of Mysore, and succeeded in converting from Jainism the then ruler of that district, Biṭṭi Deva. He lived for some time in Mysore, building temples and dedicating images. He had great success in controversies with Śaivites, Jains and Buddhists, and won many converts. On the death of the Chola persecutor, he returned to Śriraṅgam, where he died, ripe in years and great in fame.

What is most characteristic of the life of Rāmānuja is its complete dedication to religion. Whatever Rāmānuja did, be it preaching or teaching, undertaking a journey or retreating into a hermitage, was, if tradition may be believed, always done in the interests of his religion ; and it is to his religion, therefore, that we must look for the clue to all his thought and action.

Rāmānuja's religion was Vaiṣṇavism. In essence it was the worship of a Personal God, conceived as Supreme Perfection characterised by love. It is in defence of this doctrine, fundamental to his religion, but essentially impossible on the hypothesis of the prevalent advaitic philosophy, according to which pure Thought alone was ultimately real and all else was *Māyā* (illusion), that Rāmānuja's philosophy arises.

In order that a system of philosophy should obtain respectful hearing, it was necessary in Rāmānuja's day to show that it did not conflict with revealed doctrine as contained in the Vedānta sūtras (which were regarded as the summary of the teaching of the Vedas and the Upaniṣads) and the Bhagavad Gītā. It was also necessary to show that any system of thought which was opposed to it, was also opposed to the teaching of these works. It was this two-fold task, therefore, that was needed to be performed by Rāmānuja, and was performed by him in the best way possible at the time, that is, by writing two commentaries,[1] one on the Vedānta sūtras, and the other on the Bhagavadgītā, showing by a close analysis and interpretation of the sacred texts that it was, on the one hand, his own religious view of God and the universe that was taught in these works, and on the other hand, the views of his opponents were in conflict with them. The very fact that the same texts could be interpreted by different men thus to uphold opposed philosophical systems is a sufficient indication, if such indication were necessary besides the nature of the texts themselves, that the texts often were too enigmatic to teach any definite system of thought, and the commentator was free to interpret them in the light of his own prepossessions. In the case of Rāmānuja these prepossessions appear, from the predominantly religious character of his life, teachings and activities, to have been determined by his religion.

We shall find that in order to provide a catholic basis for the conception of the Deity fundamental to the religion of his sect, Rāmānuja omits tenets which are distinctively sectarian and with great insight fixes on what is essential and seeks to find support for it in the teaching of the Upaniṣads. From our account of the Upaniṣads it will be seen that the view which Rāmānuja advocates is not altogether lacking in them. But his main inspiration came, we may be sure, from the devotional religion to which he belonged.

Note.—In the work of commenting on the Vedānta sūtras from the Viśiṣṭādvaitic point of view (i.e., from the point of view of his own modified monism which admits of the reality of the material universe and finite selves) Rāmānuja regards himself as following the tradition of some earlier commentators, so that he undoubtedly profited by their labours, but to what extent

[1] Other works are also ascribed to him. Of these the more important are Vedāntadīpa, Vedāntatattvasāra and Vedārthasaṁgraha.

we are unable to say, because these works are now extant. Cf. Thibaut, S.B.E., Vol. 34, pp. xxi and xxii; T. Rājagopālācāriār—*Vaiṣṇavite Reformers*, etc., pp. 31-4.

In his Śrī Bhāṣya, Rāmānuja quotes from Dramiḍācārya, p. 487, from the Dramiḍa-bhāṣya, pp. 99, 428, from a *vṛtti*, p. 99 (usually taken to be that of Bodhāyana), a *vṛttikāra*, pp. 206, 261, 302, 337 (probably Bodhāyana), a *bhāṣyakāra*, pp. 17 and 100 (probably Dramiḍa), and a *vākyakāra*, pp. 15-18, 24, 99, 138, 317 (possibly Taṅka. See S.B.E., Vol. 34, p. xxii).

2. *The Place of empirical Reason in matters pertaining to the Deity.*

Knowledge of the Deity not obtained through empirical Reason.

A thought which may be said to have come down to Rāmānuja without break from the time of the Upaniṣads is that the Supreme Being is not knowable in terms of ordinary human experience. We noticed how in remote times Yājñavalkya exclaimed that if one seeks to describe the Imperishable one can do so only negatively, that is, by denying of Him the qualities known in experience. This scepticism with regard to the capacity of human thought to grasp the nature of the Infinite, far from declining with the development of speculation, became more and more pronounced, as we saw, in the later Upaniṣads. It is true that the later thinkers ascribed numerous perfections to the Supreme Being, but they nevertheless declared that He is more subtle than the subtle, and was to be seen only by "subtle seers," or by him whom the Deity chooses. In the Gītā this idea was further developed, and elaborate conditions in line with Sāṁkhya Yoga were laid down, whereby knowledge of the subtle *Ātman* may be obtained, and the doctrine that the Deity may be seen only by the one whom He chooses was practically demonstrated by the fact that through the grace of Kṛṣṇa Arjuna was given a special eye (XI. 8) whereby he was able to see the universal form of the Deity. In the Nārāyaṇīya we were told that Nārāyaṇa was invisible to Ekata, Dvita and Trita, but was seen by His devotees in the White Island; and the Saṁhitās postulated a *Para* or Absolute form of the Divine Being, and refused to describe[1] it in terms of any known qualities. It was thus the conviction both of philosophy and religion, for a long time prior to Rāmānuja that the supreme Being cannot be apprehended by the ordinary powers of the human mind.

This conviction Rāmānuja shares. "Brahman is not manifested by other means of proof, for Scripture says, 'His form is not to be seen, no one beholds Him with the eye' (Ka. Up. II. 6. 9)" (Ś. Bh. III., p. 617). Reason in the sense of empirical argumentation cannot, he holds, of itself yield knowledge in the noumenal realm. Hence, as we shall see, he mercilessly refutes arguments which seek purely on the ground of experience to establish the existence of God. What, he asks, are those empirical sources whereby knowledge of Brahman may be gained? "It cannot, in the first place, be Perception. Perception is two-fold, being based either on the sense-organs or on extraordinary concentration of mind (*yoga*). Of Perception of the former kind there are again two sub-species, according as Perception takes place either through the outer sense organs or the internal organ (*manas*). Now the outer sense-organs produce knowledge of their respective objects, in so far as the latter are in actual contact with the organs, but are quite unable to give rise to knowledge of the special object constituted by a supreme Self that is capable of being conscious of and creating the whole aggregate of things. Nor can internal perception give rise to such knowledge; for only purely internal things, such as pleasure and pain, fall within its cognisance, and it is incapable of relating itself to external objects apart from the outer sense-organs. Nor, again, can perception based on Yoga; for although such perception—which springs from intense imagination—implies a vivid presentation

[1] Sometimes *Para* was not regarded as the Absolute, but as the Supreme manifestation of the Absolute, and only then it was described. As the Absolute it was indescribable. See Schrader, *Introd. to the Pāñcarātra*, pp. 52 and 53.

of things, it is, after all, nothing more than a reproduction of objects perceived previously, and does not therefore rank as an instrument of knowledge; for it has no means of applying to objects other than those perceived previously. And if, after all, it does so, it is (not a means of knowledge but) a source of error" (Ś. Bh. I. I. 3, p. 162).[1]

Not only is Perception unable to give us knowledge of the Deity, but "also inference either of the kind which proceeds on the observation of special cases or of the kind which rests on generalisations. Not inference of the former kind, because such inference is not known to relate to anything beyond the reach of the senses. Nor inference of the latter kind, because we do not observe any characteristic feature that is invariably accompanied by the presence of a supreme Self capable of being conscious of, and constructing, the universe of things" (Ś. Bh. I. 1. 3, p. 162). It is this last point that Rāmānuja thinks it necessary to establish, for the others assert the quite obvious truth that the Deity cannot be proved by arguments which ultimately depend on the verdict of the senses. He accordingly seeks to show that no reasoning which is based merely on characteristics exhibited by the material world can suffice to prove the existence of a Wise and Perfect Creator.

Refutation of arguments for the existence of God

Rāmānuja considers in the main two arguments which may be put forward to establish by empirical means the existence of God. (1) It may be argued that just as from the existence of a living body, we infer the existence of a soul or intelligent principle which animates it, so from the existence of non-sentient matter in the world, we may infer the existence of an Intelligent principle which animates and supports it (Ś. Bh. I. 1. 3, p. 163).

[1] Thibaut's Translation, S.B.E., Vol. 48. Page references are to pages in this volume.

This argument Rāmānuja refutes by pointing out that the analogy on which it is based is insufficient to support it, for (*a*) the soul does not bring into existence the body which it animates, and yet this is what we wish to prove regarding the Creator in relation to non-sentient matter; (*b*) the soul does not entirely of itself support the body, for the latter depends on wife, mother or other persons for its sustenance, but what we want to prove is that matter depends for its support entirely on one Being, the Creator; (*c*) the fact that the various parts of a body cohere together may be due to other forces than to the fact that it is animated by a soul, in which case again, the analogy becomes entirely incapable of proving the conclusion; (*d*) "the existence of animated bodies, moreover, has for its characteristic mark the process of breathing, which is absent in the case of the earth, sea, mountains, etc."; (*e*) if it is argued that motion in the inanimate world, even as motion of the body, requires an animate intelligent principle to explain it, it may be pointed out there is nothing in the analogy to establish the existence of only one such principle, for even as there are many souls animating many bodies, the motion in the inanimate material world may be traced to many intelligent principles (S. Bh. I. 1. 3, p. 163). For these reasons then we may dismiss this argument as incapable of establishing the existence of a Supreme intelligent Being.

(3) Another argument may be brought forward, based on "the world's being an effected thing, it being a matter of common experience that whatever is an effect or product, is due to an agent who possesses a knowledge of the material cause, the instrumental cause, the final end, and the person meant to make use of the thing produced," as is exemplified by the case of jars and similar things (S. Bh. I. 1. 3, pp. 162 and 163).

To this Rāmānuja objects by pointing out that we

have no right to infer a Supreme Creator till we have shown that lesser beings, with limited intelligence but with religious merit, and knowledge of instrumental causes such as sacrifices and the like, are incapable of bringing about the material world.[1] "As we both admit the existence of individual souls, it will be the more economical hypothesis to ascribe to them the agency implied in the construction of the world. Nor must you object to this view on the ground that such agency cannot belong to the individual souls because they do not possess the knowledge of material causes, etc., as specified above; for all intelligent beings are capable of direct knowledge of material causes, such as earth and so on, and instrumental causes, such as sacrifices and the like. Earth and other material substances, as well as sacrifices and the like, are directly perceived by individual beings at the present time (and were no doubt equally perceived so at a former time when this world has to be planned and constructed). Nor does the fact that intelligent beings are not capable of direct insight into the unseen principle—called *apūrva* or by similar names—which resides in the form of a power in sacrifices and other instrumental causes, in any way preclude their being agents in the construction of the world. Direct insight into powers is nowhere required for undertaking work; what *is* required for that purpose is only direct presentative knowledge of the things endowed with power, while of power itself it suffices to have some kind of knowledge. Potters apply themselves to the task of making pots and jars on the strength of the direct knowledge they possess of the implements of their work—the wheel, the staff, etc.—without troubling about a similar knowledge of the powers inherent in those implements; and in the same way intelligent beings may apply themselves to their work (to be effected by means of sacrifices,

[1] It is only with the material world as a product like a jar that the argument is concerned.

etc.) if only they are assured by sacred tradition of the existence of the various powers possessed by sacrifices and the like " (Ś. Bh. I. 1. 3, p. 164). If to this objection it is replied that individual souls cannot have constructed the material world, " for on the testimony of observation we must deny to those souls the power of seeing what is extremely subtle or remote in time or place (while such power must necessarily be ascribed to a world-constructing intelligence," (P. 167), Rāmānuja points out that even so, it is not inconceivable that individual souls constructed the material world, " For we observe that individual beings acquire more and more extraordinary powers in consequence of an increase of religious merit; and as we may assume that through an eventual supreme degree of merit they may in the end qualify themselves for producing quite extraordinary effects, we may have no right to assume a highest soul of infinite merit, different from all individual souls " (Ś. Bh. I. 1. 3, p. 170).

Further, Rāmānuja points out that " experience teaches that agents having a knowledge of the material and other causes must be inferred only in the case of those effects which can be produced, and the material and other causes of which can be known; such things, on the other hand, as the earth, mountains, and oceans, can neither be produced, nor can their material and other causes ever be known; we therefore have no right to infer for them intelligent producers. Hence the quality of being an effected thing can be used as an argument for proving the existence of an intelligent causal agent, only where that quality is found in things, the production of which, and the knowledge of the causes of which, is possible at all " (Ś. Bh. I. 1. 3, pp. 164 and 165). This, however, not being possible in the case of the material world, it is impossible to establish a Supreme intelligent Being as its cause.

" Experience further teaches that earthen pots and similar things are produced by intelligent agents possessing material bodies, using implements, not endowed with the power of a Supreme Lord, limited in knowledge and so on; the quality of being an effect therefore supplies a reason for inferring an intelligent agent of the kind described only, and this is opposed to the inference of attributes of a contrary nature, viz., omniscience, omnipotence, and those other attributes that belong to the highest soul—whose existence you wish to establish" (Ś. Bh. I. 1. 3, p. 165). Rāmānuja admits—or at least raises no objection to the view—that inference on the basis of finite agency need not necessarily establish that the Creator of the material world suffers from all the limitations of a finite agent (cf. pp. 167-9). Nevertheless, he contends, it cannot warrant our predicating of the Creator perfections to which there is no analogy in what we know of finite agents.

Besides, he argues, empirical proof proceeds by testing what logically follows from some one idea, in the light of considerations obtained from other sources than mere inference (e.g., from sense perception or experimentation); but this is clearly impossible in the case of a concept such as that of a Supreme Creator, for it rests purely on inference, and cannot be tested by empirical methods. "Where the thing to be inferred is known through other means of proof also, any qualities of an opposite nature which may be suggested by the inferential mark (*liṅga*) are opposed by those other means of proof, and therefore must be dropped. In the case under discussion, however, the thing to be inferred is something not guaranteed by any other means of proof, viz.: a person capable of constructing the entire universe; here there is nothing to interfere with the ascription to such a person of all those qualities which, on the basis of methodical inferences, necessarily belong to it." Empirical proof of the existence of a Supreme Creator is therefore clearly impossible (Ś. Bh. I. 1. 3, p. 165).

Having thus considered arguments which claim

empirically to establish the existence of a Supreme Creator, Rāmānuja summarily marshals all his objections[1] to such efforts. "That the world is an effected thing because it consists of parts; and that, as all effects are observed to have for their antecedents certain appropriate agents competent to produce them, we must infer a causal agent competent to plan and construct the universe, and standing towards it in the relation of material and operative cause—this would be a conclusion altogether unjustified. There is no proof to show that the earth, oceans, etc., although things produced, were created at one time by one creator. Nor can it be pleaded in favour of such a conclusion that all those things have one uniform character of being effects, and thus are analogous to one single jar; for we observe that various effects are distinguished by difference of time of production and difference ot producers. Nor again may you obtain the oneness of the creator on the ground that individual souls are incapable of the creation of this wonderful universe, and that if an additional principle be assumed to account for the world—which manifestly is a product—it would be illegitimate to assume more than one such principle. . . . Nor also can it be proved that all things are destroyed and produced all at once; for no such thing is observed to take place, while it is, on the other hand, observed that things are produced and destroyed in succession; and if we infer that all things are produced and destroyed because they are effects, there is no reason why this production and destruction should not take place in a way agreeing with ordinary experience. If, therefore, what it is desired to prove is the agency of one intelligent being, we are met by the difficulty that the proving reason (viz., the circumstance of something being an effect) is not invariably connected with what it is desired to prove; there, further, is the fault of qualities not met with in experience being attributed to the subject

[1] We shall in what follows enumerate only the more significant of these.

about which something has to be proved; and lastly there is the fault of the proving collateral instances being destitute of what has to be proved—for experience does not exhibit to us an agent capable of producing everything" (Ś. Bh. I. 1. 3, pp. 169 and 171).

"Moreover, if you use the attribute of being an effect (which belongs to the totality of things) as a means to prove the existence of one omniscient and omnipotent creator, do you view this attribute as belonging to all things in so far as produced together, or in so far as produced in succession? In the former case the attribute of being an effect is not established (for experience does not show that all things are produced together); and in the latter case the attribute would really prove what is contrary to the hypothesis of one creator (for experience shows that things produced in succession have different causes). In attempting to prove the agency of one intelligent creative being only, we thus enter into conflict with Perception and Inference" (Ś. Bh. I. 1. 3, p. 171).

"Consider the following point also. Does the Lord produce his effects, with his body or apart from his body? Not the latter, for we do not observe causal agency on the part of any bodiless being; even the activities of the internal organ are found only in beings having a body, and although the internal organ be eternal we do not know of its producing any effects in the case of released disembodied souls. Nor again is the former alternative admissible; for in that case the Lord's body would either be permanent or non-permanent. The former alternative would imply that something made up of parts is eternal; and if we once admit this we may as well admit that the world itself is eternal, and then there is no reason to infer a Lord. And the latter alternative is inadmissible because in that case there would be no cause of the body, different from it (which would account for the origination of the body). Nor could the Lord himself be assumed as the cause of the body, since a bodiless being cannot be the cause of a body. Nor could it be maintained that the Lord can be assumed to be 'embodied' by means of some other body; for this leads us into a *regressus in infinitum*" (Ś. Bh. I. 1. 3, pp. 172 and 173).

"Should we, moreover, represent to ourselves the Lord (when productive) as engaged in effort or not?—The former is inadmissible, because he is without a body. And the latter alternative is excluded because a being not making an effort does not produce effects; and if it be said that the effect, i.e., the world, has for its causal agent one whose activity consists in mere desire, this would be to ascribe to the subject of the conclusion (i.e., the world) qualities not known from experience; and moreover the attribute to be proved would be absent in the case of the proving instances (such as jars, etc., which are not the work of agents engaged in mere wishing)" (Ś. Bh. I. 1. 3, p. 173).

"Thus," Rāmānuja concludes, "the inference of a creative Lord which claims to be in agreement with observation is refuted by reasoning which itself is in agreement with observation" (Ś. Bh. I. 1. 3, p. 173). Whether, then, on the analogy of the fact that a body presupposes a presiding intelligent principle, or on the analogy of the fact that a product presupposes a producing agent, Rāmānuja contends that it is impossible empirically to establish that the world presupposes the Supreme Being as its Creator and animating principle.

If then empirical reasoning of itself cannot give us any certain knowledge concerning the Deity, we must ask, on what, according to Rāmānuja, we may rely for this knowledge? Following the opinion of the Sūtra Kāra (I. 1. 3) Rāmānuja declares that Scripture is the source of our knowledge of Brahman. "Brahman, being raised above all contact with the senses, is not an object of perception and the other means of proof, but to be known through Scripture only" (Ś. Bh. I. 1. 3, p. 161).

Scripture as the Source for knowledge of Brahman

This seems so much like abandoning Reason in the interests of the written Word, that we must enquire what exactly Rāmānuja means by regarding Scripture as his source in matters pertaining to Brahman. His view becomes intelligible when we consider it in relation to the conviction, to which we have already referred, of philosophy and religion prior to his day, that Brahman is not to be known except by "subtle seers" and by those whom the Deity chooses. Accepting this position in principle, Rāmānuja declares that Brahman may not, as demonstrated above, be known by natural processes of thought, but by *Bhakti* or *Upāsanā* (devout meditation) and through the grace of the Deity. "What we have to understand by knowledge in this connection has been repeatedly explained, viz., a mental energy different in character from the mere cognition of the sense of texts, and more specifically denoted by such terms as *Dhyāna* or *Upāsanā*, i.e., meditation, which is of the nature of remembrance (i.e., representative thought), but in intuitive clearness is not inferior to the clearest presentative thought (*pratyakṣa*) which by constant daily practice becomes ever more perfect" (Ś. Bh. III. 4. 26, p. 699). "Steady remembrance of this kind is designated by the word 'devotion' (*bhakti*), for this term has the same meaning as *upāsanā* meditation)" (Ś. Bh. I. 1. 1, p. 16). "Such meditation is originated in the mind through the grace of the Supreme Person, who is pleased and conciliated by the different kinds of acts of sacrifice and worship duly performed by the devotee day by day" (Ś. Bh. III. 4. 26, p. 699). "It is only in the state of perfect conciliation or endearment, i.e., in meditation bearing the character of devotion, that an intuition of Brahman takes place, not in any other state" (Ś. Bh. III. 2. 23, p. 617).

If, then, knowledge of Brahman requires on the part

of man devotion, meditation and the doing of His will, and on the part of Brahman loving grace, it is not surprising that the mere logical understanding or empirical Reason does not suffice for a knowledge of Brahman. The Scriptures,[1] being a record of the vision of God granted to holy men in the past, must be our guide in matters concerning Him. Vāmadeva and others 'saw' (God by means of *bhakti* (devotion) (Ś. Bh. III. 2. 24, p. 618), and our doctrine with regard to God must rely on the religious intuition of such men, as that is recorded for us in the Scriptures. But that Rāmānuja does not mean by this to imply that Divine revelation is confined to the Scriptures, and that we can never know God first hand, is clear from the words above cited, which declare that *Upāsanā* whereby the individual realises Brahman, is in point of directness and intuitive clearness not inferior to the clearest presentative thought (*pratyakṣa*). His contention that Scripture is our source for knowledge of Brahman, when taken in the light of this fact, must be understood it would seem in the sense that ultimately we must rely for matters concerning the Deity on religious experience, whether that be of men of the past, as that is recorded in the Scriptures, or of one's own direct vision of the Deity. But since both are revelations of the Supreme Being, they cannot vary in essence, and since Scripture provides us with an objective criterion, we must regard Scripture as our guide. But Scripture, Rāmānuja makes it quite clear, is only a means to the higher knowledge which consists in direct intuition of Brahman. " 'The lower knowledge is the Ṛg. Veda,' etc.; this knowledge is the means towards the intuition of Brahman, while the higher kind of knowledge, which is called '*upāsanā*' has the character of devout meditation (*bhakti*) and

[1] That is Śruti (Vedas, Upaniṣads and Vedānta sūtras) and Smṛti (i.e., authoritative works such as the Gītā) which do not contradict Śruti (see p. 411, Ś. Bh.) Rāmānuja regards portions of the Mahābhārata and the Viṣṇu Purāṇa also as authoritative (cf. p. 91 and p. 126, Ś. Bh.).

consists in direct intuition of Brahman" (p. 284). It is direct religious experience therefore that gives us true knowledge of Brahman. But Scripture provides the necessary preliminary information regarding Brahman, and is hence authoritative.

If then Scripture or religious experience is to be our primary guide in matters concerning the Deity, we have still to ask, what part empirical reason or the logical understanding may legitimately play in developing a systematic view regarding God and His relation to the universe. It is clear that its function is not that of determining what one must believe and what one must not believe in regard to the Deity, for, as Rāmānuja indicated in his criticism of the arguments for the existence of a Supreme Creator, Reason is quite unable of itself to establish anything in this realm. But, for this reason, argumentation is not to be discarded. It is to be used to support revelation. "The conclusion from all this is that, with regard to supersensuous matters, Scripture alone is authoritative, and that reasoning is to be applied only to the support of Scripture" (Ś. Bh. II. 1. 12, p. 426).

The place which Rāmānuja thus assigns to Reason in regard to doctrines concerning the Deity is not in practice as scholastic as it seems in theory for, as we have already seen, Revelation is not confined by him to Scripture, but is admitted as possible to the individual in his own direct experience of the Deity. Moreover, the Scriptures, that is, the Upaniṣads and the Vedānta sūtras, teach no clear or consistent body of doctrine. Consequently, as it happens, Reason in the case of Rāmānuja is not bound by any hard and fast dogma, which it is its sole task to defend. Indeed, so free does Rāmānuja feel in the employment of Reason, that he at times employs reason, not to support Scripture, but to make Scripture support him. Nevertheless it must be admitted that the function which Rāmānuja assigns to Reason in matters pertaining to the Deity is that of supporting revealed truths.

Since however the Scriptures give no definite and consistent guidance, the truths upon which Rāmānuja relies are, as we shall see, those which came to him from his own sectarian religion, Vaiṣṇavism. It is the Vaiṣṇava view of Deity, therefore, that ultimately Reason must seek to support, but it must do so in the words of the Scriptures. Consequently sectarian details, which naturally are not found in the Scriptures, are to be omitted, but the main doctrines of theism are to be retained and defended in the light of Scriptural teaching. This, then, is Reason's special task in Rāmānuja's system, and in performing it, it is needless to say, it will be concerned mainly with quoting chapter and verse from the Scriptures; but it must also seek to defend itself by independent arguments. It is on these arguments that we shall chiefly fix our attention, for the others—and unfortunately they constitute the major part of Rāmānuja's arguments—being purely textual, have no philosophical value.

CHAPTER I

THE NATURE OF THE DEITY

SINCE Rāmānuja's chief purpose in philsoophy is to justify the religious view of life as against the pure monism or advaitism, which Śaṁkara had made popular among philosophers, and according to which the basic assumptions of religion were to be regarded as ultimately false, his doctrine regarding the nature of the Deity is developed in opposition to, and by way of a criticism of, the advaitic view of the nature of Ultimate Reality.

Brahman not pure unity

In his Śrībhāṣya, in which Rāmānuja is concerned with laying the philosophical foundations of his faith, he examines carefully the advaitin's view that Brahman or Ultimate Reality is *advaita* or one without a second, that is, a pure One which excludes all differences. His contention is that such a pure non-differenced Being cannot be established by an appeal to experience, for the verdict of (*a*) consciousness in general, and in particular, in (*b*) speech (*śabda*), (*c*) perception, and (*d*) inference is that the experienced is always a content characterised by differences.

(*a*) *No proof of non-differenced substance in consciousness*

" Should anyone, taking his stand on the received views of his sect, assert that the theory of a substance free from all difference (does not require any further means of proof but) is immediately established by one's own consciousness; we reply that he also is refuted by the fact, warranted by the witness of the Self, that all consciousness implies difference: all states of consciousness have for their object something that is marked by some difference, as appears in the case of judgments like 'I saw this.'"

If to this it is replied that appeal to direct consciousness is of little value, for the verdict of immediate consciousness may often be falsified by investigation, Rāmānuja points out that such is not the case in the matter under discussion, for in order to prove the falsity of the view that consciousness reveals differences it would have to be shown that consciousness reveals something different from differences, and in that very fact it would be admitted that consciousness does reveal differences. "Should a state of consciousness—although directly apprehended as implying difference—be determined by some fallacious reasoning to be devoid of difference, this determination could be effected only by means of some special attributes additional to the quality of mere Being; and owing to these special qualities on which the determination depends, that state of consciousness would clearly again be characterised by difference. The meaning of the mentioned determination could thus only be that of a thing affected with certain differences some other differences are denied; but manifestly this would not prove the existence of a thing free from all differences."

Further, consciousness has attributes such, for example, as self-illuminatedness, and thus itself presupposes differences. "To thought there at any rate belongs the quality of being thought and self-illuminatedness, for the knowing principle is observed to have for its essential nature the illumining (making to shine forth) of objects. . . . Moreover you yourself admit that to consciousness there actually belong different attributes such as permanency (oneness, self-luminousness, etc.), and of these it cannot be shown that they are only Being in general."

"And," he continues, "even if the latter point were admitted, we observe that there takes place a discussion of different views, and you yourself attempt to prove your theory by means of the differences between those views and your own. It therefore must be admitted that reality is affected with difference well established by valid means of proof" (Ś. Bh. I.1. 1, pp. 39 and 40).

(b) No proof of non-differenced substance in speech

As to sound (speech, *śabda*) it is specially apparent that it possesses the power of denoting only such things as are affected with difference. Speech operates with words and sentences. Now a word (*pada*) originates from the combination of a radical element and a suffix, and as these two elements have different meanings it necessarily follows that the word itself can convey only a sense affected with difference."

"And further, the plurality of words is based on plurality of meanings; the sentence therefore which is an aggregate of words expresses some special combination of things (meanings of words), and hence has no power to denote a thing devoid of all difference."

Speech, therefore, which consists of words (composed of roots and varying suffixes) and of sentences (composed of several words) clearly cannot testify to a thing devoid of all difference (Ś. Bh. I. 1. 1, pp. 40 and 41).

(c) No proof of non-differenced substance in perception

Perception, according to Rāmānuja, is of two kinds —determinate and indeterminate. Determinate perception is the apprehension of an object, for example, a cow as having numerous qualities, and as similar to other cows already perceived. Indeterminate perception, on the other hand, is the apprehension of an object, for example, a comet, which is the first of its class to be perceived, and which, though perceived as having definite qualities, is not perceived in relation to other members of the same class. In both cases, it is obvious that the object is perceived as having various qualities, and therefore perception, whether determinate or indeterminate, Rāmānuja concludes, is only of objects characterised by differences, and never of pure Being. "All apprehension by consciousness takes place by means of some distinction. 'This is such and such.' Nothing can be apprehended apart from some special feature of make or structure, as, e.g., the triangularly shaped dewlap in the case of cows. The true distinction between non-determinate and determinate perception is that the former is the apprehension of the first individual among a number of things belonging to the same class, while the latter is the apprehension of the second, third, and so on, individuals. On the apprehension of the first individual cow the perceiving person is not conscious of the fact that the special shape which constitutes the genuine character of the class 'cows' extends to the present individual also; while this special consciousness arises in the case of the perception of the second and third cow." Non-determinate perception, or perception of the first individual of a class, is never, Rāmānuja emphasizes, of an object free from all determinations. "That it is such (i.e., non-determinate)[1] is not due to non-apprehension of structure, colour, generic character and so on, for all these attributes are equally objects of sensuous perception (and hence perceived as belonging to the first individuals also). From this Rāmānuja concludes that perception—"with its two subdivisions of non-determinate and determinate perception—also cannot be a means of knowledge for things devoid of difference" (S. Bh. I. 1. 1, pp. 41 and 42).

The conclusion is so important for the metaphysical structure which he hopes to erect on it, that Rāmānuja is not content to leave the matter thus. He wishes to make it perfectly clear that the experienced real—

[1] Words in parenthesis are mine.

in this case, the perceived real—is always a content characterised by differences. And it is the differences, thus always found to cohere in the unity of the experienced real that Rāmānuja would emphasize. Accordingly, not satisfied with demolishing the advaitin's non-differenced Substance, he proceeds to attack the Bhedābhedavādin, who goes half way towards admitting the reality of differences, but is afraid to go all the way and to say that differences *are* differences. The Bhedābhedavādin is, according to Rāmānuja, one who says that differences are differences and yet also are not differences. The qualities are, and yet also are not, different from the objects in which they are found. This view Rāmānuja finds to be quite unacceptable. " Take the judgment 'This is such and such,' how can we realise here the non-difference of 'being thus' and 'being such and such'? The 'such and such' denotes a peculiar make characterised, e.g., by a dewlap, the 'this' denotes the thing distinguished by that peculiar make; the non-difference of these two is thus contradicted by immediate consciousness." To state Rāmānuja's view in modern philosophical language the 'that' is not the same as the 'what.'

In insisting thus on the difference of the 'what' from the 'that,' Rāmānuja, it is necessary to note, does not mean to assert that the 'what' as generic quality falls entirely outside the 'that' or object to which it belongs. Indeed, his whole contention has been that the 'that' as already demonstrated, is never a pure 'that' as the advaitin, according to him, maintains, but always and only a 'that-what,' so that the 'what' is found contained in the 'that.' But, and this is quite important for his Metaphysics, the 'what' is essentially different from the 'that' although it may be contained in the 'that.' It is this essential difference between the 'what' and the 'that' that Rāmānuja wishes to emphasize as against the Bhedābhedavādin, when he declares that "wherever we cognise the relation of distinguishing attribute and thing distinguished thereby, the two clearly present themselves to our mind as absolutely different."

It must, however, be admitted that Rāmānuja is willing to carry his distinction between the 'what' and the 'that' further than this. For he claims—again, one suspects, in the interests of his metaphysical theory—that the 'what' may include, besides generic qualities, other things which are capable of existing independently of the 'that' to which they belong. "Some things—e.g., staffs and bracelets—appear sometimes as having a separate, independent existence of their own; at other times they present themselves as distinguishing attributes of other things or beings (i.e., of the persons carrying staffs or wearing bracelets). Other entities—e.g., the generic character of cows—have a being only in so far as they constitute the form of substances and thus always present themselves as distinguishing attributes of those substances. In both cases there is the same relation of distinguishing attribute and the things distinguished thereby, and these two are apprehended as absolutely different. The difference between the two classes of entities is only that staffs, bracelets and similar things are capable of being apprehended in separation from other things, while the generic characteristics of a species are absolutely incapable thereof" (S. Bh. I. 1. 1, pp. 42 and 43. Whether Rāmānuja is justified or not in stretching the substance-attribute relation to cover cases which are not generally regarded as cases of that relationship, his point is clear that the distinguishing attribute is quite distinct from the substance to which it belongs.

But in thus establishing as against the Bhedābhedavādin that perception always reveals attributes which are entirely different from the substance to which they belong, Rāmānuja finds himself exposed to two objections. It might be said that, if the attribute is entirely different from the substance, then a third term is required to relate them to each other, and that term needs still another and so on *ad infinitum*. Besides, it might be said that we are committed to a logical see-saw, for we declare that the qualities are known by knowing the object, and at the same time we also declare that the thing is known by knowing its qualities (Ś. Bh. I. 11, p. 32). Rāmānuja meets both objections by pointing out that they rest on an artificial separation of qualities from things; in reality qualities and the objects in which they inhere exist inseparably united together. Consequently at the very moment that the quality is perceived the object is also perceived, and at the very moment that the object is perceived the quality is also perceived. There is no question, therefore, of either bringing the quality and the object together, by means of other terms *ad infinitum*, or of apprehending one first and then by means of it apprehending the other. Accordingly in answer to those who raise such objections Rāmānuja replies, "We point out that these charges are completely refuted by the fact that the only objects of perception are things distinguished by generic character and so on, and that generic character and so on—as being relative things—give at once rise to the judgment as to the distinction between themselves and the things in which they inhere. You yourself admit that in the case of knowledge and in that of colour and other qualities this relation holds good, viz., that something which gives rise to a judgment about another thing at the same time gives rise to a judgment about itself; the same may therefore be admitted with regard to difference.[1] For this reason the charge of a *regressus in infinitum* and a logical see-saw cannot be upheld. For even if perceptive cognition takes place within one moment, we apprehend within

[1] Thibaut explains in a footnote—"Colour reveals itself as well as the thing that has colour; knowledge reveals itself as well as the objects known; so difference manifests itself as well as the things that differ" (p. 44), i.e., difference or attribute in manifesting itself manifests in that very fact also the object to which it belongs.

that moment the generic character which constitutes on the one hand the difference of the thing from others, and on the other hand the peculiar character of the thing itself, and thus there remains nothing to be apprehended in a second moment" (S. Bh. I. 1. 1, p. 44). In this way Rāmānuja emphatically maintains that though the attribute is quite distinct from the substance, nevertheless what is experienced is always a substance-attribute, and never a bare substance with which an attribute has later to be artificially united. Rāmānuja regards this conclusion as so important that he piles evidence upon evidence to support it.

"If perception made us apprehend only pure Being, judgments clearly referring to different objects—such as 'here is a jar,' 'there is a piece of cloth'—would be devoid of all meaning."

"If through perception we did not apprehend difference—as marked by generic character, etc., constituting the structure or make of a thing—why should a man searching for a horse not be satifised with finding a buffalo?"

"If mere Being only were the object of all our cognitions, why should we not remember, in the case of each particular cognition, all the words which are connected with all our cognitions?" Why, in other words, do we not cognise all Being at once at any one time?

"If the cognition of a horse and that of an elephant had one object only, the later cognition would cause us to apprehend only what was apprehended before, and there being thus no difference (of object of cognition) there wou d be nothing to distinguish the later state of cognition from remembrance." Since all objects are assumed to be one, later cognition can only be a remembrance of what has already been cognised; and this is manifestly absurd. "If on the other hand a difference is admitted for each state of consciousness, we admit thereby that perception has for its objects the things affected with difference."

" If all acts of cognition had one and the same object only, it would follow that there are no persons either deaf or blind," for reality being something which is void of differences, it can make no difference in cognition to be without ear or eye.

" Nor does, as a matter of fact, the eye apprehend mere Being only ; for what it does apprehend is colour and the coloured thing, and those other qualities (viz., extension, etc.) which inhere in the thing together with colour. Nor does feeling do so ; for it has for its object things palpable. Nor have the ear and the other senses mere Being for their object ; but they relate to what is distinguished by a special sound or taste or smell. Hence there is not any source of knowledge causing us to apprehend mere Being."

" From all this we conclude that perception has for its object only what is distinguished by difference manifesting itself in generic character and so on, which constitute the make or structure of a thing " (Ś. Bh. I. 1. 1, pp. 44 and 45).

(d) *No proof of non-differenced substance in inference*

Now that it has been shown very fully that perception reveals only what is characterised by differences, and never something which is pure qualityless Being, it is easy to show that inference also does the same, for inference rests on knowledge obtained through perception. " Perception thus having for its object only what is marked by difference, inference also is in the same case ; for its object is only what is distinguished by connection with things known through perception and other means of knowledge. And thus, even in the case of disagreement as to the number of the different instruments of knowledge, a thing devoid of difference could not be established by any one of them since the instruments of knowledge acknowledged by all have only one and the same object, viz., what is marked by difference."

But if it is said that, though perception reveals differences as real, still inference may establish in opposition to perception that differences are unreal, Rāmānuja has already pointed out that in the matter under dispute inference cannot do this, for to do so inference would have to establish that Reality is *different* from what it is revealed to be in perception, and in that very fact it would be admitting the reality of differences. Moreover, he now points out that it is impossible to say that, though perception reveals differences as real, inference may come to a contrary conclusion; for to do so inference would have to contradict itself. It would have to establish that differences are unreal on the ground that they are real, i.e., on the ground of perception on which inference ultimately rests. Accordingly he declares that "a person who maintains the existence of a thing devoid of difference on the ground of differences affecting that very thing simply contradicts himself without knowing what he does" (Ś. Bh. I. 1. 1, p. 43).

From all this Rāmānuja concludes that there is no proof anywhere in experience of a substance unqualified by differences, or, stated positively, that the only Real revealed in experience, is one which is characterized throughout by differences.

Brahman not pure Thought

The Advaitin maintains that the pure qualityless Being which is according to him the only ultimate Reality is identical with pure thought or consciousness, for while all other things are seen to exist in relation to consciousness, which thus explains or illuminates all things, consciousness alone is not explained in relation to anything other than itself, for consciousness is self-illumined. It therefore proves itself as well as all other kinds of being, and is hence supremely real. And since on the Advaitin's assumptions difference is ultimately unreal all things other than pure non-differenced consciousness are ultimately unreal. Hence Brahman or ultimate Reality is identical with pure thought or consciousness (Ś. Bh. I. 1. 1, pp. 33-35).

Such a view which deprives the Supreme Being of personality and reduces Him to bare qualityless thought is the very antithesis of the soul-entrancing God of the Āḻvārs, or of the intensely human Kṛṣṇa of the Bhagavadgītā. Rāmānuja must therefore show that the view of Brahman as pure thought is false, and that the Supreme Being may be, nay more, must be, conceived as Self or Person.

To do so, Rāmānuja draws upon what he has already established with regard to the experienced real as always characterised by differences. Since everything experienced is found to display differences within itself, and since all proof rests on experience, the advaitin cannot prove his non-differenced pure thought to be real. If he attempts to prove it, it will begin to display attributes, for all things capable of proof have attributes and if he does not prove it, it is reduced to a mere fanciful hypothesis, contradicted by experience. He therefore confronts the advaitin with a dilemma. " Consciousness is either proved (established) or not. If it is proved, it follows that it possesses attributes ; if it is not, it is something absolutely nugatory, like a sky-flower, and similar purely imaginary things " (Ś. Bh. I. 1. 1, p. 55).

Moreover the advaitin himself predicates certain attributes such as eternity, oneness and self-luminousness of ultimate Thought, so that even on his hypothesis Brahman is not pure attributeless thought. " Nor may you urge against this that all these alleged attributes are in reality mere consciousness or ' knowing ' for they are essentially distinct." For example, eternity means ' being present in all time ' ; one-ness means ' being defined by the number one ' ; and these are not the same as what consciousness means. Similarly self-luminousness is not the same as luminousness or knowing; for while luminousness means the capacity to illuminate other objects, self-luminousness means the capacity to illuminate itself. Consequently the Thought which the advaitin claims to be ultimate is not after all qualityless. It has several distinct attributes. Further Rāmānuja adds, even if it is said that these qualities are not positive attributes existing within the nature of thought, but merely indicate the absence in thought of qualities opposed to them, and hence are to be described as negative attributes, "you still cannot avoid the admission that they are attributes of consciousness"; for as negative attributes, they qualify the nature of consciousness as being the opposite of non-eternal, non-one, and such like. That they do qualify the nature of consciousness, and hence are attributes, is proved by the fact, that otherwise it would be possible to ascribe non-eternality, non-oneness and such like to consciousness (Ś. Bh, I. 1, 1, p. 55). For these reasons, then, it must be admitted that even the advaitin does not regard Brahman as qualityless Thought.

So far it has been shown that Brahman cannot be regarded as pure non-differenced consciousness. Now it remains to establish as against the advaitin that Brahman must be regarded as Self or Person. We may do so by considering what is presupposed by consciousness, with which the advaitin equates Brahman.

Consciousness is regarded as proof (*siddhi*) itself. If it is proof, then it must be proof of something to someone; that is, consciousness inevitably presupposes a self on the one hand and objects on the other. And if it thus presupposes a self to which it belongs, it is clear that it is this self which is the Agent in consciousness, and not consciousness itself. "To explain: the essential character of consciousness or knowledge is that by its very existence it renders things capable of becoming objects, to its own substrate, of thought and speech. This consciousness (*anubhūti*), which is also termed *jñāna*, *avagati*, *saṁvid*, is a particular attribute belonging to a conscious self and related to an object; as such it is known to everyone on the testimony of his own self—as appears from ordinary judgments such as 'I know the jar,' 'I understand this matter.' . . . That such is the essential nature of consciousness you yourself admit; for you have proved thereby its self-luminousness. Of this consciousness which thus clearly presents itself as the attribute of an agent and as related to an object it would be difficult indeed to prove that at the same time it is itself the agent, as difficult as it would be to prove that the object of action is the agent." That is, since consciousness is only the activity or function of a self, it is the self that is ultimate, not consciousness.

That consciousness is the activity of a self which is other than its conscious states is seen from the fact that consciousness consists of momentary mental states. which require a permanent self as their substrate and relating principle. Recognition, for example would clearly be impossible unless there were a permanent self, not to be identified with any of its mental states, but persisting through all its experiences and relating its present state of consciousness with its previous conscious states. "For we clearly see that this agent (the subject of consciousness) is permanent (constant), while its attribute, i.e., consciousness, not differing herein from joy, grief, and the life, rises, persists for some time, and then comes to an end. The permanency of the conscious subject is proved by the fact of recognition. 'This very same thing was formerly apprehended by me.' The non-permanency of consciousness, on the other hand, is proved by thought expressing itself in the following forms: 'I know at present.' 'I knew at a time,' 'I, the knowing subject, no longer have knowledge of this thing.' How then should consciousness and the conscious subject be one? If consciousness which changes every moment were admitted to constitute the conscious subject, it would be impossible for us to recognise the thing seen to-day as the one we saw yesterday, for what has been perceived by one cannot be recognised by another. . . . For recognition implies a conscious subject persisting from the earlier to the later moment, and not merely consciousness" (Ś. Bh. I. 1. 1, pp. 56 and 57). Therefore we may conclude that consciousness presupposes a conscious self which is not identifiable with consciousness itself.

"In general we may say that where there is light it must belong to something, as shown by the light of a lamp. The Self thus cannot be mere consciousness. The grammarians moreover tell us that words such as 'consciousness,' 'knowledge,' etc., are relative; neither ordinary nor Vedic language uses expressions such as 'he knows' without reference to an object known and an agent who knows. "All which shows that the self-luminous Self is a knower, i.e., a knowing subject; and not pure light (non-personal intelligence)" (Ś. Bh. I. 1. 1, p. 60).

His analysis of consciousness thus leads Rāmānuja to the conclusion that consciousness presupposes a conscious self, and that this self cannot, as the advaitin claims, be identified with mere consciousness. Applying this conclusion to Brahman, it is clear that if consciousness is predicated of Brahman, He cannot be mere non-differenced consciousness, but must be a self which is characterised by consciousness.

Further Rāmānuja points out that the consciousness which the advaitin is anxious to predicate of Brahman is impossible and hence unreal, and that therefore Brahman is in the end reduced by the advaitin to something not unlike the unconscious *Pradhāna*. For the advaitin predicates of Brahman distinctionless consciousness; but can consciousness exist where all distinctions are unreal? "On the theory of . . . a Brahman that is nothing but distinctionless intelligence even the witnessing function of consciousness would be unreal." "To be intelligent means to possess the quality of intelligence; a being devoid of the quality of thought would not differ in nature from the *Pradhāna.*"

"Further, on the theory of Brahman being mere non-differenced light it would be difficult to prove that Brahman is self-luminous. For by light we understand that particular thing which renders itself, as well as other things, capable of becoming the object of ordinary thought and speech; but as a thing devoid of all difference does not, of course, possess these two characteristics, it follows that it is as devoid of intelligence as a pot may be."

"Let it then be assumed that although a thing devoid of all distinction does not actually possess these characteristics, yet it has the potentiality of possessing them! But if it possesses the attribute of potentiality it is clear that you abandon your entire theory of a substance devoid of all distinction! . . . Moreover, potentiality means capability to produce certain special effects, and hence can be determined on the ground of those special effects only. But if there are no means of knowing these particular effects, there are also no means of cognising potentiality."

"It therefore remains a settled conclusion that the Brahman to be known is nothing else but the highest Person" (Ś. Bh. I. 1. 12, pp. 207 and 208).

So far we have sought merely by empirical reasoning to show that Brahman cannot be qualityless Being nor pure Thought, but must be a Self characterised by thought as well as by several other attributes. But empirical reasoning cannot of itself avail, as we have already shown, to establish anything with regard to Brahman; for, in regard to such matters Scripture is our ultimate authority. If, therefore, Scripture teaches that Brahman is pure qualityless Thought, we must agree that all our reasoning is futile, and that the advaitin's view regarding the nature of Brahman is the only one that can be accepted. But what does Scripture teach? And herein we come upon our supreme and final argument against the advaitin, for his view regarding the nature of Brahman is contradicted by Scripture.

Brahman is highest Self characterised by excellent attributes

The advaitin seeks to maintain his views that Brahman is pure non-differenced substance by fixing on Scriptural texts such as 'Being only this was in the beginning,' 'one only without a second,' and such like. Rāmānuja declares that to fix only on such texts and to overlook or explain away texts which predicate attributes of Brahman is entirely unjustified. What is necessary, he contends, is to arrive at a view where all texts receive a consistent interpretation, but where none are sacrificed for the sake of upholding teaching derived from some texts to the exclusion of others. The principle which he lays down for interpreting scriptural texts is "that the qualities attributed in all Śākhās to Brahman . . . should be taken over into the passage under discussion also" (Ś. Bh. I. 1. 1, p. 80). That is, no passage should be interpreted purely in the light of what it itself seems to say, but its meaning should be gathered also from the general teaching of the Scriptures, as that is obtained from a consideration of all other texts. This principle the advaitin also accepts; but, Rāmānuja complains, he makes wrong use of it (p. 80), for though he also interprets individual texts in the light of what he regards as the general teaching of the Scriptures, his view as to what is the general teaching of the Scriptures is based on a consideration of only some texts to the exclusion of all others. For example, the advaitin interprets the text, 'one only without a second,' to mean that Brahman is a pure unity devoid of all differences. But Rāmānuja asks, if this be true, what about other passages which predicate "eternity and other attributes of Brahman which you yourself assume?" When these passages are also taken into consideration, the text that Brahman is 'one only without a second' will have to be viewed as teaching, not that Brahman is devoid of qualities, but that He is one, like whom there is none other. "What the phrase 'without a second' really aims at intimating is that Brahman possesses manifold powers, and this it does by denying the existence of another ruling principle different from Brahman. . . . The clause 'Being only this was in the beginning, one only,' teaches that Brahman when about to create constitutes the substantial cause of the world. Here the idea of some further operative cause capable of giving rise to the effect naturally presents itself to the mind, and hence we understand that the added clause, 'without a second,' is meant to negative such an additional cause" (Ś. Bh. I. 1. 1, p. 80).

Similarly when some texts declare that Brahman is free from qualities, the advaitin makes the mistake of interpreting them in isolation, without considering other texts which describe Brahman as having several qualities. When these texts are also considered, Rāmānuja says, we shall have to conclude that the passages which declare that Brahman is without qualities "are meant to negative the evil qualities depending on *Prakṛti*," and not all qualities as such (Ś. Bh. I. 1. 1, p. 81).[1] We may therefore conclude in the light of both sets of passages, that what the Scripture means to teach is that Brahman has many excellent qualities, but is devoid of all evil qualities.

Further, Rāmānuja argues, the advaitin himself admits that the Scripture teaches that Brahman has some qualities, for he accepts the text which declares, 'true knowledge, infinite is Brahman,' and "the co-ordination of the terms of which it (viz., this text)[2] consists explains itself in so far only as denoting one thing distinguished by several attributes. For co-ordination (*sāmānādhikaraṇya*, lit., 'the abiding of

[1] Cf. Also his long comment on Bhg. XIII. 2, pp. 411 and 412, in Govindācārya's Translation.
[2] The words in parenthesis are mine.

several things in a common substrate') means the reference (of several terms) to one thing, there being a difference of reason for the application (of several terms to one thing). Now whether we take the several terms, 'True,' 'Knowledge,' 'Infinite,' in their primary sense, i.e., as denoting qualities, or as denoting modes of being opposed to whatever is contrary to those qualities; in either case we must needs admit a plurality of causes for the application of those several terms to one thing. There is, however, that difference between the two alternatives that in the former case the terms preserve their primary meaning, while in the latter case their denotive power depends on so-called 'implication' (*lakṣaṇā*). Nor can it be said that the opposition in nature to non-knowledge, etc. (which is the purport of the terms on the hypothesis of (*lakṣaṇā*) constitutes nothing more than the essential nature (of one non-differenced substance, the three terms thus having one purport only); for as such essential nature would be sufficiently apprehended through one term, the employment of further terms would be purposeless. This view would moreover be in conflict with co-ordination, as it would not allow of difference of motive for several terms applied to one thing. On the other hand it cannot be urged against the former alternative that the distinction of several attributes predicated of one thing implies a distinction in the thing to which the attributes belong, and that from this it follows that the several terms denote several things—a result which also could not be reconciled with 'co-ordination'; for what 'co-ordination' aims at is just to convey the idea of one thing being qualified by several attributes. For the grammarians define 'co-ordination' as the application, to one thing, of several words, for the application of each of which there is a different motive." Scripture, therefore, must be admitted by the advaitin to teach that Brahman is not a pure non-differenced unity, devoid of all attributes.

Nor may the advaitin claim that Scripture teaches that Brahman is pure thought or knowledge. "Those texts . . . which refer to mere knowledge declare indeed that knowledge is the essential nature of Brahman, but this does not mean that mere knowledge constitutes the fundamental reality. . . . That Brahman is a knowing subject all scriptural texts declare; cf. 'He who is all knowing' (Muṇḍ. Up. I. 1. 9.) . . . 'This divine being thought' (Chānd. Up. VI. 3. 2). . . . 'He who arranges the wishes—as eternal of those who are not eternal, as thinker of (other) thinkers . . .' (Ka. Up. II. 5. 13); 'Let us know Him the highest of Lords, the great Lord, the highest deity of deities, the master of masters, the highest above the God, the lord of the world, the adorable one' (Śvet. Up. VI. 7); 'No one is seen like unto him or better, his high power is revealed as manifold, forming his essential nature, as knowledge strength, and action' (Śvet. Up. VI. 8); 'That is the Self, free from sin, ageless, deathless, griefless, free from hunger and thirst whose wishes are true, whose purposes are true' (Chānd. Up VIII 1. 5). These and other texts declare that to Brahman, whose essential nature is knowledge, there belong many excellent qualities—among which that of being a knowing subject stands first" (Ś. Bh. I. 1. 1, p. 81).

Nor may the advaitin say that Scripture teaches that Brahman is pure Bliss. "Your assertion that the text 'Bliss is Brahman' (Taitt. Up. III. 6. 1) proves pure Bliss to constitute the essential nature of Brahman is already disposed of by the refutation of the view that knowledge (consciousness) constitutes the essential nature of Brahman; Brahman being in reality the substrate only of knowledge. For by bliss we understand a pleasing state of consciousness. Such passages as 'consciousness, bliss is Brahman' therefore mean 'consciousness the essential character of which is bliss—is Brahman.' On this identity of the two things there rests that homogeneous character of

Brahman, so much insisted upon by yourself. And in the same way as numerous passages teach that Brahman, while having knowledge for its essential nature, is at the same time a knowing subject, so other passages, speaking of Brahman as something separate from mere bliss, show it to be not mere bliss but a subject enjoying bliss; cf. 'That is one bliss of Brahman' (Taitt. Up. II. 8. 4); 'he knowing the bliss of Brahman' (Taitt. Up. II. 9. 1). To be a subject enjoying bliss is in fact the same as to be a conscious subject" (Ś. Bh. I. 1. 1, p. 84).

Moreover, Rāmānuja adds, the bliss of Brahman may be said to indicate His excellent qualities, for in the Scriptural section which speaks of the relative bliss enjoyed by souls in different worlds, the highest bliss is said to be the bliss of Brahman; that is, the soul which realises Him finds Him to have auspicious qualities which fulfil all its desires and thus produce in it supreme bliss. Accordingly Rāmānuja writes: "the section 'one hundred times that human bliss,' etc., makes statements as to the relative bliss enjoyed by the different classes of embodied souls; the concluding passage, 'He who knows the bliss of that Brahman from whence all speech together with the mind, turns away unable to reach it,' hence must be taken as proclaiming with emphasis the infinite nature of Brahman's auspicious qualities. Moreover, a clause in the chapter under discussion—viz., 'he obtains all desires, together with Brahman the all-wise' (Taitt. II. 1)—which gives information as to the fruit of the knowledge of Brahman clearly declares the infinite nature of the qualities of the highest all-wise Brahman. The desires are the auspicious qualities of Brahman which are the objects of desire; the man who knows Brahman obtains, together with Brahman, all qualities of it. The expression 'together with' is meant to bring out the primary importance of the qualities" (Ś. Bh. I. 1. 1, p. 82). Thus when Brahman is spoken of as bliss, reference is to the many bliss-producing, auspicious qualities which belong to the nature of Brahman. Far from teaching that Brahman is void of qualities, Scripture is thus found to maintain that Brahman has many excellent qualities.

But it may be asked, why if Brahman is known to have such auspicious qualities does Scripture nevertheless teach, as in the Kena Upaniṣad, 'By whom it is not thought, by him it is thought,' 'not understood by those who understand' (II. 3). In answer Rāmānuja declares that the passage when understood in relation to the Taittirīya text above discussed explains itself thus. "We are informed by the passage 'from whence speech together with mind turns away, being unable to reach it' that the infinite Brahman with its unlimited excellences cannot be defined either by mind or speech as being so or so much, and from this we conclude the Kena text to mean that Brahman is not thought and not understood by those who understand it to be of a definitely limited nature, Brahman in truth being unlimited" (Ś. Bh. I. 1. 1, p. 83).

Similarly in commenting on the Bṛhadaraṇyaka text which declares that Brahman is 'not so, not so,' Rāmānuja argues that the passage is not intended to teach that Brahman has no qualities, but only that He is not to be regarded as limited to the qualities already enumerated. "The passage denies that limited nature of Brahman which would result from Brahman being viewed as distinguished by the previously stated attributes only. The word *so* refers to that limited nature and the phrase *not so* therefore means that Brahman is not distinguished by the previously stated modes *only*. This interpretation is further confirmed by the fact that after that negative phrase, further qualities of Brahman are declared by the text: 'For there is not anything higher than this *not so*. Then comes the name, the *True of the True*: for the *prāṇas* are the True, and he is the True of them.' That means: Than that Brahman which is expressed by the phrase 'not so' there is no other thing higher, i.e., there is nothing more exalted than Brahman either in essential nature or in qualities. And of that Brahman the name is 'True of the True.' As thus the complementary passage declares Brahman to be connected with certain qualities, the clause 'not so, not so' (to which that passage is complementary) cannot deny that Brahman possesses distinctive attributes, but only that Brahman's nature is to be confined to the attributes previously stated" (Ś. Bh. III. 2. 22, pp. 616 and 617).

Accordingly it would seem that the teaching of Scripture is not that Brahman is a substance void of qualities, nor thought void of attributes, but that He is highest Self, whose essential attribute is knowledge characterised by bliss, who is possessed of an unlimited number of auspicious qualities but excludes all evil qualities, and similar to, or higher than, whom there is no other. Empirical reasoning points to a view of Reality as characterised by differences; Scripture confirms it by describing Brahman as having excellent qualities. Hence this view is undoubtedly true.

But it may be asked—Whence did Rāmānuja obtain this doctrine? He claims that Scripture (i.e., in this case, the Upaniṣads) teaches it. But our account of the Upaniṣads has already shown that no such clearly formulated doctrine is to be found in them. Moreover Rāmānuja himself is aware of this fact, as is clear from the great pains he takes, as we have briefly indicated above, to explain Upaniṣadic texts which conflict with his view. Further, the Upaniṣadic passages which he cites (cf. Ś. Bh., pp. 81-84) as teaching his view of the nature of Brahman are so few and uncertain in meaning that we may be sure that he did not derive his doctrine from them. Besides his very eagerness to claim support for his view from Scripture seems to reveal the fact that he obtained his doctrine from other sources. What those sources were, we have already suggested, viz., the beliefs of the religious sect, Vaiṣṇavism, to which he belonged. In this view we are now confirmed, for after showing that his doctrine regarding the nature of Brahman is taught by Scripture, Rāmānuja proceeds to show that it is also taught by the Viṣṇu Purāṇa, and the passages which he cites so fully reflect the view which he advocates throughout the Śrībhāṣya, that Brahman is highest Person, characterised by the most blessed attributes, and free from all evil qualities, that it is not by any means improbable that it is to the Viṣṇu Purāṇa in particular, and to Vaiṣṇavism in general, that Rāmānuja turned for his doctrine regarding the nature of the Deity. He at any rate found in the Viṣṇu Purāṇa a description of the blessed qualities of the Deity, which description he failed to find except in very meagre form in the Upaniṣads. He accordingly depends, chiefly on the Viṣṇu Purāṇa for an enumeration of the attributes which belong to the Divine nature. What these are we shall see if we follow Rāmānuja in his citation of passages from the Viṣṇu Purāṇa.

"'He transcends the fundamental matter of all beings its modifications, properties and imperfections . . . all auspicious qualities constitute his nature. The whole creation of beings is taken out of a small part of his power. Assuming at will whatever form he desires he bestows benefits on the whole world effected by him. Glory, strength, dominion, wisdom, energy, power and other attributes are collected in him, Supreme of the supreme in whom no troubles abide, ruler over high and low, lord in collective and distributive form, non-manifest and manifest, universal lord, all-seeing, all-knowing, all-powerful, highest Lord. The knowledge by which that perfect, pure, highest, stainless homogeneous (Brahman) is known or perceived or comprehended—that is knwoledge ; all else is ignorance' (Viṣṇu Purāṇa VI. 5. 82-87). 'To that pure one of mighty power the highest Brahman to which no term is applicable, the cause of all causes, the name Bhagavat is suitable. The letter *bha* implies both the cherisher and supporter, the letter *ga* the leader, mover and creator. The two syllables *bhaga* indicate the six attributes dominion, strength, glory, splendour, wisdom, dispassion. That in him—the universal Self, the Self of the beings—all beings dwell and that he dwells in all, this is the meaning of the letter *va*. Wisdom, might, strength, dominion, glory, without any evil qualities, are all denoted by the word *bhagavat*. This great word *bhagavat* is the name of Vāsudeva, who is the highest Brahman—and of no one else. This word which denotes persons worthy of reverence in general is used in its primary sense with reference to Vāsudeva only; in a derived sense with regard to other persons' (Viṣ. P. VI. 5. 72). . . ".

" 'Him who is of this kind, stainless, eternal, all pervading, imperishable, free from all evil, named Viṣṇu, the highest abode' (Viṣ. P. I. 22. 53); 'He who is the highest of the high, the Person, the highest Self, founded on himself; who is devoid of all the distinguishing characteristics of colour, caste and the like; who is exempt from birth, change, increase, decay and death; of whom it can only be said that he ever is. He is everywhere and in him everything abides, hence he is called Vāsudeva by those who know. He is Brahman, eternal, supreme, imperishable, undecaying, of one essential nature and ever pure, as free from all defects' (Viṣ. P. I. 2. 10-14)."

"These and other texts," Rāmānuja concludes, "teach that the highest Brahman is essentially free from all imperfection whatsoever, (and) comprises within itself all auspicious qualities" (Ś. Bh. I. 1. 1, pp. 86-88).

There are two points which are worthy of note in connection with the qualities above enumerated, for they reveal ideas not to be found in the Upaniṣads, and hence are to be regarded as distinctly sectarian. Rāmānuja accepts them, though there is no warrant for them in the Upaniṣads, and they form a fundamental part of his view regarding the Deity. One of them is the enumeration of six qualities—glory, strength, dominion, wisdom, energy and power—as belonging to Brahman. It is significant that in the few citations given by Rāmānuja from the Viṣṇu Purāṇa, these qualities are repeated as many as three times. It will be remembered that these six qualities play an important part in Pāñcarātra philsoophy. Rāmānuja refers to them repeatedly in his works,[1] and it must therefore be concluded that they formed a fundamental part of his conception regarding the Deity. The other point worthy of note is the description of the Deity as assuming various forms for the benefit of the world. This again, as we have seen, is a doctrine of long standing among the Vaiṣṇavas, and very central in their thought of the Deity, but not to be found in the Upaniṣads. The attributes which it presupposes in the Supreme Being is love, and Rāmānuja, as we shall see, does not hesitate to dwell with great feeling on this attribute of the Deity, when he deals with the topic of incarnation.

Another point is also noticeable, though it cannot be said to be peculiarly Vaiṣṇava, for, as we have seen, it is not lacking entirely even in the Upaniṣads—the view, namely that the Deity is a Perfect being, in whom there is no evil. But while in the Upaniṣads this doctrine is never clearly or consistently formulated, the Śrī Bhāṣya passages we have cited show Rāmānuja consistently maintaining that Brahman has only auspicious qualities, and that He is entirely free from evil qualities. It is significant that the passages from the Viṣṇu Purāṇa which he selects to support his view also make it very clear that Brahman is free from all defects, and that nothing but auspicious qualities constitute His nature. So central in Rāmānuja's view of the Deity is the doctrine that Brahman is altogether perfect and excludes everything that is evil, that he

[1] Cf., e.g., Ś. Bh., pp. 324, 608; Bhg. Bh., pp. 6, 221, 236, 331, 349, 357, 381, 385, 568 (Govindācārya's Translation).

introduces this teaching wherever possible, even for example when he is discussing passages which by no stretch of imagination can be thought to imply it. Thus in regard to Upaniṣadic passages which describe Brahman as "made of Mind"[1] he writes, "'made of mind' means to be apprehended by a purified mind only. The highest Self can be apprehended only by a mind purified by meditation on that Self. . . . This intimates that the highest Self is of pure goodness, precluding all evil, and therefore different in nature from everything else; for by the impure minded impure objects only can be apprehended" (Ś. Bh. I. 2. 2, p. 261). In regard to texts which declare that Brahman has light for his form, Rāmānuja says that that light is not to be confused with any quality belonging to matter (*prakṛti*). 'Whose form is light' means "who is of supreme splendour, his form being a divine one of supreme excellence peculiar to him, and not consisting of the stuff of *prakṛti*." 'To whom all wishes belong' Rāmānuja similarly interprets to mean "He to whom all pure objects and means of desire and enjoyment belong." 'He to whom all odours and tastes belong' he says means "he to whom there belong, as objects of enjoyment, all kinds of uncommon, special, perfect, supremely excellent odours and tastes; ordinary smells and tastes being negatived by another text, viz., 'That which is without sound, without touch, without taste, etc.' (Ka. Up. III. 15)" (Ś. Bh. I. 2. 2, p. 262). Similarly in regard to meditating on Brahman as bliss, Rāmānuja says it is not enough to think of Brahman as bliss, for bliss when ascribed to Him must be purged of all grossness. "The apprehension of a thing means the apprehension of its specific character. But mere bliss

[1] Rāmānuja's unwillingness to regard Brahman as 'made of mind' arises from the fact that 'mind' (*manas*) was regarded by him in accordance with Sāṁkhyan philosophy as a material principle; and, of course, Brahman, according to Rāmānuja cannot be regarded as made of anything so evil as matter. The Upaniṣadic passage is apparently innocent of this implication of *manas*.

and so on, does not suggest the specific character of Brahman, since those qualities belong also to the individual soul. What is specifically characteristic of Brahman is bliss, and so on, in so far as fundamentally opposed to all evil and imperfection. . . . Now being fundamentally opposed to evil implies having a character the opposite of grossness and all similar qualities which belong to the empirical world. . . . He therefore who thinks of Brahman must think of it as having for its essential nature bliss, knowledge, and so on, in so far as distinguished by absence of grossness and the like" (Ś. Bh. III. 3. 33, pp. 653 and 654). In this way Rāmānuja brings to full fruition the tendency of some of the Upaniṣads to ascribe numerous perfections to the Supreme Being. His inspiration in this regard probably came from his religion, which as we saw throughout its history was inclined, in spite of its alliance with advaitism, to regard the Supreme Being as characterised by several perfections, especially the perfection of goodness and love. Rāmānuja was one of the first, it would appear who clearly perceived that if all that was distinctive of his religion, especially as it expressed itself in the intense God-devotion of the Āḻvārs, was to be preserved, the unholy alliance of his sect with advaitism, of however long standing, must be terminated. He accordingly set himself to this task, and in breaking away from advaitism it would seem Rāmānuja is enabled to teach in clear, unmistakable language, unlike any of his predecessors, that Brahman's nature is constituted by an infinite number of blessed qualities, entirely excludes all evil, and is above all characterised by love.

So far we have followed Rāmānuja in establishing as against the advaitin that Perception, Inference, Scripture and works of authority like the Viṣṇu Purāṇa, indicate that Brahman is not pure Being, nor pure Thought, but a highest Person, characterised by knowledge and bliss, as well as by an infinite number of excellent qualities. We have also seen how in the light of the distinctive tenets of his religion Rāmānuja was enabled to go beyond the teaching of the Scripture, that is, the Upaniṣads, and to enumerate six qualities of Brahman as in Pāñcarātra philosophy, as well as to ascribe to Him the quality of love, which leads Him to assume various forms for the benefit of the world. But so far we have confined ourselves to the Śrībhāṣya, where Rāmānuja is manifestly concerned to expound Vedānta philosophy. It is true that he does not hesitate to read his own view into texts, so that even in his Śrībhāṣya he succeeds, as we have seen, in presenting his main tenets regarding the nature of the Deity. If, however, we would obtain a fuller idea of his own sectarian beliefs regarding the nature and attributes of the Deity we must turn to his commentary[1] on the Bhagavadgītā, for dealing as he does there with a literary work of his own sect, he is at liberty to give expression to sectarian ideas without let or hindrance.[2] One or two typical passages should suffice by way of illustration.

Rāmānuja begins his commentary on the Bhagavadgītā with a description of the Deity, His attributes, His ornaments, His consort Śrī, His heavenly abode with a host of celestials hymning His praise, and a brief allusion to His incarnations. All this is essentially Purāṇic, and has little philosophical significance. We shall therefore concern ourselves merely with that part of it which describes the nature and attributes of the Supreme Being. It runs thus: "The Lord of Śrī, whose essential nature is the being the sole Reservoir of all illustrious attributes, the antithesis to all evil (*heya*)—such attributes as Wisdom (*jñāna*) and Bliss (*ānanda*); who is the great ocean of the legions of the boundless, exalted and countless glorious qualities, behoving His nature, such as Omniscience

[1] Passages cited here and elsewhere from this work are taken from A. Govindācārya's translation. Page references are to pages in the translation.

[2] Cf. also the description of the Deity given in the Śaraṇāgati-gadya. Brahmavādin, Vol. 1, p. 221.

(*jñāna*), Strength (*bala*), Sovereignty (*aiśvarya*), constancy (*vīrya*), Power (*śakti*) and Lustre (*tejas*); whose Divine form is a mine of effulgence, beauty, comeliness, youth and other perfections of the Person" (Bhg. Bh., pp. 6 and 7). Again, commenting on Bhagavadgītā IX. 34, where Kṛṣṇa says to Arjuna, Fix thy heart on me, Rāmānuja imagines Kṛṣṇa to mean, Fix thy heart on me—" me, the sole asylum of all excellences, exempt from fault; me, the omniscient; me, of indomitable will; me, of the lotus-like clear and large eyes, and of uniform blue cloud-hue; me, of a resplendence as if a thousand suns had simultaneously shone; me, the nectar-ocean of loveliness, of arms four . . . me, again, the ocean of infinite mercy, compassion, beauty, sweetness, dignity, bounty, affection, etc." (Bhg. Bh., pp. 314 and 315). Also later, in regard to a similar passage (xiii. 9), he writes: " Me, the natural boundless ocean of all the exalted countless glorious attributes, such as beauty, compassion and condescension, love and clemency, sweetness and dignity and bounty, courage, valour, and daring, wisdom, lordship; me, the antithesis (or antidote) of all vice" (p. 385).

What these passages reveal are the same two sectarian doctrines already noticed in connection with the Viṣṇu Purāṇa texts cited above, viz., that the Deity is characterised by the six attributes enumerated in Pāñcarātra philosophy, and that He is full of love and tender mercy. The love of the Deity is, however, as we should expect, more particularly emphasized, and in addition the beauty of the Lord (envisaged as Kṛṣṇa) receives special mention, and once again Rāmānuja reiterates his belief that the Deity is all-perfect and free from all evil.

We may conclude, therefore, by saying that according to Rāmānuja the Supreme Being is not, as the advaitin asserts, pure non-differenced Substance, nor characterless Thought, but highest Self, characterised essentially by thought and bliss as well as by the six attributes of wisdom (*jñāna*), strength (*bala*), lordship (*aiśvarya*), might (*vīrya*), energy (*śakti*) and glory (*tejas*), of great beauty, absolutely unrivalled, free from all evil, filled with an infinite number of excellent qualities, and abounding in love.[1]

[1] It is obvious from the foregoing that Rāmānuja obtains most of his doctrines regarding the nature of the Deity from his own religious sect. That part of his teaching, however, which may be said primarily to reveal Upaniṣadic influence is that which describes thought and bliss as constituting the essential nature of Brahman, although, as our account of the Upaniṣads shows, the conception of Brahman as an all-perfect Being characterised by grace is not altogether absent even in the Upaniṣads.

CHAPTER II

RELATION OF THE DEITY TO THE WORLD

WE have seen how by empirical reasoning and by an appeal to Scripture and authoritative works, Rāmānuja established that Brahman cannot be regarded as pure unity, but must be thought of as a unity which includes differences within itself. In the last chapter, we saw how this conclusion was applied to show that Brahman cannot be defined as mere Thought, but must be regarded as Self characterised by an infinite number of excellent qualities. This was an important accomplishment, for in place of the advaitin's characterless Absolute, Rāmānuja was able to substitute the Adorable One of the Vaiṣṇavas, loving and lovable, filled with every perfection and stealing away the heart of His worhsippers. But this is not the only use that Rāmānuja makes of the principle that Brahman is a unity characterised by differences. We have already hinted that a metaphysical edifice will be constructed by him on this foundation. We are now to see this edifice being built. Perhaps the metaphor of building is not quite the right one in this connection, for all that is necessary is the wave of the logician's wand whereby the substance-attribute relation is given a new meaning, and lo, the building appears, firm and impregnable.

We noticed that while dealing with the advaitin's view of reality as attributeless substance, Rāmānuja prepared the soil by telling us that the substance-attribute relationship holds not only in the case of objects and the generic qualities which they possess, but also in the case of two distinct objects such as man and the staff which he carries. The staff may be regarded as the quality of the man, in so far as it is dependent on him and qualifies him for he is not just man, but a staff-bearing man, even as a man who is qualified by strength is not just man, but a strong man. The difference in the two cases, namely that the man's strength cannot exist apart from him, whereas the staff can, Rāmānuja was aware of; but he declared that the difference did not alter the relationship, for in both cases it was a matter of one thing depending on and qualifying another. Grant this and you grant all that Rāmānuja wants for establishing the reality of the world and its relationship to the Deity; for, seeing that it has been shown that Brahman must be regarded as a substance qualified by attributes, and seeing that it is now granted that an attribute need not necessarily mean only abstract qualities such as were predicated of Brahman in the last chapter, there can be no objection to saying that the world is an attribute or mode of Brahman, though it, even like the staff, is in a sense substantive, and not merely qualitative. In this way, the world with all its plurality may be accepted as real, and yet at the same time, it may be regarded as not endangering the unity of ultimate Reality, for it stands to the latter in the relation of attribute to substance.

Here again, as in the last chapter, it is clear that Rāmānuja is seeking to provide what is essential to religion as against the advaitin, who dismisses the world and all that is therein as ultimately an illusion. If the world is illusion, the soul which belongs to it is illusion, and if the soul is illusion, religion is illusion. Very necessary it is, therefore, for Rāmānuja to discover a way of conceiving the unity of Brahman, compatible with the reality of the world. But before this is attempted the advaitin's method of relating Brahman to the world, whereby, as already said, the world is proclaimed ultimately to be unreal, must first be refuted. Rāmānuja uses all his ingenuity against the unfortunate advaitin, and employs several forceful arguments, of which we may mention a few.

Refutation of the Doctrine of Māyā[1]

The advaitin's position according to Rāmānuja is this : " The entire world, with its distinctions of gods, men, animals, inanimate matter, and so on, is, owing to an imperfection, wrongly imagined in the highest Brahman whose substance is mere intelligence, and therefore is false in so far as it may be sublated by the cognition of the nature of the real Brahman. What constitutes that imferpection is beginningless Nescience (*avidyā*), which, hiding the truth of things, gives rise to manifold illusions, and cannot be defined either as something that is or as something that is not " (Ś. Bh. I. 1. 1, p. 22) ; " this Nescience comes to an end through the cognition of the essential unity of the Self with Brahman which is nothing but non-differenced substance " (Ś. Bh. I. 1. 1, p. 23). The appearance of the world, then, is due to Nescience, and since nothing really exists beyond Brahman, the Nescience must be regarded as an imperfection residing in Brahman, or somehow associated with Him, and bringing about the apparent existence of the world. When this Nescience is brought to an end, the false appearance of the world will cease. It is obvious that since the theory seeks to relate Brahman to the world by means of Nescience, which leads Him, as it were, to project a phenomenal world, a criticism of it must ultimately focus on the postulated relationship between Brahman and Nescience. It is on this alone that we shall fix our attention in the sequel, although Rāmānuja himself attacks the theory from every possible angle showing (Ś. Bh., pp. 437-41 ; I. 1. 1, p. 103) for example that Nescience cannot belong to the individual soul ; can never be an object of know-

[1] I confine myself to the Ś. Bh., Rāmānuja's arguments in his other works, E.g., the Vedāntatattvasāra, being in essence the same as those developed by him in the Ś. Bh.

ledge (Ś. Bh. I. 1. 1, pp. 109 f.); and, if a positive existence, can never be terminated by knowledge (Ś. Bh. I. 1. 1, p. 116).

Brahman, Rāmānuja declares, as pure Intelligence can have nothing to do with Nescience. He cannot be its substrate, "for Brahman is nothing but self-luminous intelligence, and hence contradictory in nature to Nescience" (p. 103).[1]

Nor can Nescience be admitted as a second principle on the advaita hypothesis. "If non-duality constitutes the true nature of Brahman, and is proved by Brahman's own consciousness, there is room neither for what is contradictory to it, viz., that non-knowledge which consists in the view of duality, nor for the sublation of that non-knowledge.—Let then non-duality be taken for an attribute (not the essential nature) of Brahman!—This too we refuse to admit; for you yourself have proved that Brahman which is pure Consciousness, is free from attributes" (p. 105).

"When, in the next place, you maintain that Brahman, whose nature is homogeneous intelligence, is invested and hidden by Nescience, you thereby assert the destruction of Brahman's essential nature. Causing light to disappear means either obstructing the origination of light, or else destroying the light that exists. And as you teach that light (consciousness) cannot originate (for consciousness is eternal and beginningless, see pp. 35 and 36)[2] the 'hiding' or 'making to disappear' of light can only mean its destruction" (p. 105).

"Consider the following point also. Your theory is that self-luminous consciousness, which is without object and without substrate, becomes, through the influence of an imperfection residing within itself, conscious of itself as connected with innumerous substrata and innumerous objects.—Is then, we ask,

[1] Page references in what follows are to pages in Thibaut's translation of the Ś. Bh. in S.B.E. Series, Vol. 48.

[2] The words in parenthesis are mine.

that imperfection residing within consciousness something real or something unreal? The former alternative is excluded, as not being admitted by yourself. Nor can we accept the latter alternative," for if we regard the imperfection which inheres in Consciousness as itself, say, some form of consciousness, which while unreal, resides in Consciousness, we should have to admit two kinds of consciousness and this is contrary to the fundamental doctrine of the oneness of consciousness. If, on the other hand, we say 'that the consciousness in which the imperfection inheres is of the same nature as the latter, i.e., unreal, we are landed in the view of universal unreality' (pp. 105 and 106).[1]

Further, the theory leads to an infinite regress. It postulates that Brahman owing to an imperfection residing within itself becomes conscious of a world of plurality. The imperfection then is the cause of the unreal world; but this imperfection, according to the advaitin is unreal. If so, another imperfection would have to be postulated in order to account for this unreal existence, called imperfection, and so on *ad infinitum* (pp. 105 and 106). "To avoid this difficulty, it might now be said that that real consciousness itself, which constitutes Brahman's nature, is that imperfection. But if Brahman itself constitutes the imperfection, then Brahman is the basis of the appearance of a world, and it is gratuitous to assume an additional *avidyā* to account for the world. Moreover, as Brahman is eternal, it would follow from this hypothesis that no release could ever take place. Unless, therefore, you admit a real imperfection apart from Brahman, you are unable to account for the great world-error" (p. 106).

"Further, your view implies on the one hand that this non-knowledge which is the cause of the concealment of Brahman's nature hides Brahman in so far Brahman is conscious of it, and on the other hand that having hidden Brahman, it becomes the object

[1] The words quoted are Thibaut's in a footnote explaining the text, p. 106.

of consciousness on the part of Brahman; and this evidently constitutes a logical see-saw. You will perhaps say that it hides Brahman in so far only as Brahman is conscious of it. But, we point out, if the consciousness of *ajñāna* takes place on the part of a Brahman whose nature is not hidden, the whole hypothesis of the 'hiding' of Brahman's nature loses its purport, and with it the fundamental hypothesis as to the nature of *ajñāna*; for if Brahman may be conscious of *ajñāna* (without a previous obscuration of its nature by *ajñāna*) it may as well be held to be in the same way conscious of the world, which, by you, is considered to be an effect of *ajñāna*" (pp. 111 and 112).

"Let it then be said that *ajñāna* having first hidden Brahman then becomes the object of its consciousness. This, we rejoin, would imply that *ajñāna*—acting like a defect of the eye—by its very essential being hides Brahman and then *ajñāna* could not be sublated by knowledge," any more than a real defect of the eye can be cured by a mere act of knowledge (p. 112).

"Let us then put the case as follows:—*Ajñāna*, which is by itself beginningless, at the very same time effects Brahman's witnessing it (being conscious of it), and Brahman's nature being hidden. . . . But this also we cannot admit; for Brahman is essentially consciousness of Self, and cannot become a witnessing principle (i.e., become conscious of *ajñāna*)[1] unless its nature be previously hidden.—Then let Brahman be hidden by some other cause!—This, we rejoin, would take away from *ajñāna* its alleged beginninglessness, and further would also lead to an infinite regress" (p. 112).

"If, moreover, Brahman is hidden by *avidyā*, does it then not shine forth at all, or does it shine forth to some extent? On the former alternative the not shining forth of Brahman—whose nature is mere light—reduces it to an absolute non-entity. Regarding

[1] The words in parenthesis are mine.

the latter alternative we ask, 'of Brahman, which is of an absolutely homogeneous nature, which part do you consider to be concealed, and which to shine forth?' To that substance which is pure light, free from all division and distinction, there cannot belong two modes of being, and hence obscuration and light cannot abide in it together" (p. 113).

"Let us then say that Brahman, which is homogeneous being, intelligence, bliss, has its nature obscured by *avidyā*, and hence is seen indistinctly as it were.—But how, we ask, are we to conceive the distinctness or indistinctness of that whose nature is pure light? When an object of light which has parts and distinguishing attributes appears in its totality, we say that it appears distinctly; while we say that its appearance is indistinct when some of its attributes do not appear. . . . But in Brahman, which is not an object, without any distinguishing attributes, pure light, the essential nature of which it is to shine forth, indistinctness which consists in the non-apprehension of certain attributes can in no way be conceived" (p. 113).

So far we have contented ourselves with showing that the concept of Nescience is entirely contradictory of the non-duality of Brahman and His nature as pure Consciousness. It may now be shown that the concept itself is unintelligible and hence incapable of being used as a principle of explanation. No lengthy argument is necessary in this connection, for the advaitin himself describes Nescience as inexplicable (*anirvacanīya*), in that it is different in nature from that which *is*, as well as from that which *is not*.—"A thing of such kind would be inexplicable indeed; for none of the means of knowledge apply to it" (p. 106).

But the advaitin replies that, though Nescience is inexplicable, it must be admitted as a fact, on the ground of erroneous apprehension, as for instance, when a man mistakes shell for silver, and by further knowledge sees his mistake, or in other words becomes aware of his former Nescience. Nescience, therefore, however, inexplicable, is attested in experience (p. 107). To this Rāmānuja answers that even in erroneous perception there is no evidence of any such thing as Nescience, for when a man mistakes shell for silver, there is an apprehension of the qualities which the shell has in common with silver. The apprehension is regarded as erroneous, not because it is a case of non-apprehension or Nescience, but because, though it apprehends some qualities of the shell, it does not apprehend all; and the mistake is terminated, not by substituting knowledge in the place of Nescience, but by perfecting the former knowledge. "We observe that shells are similar to silver; thus perception itself informs us that some elements of the latter actually exist in the former. Sometimes it happens that . . . the silver-element only is apprehended, not the shell-element, and then the percipient person, desirous of silver, moves to pick up the shell. If, on the other hand . . . he apprehends the shell-element (also he) then refrains from action. Hence the cognition of silver in the shell is a true one. In the same way the relation of one cognition being sublated by another explains itself through the preponderant element, according as the preponderance of the shell-element is apprehended partially or in its totality, and does not therefore depend on one cognition having for its object the false thing and another the true thing" (p. 120). Nescience, therefore, is not only inexplicable in theory, but is also not vouched for as a fact of experience.

Consequently we must conclude that the theory of Nescience whereby the advaitin claims to relate Brahman to the world is not capable of being defended by any means of argument, Nescience being undefinable, not warranted in experience, and quite in conflict with the advaitin's definition of the nature of Brahman.

Nor may the theory of Nescience claim support from Scripture, Smṛti or Purāṇa (pp. 124-129). It is true that *Prakṛti* is in some texts declared to be *Māyā*, and *Māyā* may be synonymous with '*mithyā*' or falsehood. But, Rāmānuja declares, "'*Māyā*' does not in all places refer to what is false; we see it applied, e.g., to such things as the weapons of Asuras and Rākṣasas, which are not false but real. '*Māyā*,' in such passages, really denotes that which produces various wonderful effects, and it is in this sense that *Prakṛti* is called *Māyā*. This appears from the passage (Śvet. Up. IV. 9): 'From that the *Māyin* creates all this, and in that the other one is bound up by *Māyā*.' For this text declares that *Prakṛti*—there called *Māyā*—produces manifold wonderful creations, and the highest Person is there called '*māyin*' because he possesses that power of *māyā*; not on account of any ignorance or nescience on his part. . . . All this shows that Scripture does not teach the existence of a 'principle called Nescience, not to be defined either as that which is or that which is not'" (pp. 125 and 126).

Again, when in certain texts it is said that "'Then there was neither non-Being nor Being' (R. Saṁh. X. 129. 1) the terms 'being' and 'non-being' denote intelligent and non-intelligent beings in their distributive state" (p. 125), that is, souls and material objects, and there is "no reference whatever to something 'not definable either as being or non-being'" or Nescience (p. 125).

Nor when Scripture describes material objects as non-being, does it mean to teach that the material world is false and non-existent, as the advaitin wrongly concludes. It means to assert only that the material object is changeable and perishable, and hence while existing it does not have that permanent, unchangeable existence which characterises Brahman. "By 'that which is not' or 'which is untrue,' we have to understand not what is undefinable, but that which has no true being, in so far as it is changeable and perishable. Of this character is all non-intelligent matter. This also appears from the instance adduced in *śl.* 42: the jar is something perishable, but not a thing devoid of proof or to be sublated by true knowledge. 'Non-being' we may call it, in so far as while it is observed at a certain moment in a certain form it is at some other moment observed in a different condition. But there is no contradiction between two different conditions of a thing which are perceived at different times; and hence there is no reason to call it something futile (*tuccha*) or false (*mithyā*), etc." (p. 129). Rāmānuja's view here is significant as disclosing the kind of reality which he is willing to concede to the material world as compared with that of Brahman, and also as offering a very telling criticism of the advaitin's view regarding the complete unreality of the world. We may therefore be allowed to dwell on it a little longer. His contention here must be understood, it would seem, in the light of a previous passage (pp. 46 and 47), where he is concerned to refute the advaita view that plurality is unreal. He there makes a distinction between 'sublation' and 'non-persistence,' and claims that it is the failure on the part of the advaitin to make this distinction that is responsibile for his view that the world of plurality is entirely unreal. By 'sublation' he means the process whereby one element in our experience is contradicted by our wider system of experiences, and is thus proved to be unreal or false, for example, the rope that is mistaken for the snake. At the moment of perception the rope appears to be a snake, but this judgment of ours is 'sublated' by further experiences of that object, when we discover that what we took for a snake was only a rope. The judgment, 'This is a snake,' is thus proved to be unreal and false. But, Rāmānuja points out, such sublation is very different from non-persistence of an object in experience. A real object, for example, the rope, may exist in our experience for only a brief period of time; nevertheless it is real, so long as it is not 'sublated' or contradicted by the wider whole of experience. That an object exists thus only for a short time in experience does not, Rāmānuja claims, condemn it as false. The world of plurality may be fleeting and changeful, but that does not mean that it is on that account mere illusion. Accordingly Rāmānuja writes, " As to the assertion that all difference presented in our cognition—as of jars, pieces of cloth and the like—is unreal because such difference does not persist. This view, we maintain, is altogether erroneous, springs in fact from the neglect of distinguishing between persistence and non-persistence on the one hand, and the relation between what sublates and what is sublated on the other hand, Where two cognitions are mutually contradictory, there the latter relation holds good, and there is non-persistence of what is sublated. But jars, pieces of cloth and the like, do not contradict one another, since they are separate in place and time. If on the other hand the non-existence of a thing is cognised at the same time and the same place where and when its existence is cognised, we have a mutual contradiction of two cognitions, and then the stronger one sublates the other cognition which thus comes to an end. But when of a thing that is perceived in connection with some place and time, the non-existence is perceived in connection with some other place and time, there arises no contradiction ; how then should one cognition sublate the other ? or how can it be said that of a thing absent at one time and place there is absence at other times and places also ? In the case of the snake-rope, there arises a cognition of non-existence in connection with the given place and time ; hence there is contradiction, one judgment sublates the other and the sublated cognition comes to an end. But the circumstance of something which is seen at one time and in one place not persisting at another time and in another place is not observed to be invariably accompanied by falsehood, and hence mere non-persistence of this kind does not constitute a reason for unreality " (pp. 46 and 47). Thus Rāmānuja admits that the material world may, as compared with Brahman, be described as non-being although it is existent. This according to him is what Scriptural texts also mean by non-being.

It would be ridiculous, he further remarks, for the Scriptures to teach that Brahman became many, as is evidenced by texts which declare that Brahman thought, 'may I become many' (e.g., Chānd. Up. VI. 2, 3), if they believed at the same time that the many do not exist. "It is an altogether laughable assertion that Scripture should at first teach the doctrine, difficult to comprehend, that plurality as suggested by perception and the other means of knowledge belongs to Brahman also, and should afterwards negative this very doctrine!" (p. 85).

Accordingly even those Scriptural texts which appear to negative the existence of plurality, Rāmānuja argues, do not really mean to do so. "What all these texts deny is only plurality in so far as contradicting that unity of the world which depends on its being in its entirety an effect of Brahman, and having Brahman for its inward ruling principle and its true Self" (pp. 84 and 85).

Scripture, then, when rightly understood, gives no support to the doctrine of Nescience or the view that the world of plurality is an illusion. We have already seen that reason also gives no support to that theory. "We thus see that there is no cognition of any kind which has for its object a Nescience of 'inexplicable' nature" (p. 117). Consequently we must conclude that the advaitin's device of relating his pure non-differenced Brahman to a world of plurality by declaring the world to be an unreal product of beginningless Nescience is void both of reason and Scriptural authority.

Scriptural teaching regarding the relationship of Brahman to the world

Now that we have shown as against the advaitin

that the world is something real, we may proceed to consider how Brahman may be regarded as related to it. Two points have been estalished so far, both fundamental to religion, one, namely, that Brahman is highest Self characterised by every perfection, and the other that the world with all its change and multiplicity is real. Whatever view we might adopt regarding the relationship of the Deity to the world, both these points must be preserved at all costs. Rāmānuja accordingly seeks for such scriptural texts as relate Brahman to the world without sacrificing either the distinctive nature of Brahman or the reality of the world. Although generally the Upaniṣads, as we have seen, naïvely assumed the reality of the world, and regarded Brahman as the subtle principle which pervades it, philosophical speculation had not advanced sufficiently at that time for those early thinkers to trouble themselves over the question which perplexes Rāmānuja. Accordingly, as we saw, they often tended to overlook all distinction between Brahman and the world. Fortunately for Rāmānuja not all of them did this, for some, as we noted, began increasingly to distinguish Brahman from the world; and the view which they advocated, though not very clearly or consistently, was that Brahman is not Himself the world but that He is the Soul of the world. The earliest, and indeed the clearest formulation of this view is the one attributed to Yājñavalkya and found in the Antaryāmin Brāhmaṇa of the Bṛhadāraṇyaka Upaniṣad (III. 7), where principle after principle belonging to the world is enumerated and is proclaimed to be the body in which Brahman dwells as the Inner Ruler (*antaryāmin*). Here all that Rāmānuja is looking for is found. The plurality of the world is recognised; the supremacy of Brahman is taught, and both are brought together into a unity where the distinctive nature of Brahman is preserved and the reality of the world is accepted. What more can Rāmānuja want? He therefore fixes on it and, as we shall see, makes it a fundamental part of his teaching regarding the relationship of the Deity to the world.

This was not all the help which the Upaniṣads could give Rāmānuja in his attempt to conceive the relation of the Deity to the world. The Śvetāśvatara, we noted, was essentially theistic in sentiment, and Rāmānuja might without doubt expect help from that quarter. He finds it in the view of the Śvetāśvatara that Reality is ultimately a triad, consisting of the Lord, the material world and the individual soul, where the distinction of each is retained, and at the same time Brahman is regarded as containing the two elements of the world, matter and soul, within Himself.

These two, then, the idea that the world forms the body of Brahman, who is other than it and controls it from within, and that ultimately Brahman is a triad, holding matter and soul within Himself, provide Rāmānuja with the general framework of his system, the details being worked out in the light of teaching to be found in the Upaniṣads and the Bhagavadgītā. Of these details, two may here be mentioned, namely, the doctrine of repeated creation which he takes from Bhagavadgītā IX. 7. 9 (see Ś. Bh., pp. 139 and 140), which is taught also in the Śvetāśvatara Upaniṣad (cf. III. 2 ; IV. 1 ; V. 3), and which possibly goes back to ancient teaching about world-cycles ; and the view that creation proceeds in the main according to the stages enumerated in Sāṁkyhan philosophy and taught also, as we saw, by some of the later Upaniṣads and the Bhagavadgītā. In consonance with his contention that Scripture is our ultimate guide in such matters, he brings together numerous texts which, it is not unlikely, provided him with his main tenets.

" The whole matter," he says, " may be summarily stated as follows. Some texts declare a distinction of nature between non-intelligent matter, intelligent beings and Brahman, in so far as matter is the object of enjoyment, the souls the enjoying subjects, and

Brahman the ruling principle" ; and all the texts which he cites in support of this, it must be noted, are from the Śvetāśvatara. Having thus obtained one of his fundamental doctrines, he proceeds, " Smṛti expresses itself similarly.—' Thus eightfold is my nature divided. Lower is this Nature ; other than this and higher know that Nature of mine which constitutes the individual soul, by which this world is supported ' (Bhg. VII. 4. 5). ' All beings at the end of a Kalpa return into my Nature, and again at the beginning of a Kalpa do I send them forth. Resting on my own nature again and again do I send forth this entire body of beings, which has no power of its own, being subject to the power of nature ' (Bhg. IX. 7. 8) ; ' With me as supervisor Nature brings forth the movable and the immovable . . .' (Bhg. IX. 10), ' The great Brahman is my womb, in which I place the embryo, and thence there is the origin of all beings ' (XIV. 3). This last passage means—the womb of the world is the great Brahman, i.e., non-intelligent matter in its subtle state, commonly called *Prakṛti* ; with this I connect the embryo, i.e., the intelligent principle. From this contact of the non-intelligent and the intelligent, due to my will, there ensues the origination of all beings from gods down to lifeless things " (pp. 138-40).

Matter and souls, which are the constituent elements of the world, exist then in Brahman. Matter is composed of various parts, and Brahman creates the world by connecting the individual soul with matter, which under His supervision evolves and produces all that is. What the relation of matter and souls is to Brahman is next stated " Non-intelligent matter and intelligent beings—holding the relative position of objects of enjoyment and enjoying subjects and appearing in multifarious forms—other scriptural texts declare to be permanently connected with the highest Person in so far as they constitute his body, and thus are controlled by him ; the highest Person thus constituting their Self. Compare the following passages: 'He who dwells in the earth and within the earth, whom the earth does not know, whose body the earth is, and who rules the earth within, he is thy Self, the ruler within, the immortal' (Br. Up. III. 7); 'Entered within, the ruler of creatures, the Self of All' (Taitt. Ār. III. 24)." Rāmānuja has thus obtained the doctrine that the world with its various forms of existence is not only contained in Brahman and evolves in all its complexity from Him, but that He exists in it as its inner Self, while it stands to Him in the relationship of body.

Since Brahman, as already noted, repeatedly creates the universe out of Himself, sending the world out into its manifest form, withdrawing it back into Himself, and then sending it out again, two distinct states of Brahman in relation to the world are recognisable, one in which Brahman has the world within Himself in its manifest or evolved state, and the other in which He has it within Him in an unmanifest or subtle state. Rāmānuja finds support for this doctrine in texts which teach that prior to creation, Brahman was one only, without a second. As a matter of fact he is not here concerned so much in finding support for his theory as in defending it in advance against possible attacks. For it might be said against his view that if the world eternally forms a part of Brahman, whether in manifest or unmanifest state, Brahman is never Being Only, while this is what some Scriptural passages actually teach. As against this Rāmānuja declares that texts which speak of Brahman as Being only in the beginning refer to a state of Brahman when the world does not exist except in a subtle or potential form, and texts which speak of His becoming many refer to the state of Brahman in which the world appears in its actual form. By recognising these two states of Brahman, Rāmānuja seeks to ward off possible objections and to press into his service texts which describe Brahman as a pure unity as well as texts which regard Him as having become a plurality. He accordingly continues, "Other texts, again, aim at teaching that the highest Self to whom non-intelligent and intelligent beings stand in the relation of body, and hence of modes, subsists in the form of the world, in its causal as well as in its effected aspect, and hence speak of the world in this its double aspect as that which is (the Real); so, e.g., 'Being only this was in the beginning, one only without a second—it desired, may I be many, may I grow forth,' etc. . . . (Chānd. Up. VI. 2-8)"—also Taitt. Up. II. 6. "The same process of evolution of names and forms is described elsewhere also, 'All this was then unevolved; it became evolved by name and form' (Bṛ. Up. I. 4, 7). The fact is that the highest Self is in its causal or in its 'effected' condition, according as it has for its body intelligent and non-intelligent beings either in their subtle or their gross state. . . . A term which denotes the highest Self in its causal condition may therefore be exhibited in co-ordination with another term denoting the highest Self in its 'effected' state, both terms being used in their primary senses. Brahman, having for its modes intelligent and non-intelligent things in their gross and subtle states, thus constitutes effect and cause" (pp. 140-2).

In other words, Rāmānuja's teaching, as derived from authoritative works, in regard to the relation of Brahman to the world, is this: The world, consisting of matter and souls is the body of Brahman. He is distinct from it and forms its Soul. It is, however, not always in its evolved condition for from age to age Brahman withdraws the evolved universe into Himself, and then it exists in Him only in an undifferentiated subtle form. After a time, combining the soul with matter, He again sends out the world of objects and souls. The details in this process of emanation of the world from Brahman may now be set forth.

Creation

When the time for creation draws near, Brahman, who has the world with its distinction of matter and souls, within Him in a " form so extremely subtle that it hardly deserves to be called something separate from Brahman . . . forms the resolve ' May I again possess a world-body constituted by all sentient and non-sentient beings, distinguished by names and forms as in the previous æon ' " (p. 403). This thought or will is indicated also by texts which speak of Brahman as ' brooding ' prior to creation. " ' Brahman swells through brooding ' ; through brooding, i.e., thought —in agreement with a later text, ' brooding consists of thought '—Brahman swells, i.e., through thought in the form of an intention, viz., ' may I become many,' Brahman becomes ready for creation " (p. 285). This brooding, consisting of thought and intention, we may here remark, signifies two things with regard to Brahman in relation to creation. Brahman creates out of free choice, there being no external force constraining Him to create. We shall speak of this at greater length later.[1] It also signifies that this creation upon which Brahman enters entirely according to His desire, is not arbitrary and irrational but intelligent and rational. What Brahman broods on Rāmānuja tells us : " The ' brooding ' referred to in this text denotes knowing, viz., reflection on the shape and character of the previous world which Brahman is about to reproduce. . . . The meaning therefore is that Brahman, having an inward intuition of the characteristics of the former world, creates the new-world on the same pattern " (p. 405). " When the period of a great *pralaya* draws towards its close, the divine supreme Person, remembering the constitution of the world previous to the *pralaya*, and forming the volition ' may I become manifold,' separates into its constituent elements the whole mass of enjoying

[1] See pages 242-245 below.

souls and objects of enjoyment " (pp. 133 and 134). Why it is so necessary that Brahman should create the new world in accordance with what existed in a previous creation, we shall see later.[1] It suffices here to have noted that creation is always preceded by intention and thought on the part of the Supreme Being.

Brahman, then, having thought, proceeds to create the world. This He does by means of *Prakṛti* which, rests in Him in subtle undifferentiated form. At this stage it begins to acquire the three *guṇas* which it did not have in its subtle state. Speaking of these two states of *Prakṛti*; one in which it does not have the *guṇas*, and the other in which it comes to be characterised by them, Rāmānuja writes: " During a *pralaya* it (*prakṛti*) unites itself with Brahman and abides in its subtle state, without any distinction of names and forms; it then is called the 'Unevolved,' and by other similar names. At the time of creation, on the other hand, there reveal themselves in *Prakṛti* Goodness and the other *guṇas*, it divides itself according to names and forms, and then is called the 'evolved,' and so on " (p. 368). In this manner some texts which declare that *Prakṛti* is unoriginated are to be reconciled with others which teach that *Prakṛti* is originated.

When *Prakṛti* has acquired its three *guṇas*, creation proceeds much as in Sāṁkhyan philosophy, by the mutual influence of matter and soul, but animated and controlled at every stage by Brahman. First, there is *Prakṛti* with its three *guṇas*, *Sattva*, *Rajas* and *Tamas*. Then there follow the " seven Principles which are the effects of *Prakṛti* and the causal substances of everything else; these seven are the *mahat*, the *ahaṁkāra*, the subtle matter (*tanmātra*) of sound, the subtle matter of touch, the subtle matter of colour, the subtle matter of taste, and the subtle matter of smell. The *ahaṁkāra* is threefold, being either modified (*vaikārika*), or active (*taijasa*), or the originator

[1] See pp. 244, 245. 262, 263, below.

of the elements (*bhūtādi*). The *vaikārika* is of *sattva*-nature and the originator of the sense-organs; the *bhūtādi* is of *tamas*-nature, and the cause of those subtle matters (*tanmātra*) which in their turn are the cause of the gross elements; the *taijasa* is of the nature of *rajas*, and assists the other two. The five gross elements are the ether and so on, the five intellectual senses are hearing and so on; the five organs of action are speech and so on. With the addition of the internal organ (*manas*) these are the sixteen entities which are mere effects" (pp. 480 and 481). It is true that Rāmānuja gives the above as an account of the principles enunciated in Sāṁkhyan philosophy. But he definitely declares that the Sāṁkhyan principles are to be accepted, and modified only by the view that Brahman underlies all the processes enumerated in Sāṁkhyan philosophy. "The Śārīraka Śāstra (i.e., the Vedānta) does not disprove the principles assumed by the Sāṁkhyas, but merely the view of their not having Brahman for their Self" (p. 531). This is not merely the teaching of the Vedānta according to him, but also his own view. "We by no means wish to deny unevolved matter and all its effects in themselves, but in so far only as they are maintained not to have their Self in the Supreme Person. For the fact is that they constitute His body and He thus constitutes their Self; and it is only through this their relation to Him that the *Pradhāna*, and so on, are capable of accomplishing their several ends. Otherwise the different essential natures of them all could never exist—nor persist, nor act. It is just on the ground of this dependence on the Lord not being acknowledged by the Sāṁkhyas that their system is disproved by us" (pp. 358 and 359).

Although in the main Rāmānuja accepts the Sāṁkhyan account of the evolution of the universe, with the important proviso that Brahman is the author, sustainer, and controller of the whole process, he sometimes tacks on to this the idea of a Cosmic

Egg in which all the elements of matter and souls after they have been evolved are combined together, and in which is born the creator-Brahmā, who brings about the world as we know it. Thus in upholding the eternity of the Veda he writes: the Supreme Person "emits the entire world just as it had been before, from the so-called *Mahat* down to the Brahman-egg, and Hiraṇyagarbha (Prajāpati). Having thereupon manifested the Vedas in exactly the same order and arrangement they had had before, and having taught them to Hiraṇyagarbha, He entrusts to him the new creation of the different classes of beings, gods, and so on, just as it was before; and at the same time abides Himself within the world so created as its inner Self and Ruler" (p. 334). For this view he quotes as his authority Śvet. VI. 18, which runs, 'He who first creates Brahmā and delivers the Vedas to him,' and also cites passages from Manu Smṛti and the Purāṇas, which speaks of Brahmā being born in a golden egg, or springing out of a lotus from the navel of Nārāyaṇa reposing on the waters (pp. 334 and 335). The reason why the various elements when once evolved need to combine into an egg he borrows from a Smṛti text which says, 'possessing various powers these (elements), being separate from one another, were unable to produce creatures without combining. But having entered into mutual conjunction they, from the Mahat down to individual beings, produce the Brahmā egg' (p. 731).

It is significant that, although this doctrine with regard to the evolved elements combining to form an egg out of which the creator-Brahmā is born to create the actual world, is to be found in the Pāñcarātra Saṁhitās, as we have already seen, Rāmānuja does not seek their support.

With regard to the relation of the Supreme Brahman to the creator-Brahmā, Rāmānuja makes it quite plain that Hiraṇyagarbha the creator-Brahmā, is only as it were the instrument of the Supreme Being, who dwells within him and uses him even as the soul uses the body. So, ultimately, it is the Supreme Brahman who creates. In this connection he says, " A question now arises with regard to the creation of the world in its discrete aspect (*vyaṣṭi*) which consists in the differentiation of names and forms (i.e., individual beings). Is this latter creation the work of Hiraṇyagarbha only . . . or, fundamentally the work of the highest Brahman having Hiraṇyagarbha for its body? . . . The Pūrvapakṣin maintains the former alternative. . . . Against this view the Sūtra declares itself. The differentiation of names and forms belongs to . . . the highest Brahman; since it is assigned by Scripture to the latter only. . . . The work of differentiating names and forms thus belongs to the highest Brahman which has for its body Hiraṇyagarbha. . . ." (pp. 578-80).

Obviously then the theory of world-creation by the god Brahmā or Hiraṇyagarbha has little philosophical significance in Rāmānuja's system. If the Supreme Being Himself creates through Hiraṇyagarbha, the theory of the creator-Brahmā may as well be dispensed with. But the theory was long in vogue in Pāñcarātra philosophy. It is to be found, as we saw, in the Nārāyaṇīya, the Pāñcarātra Saṁhitās and the Purāṇas, and Rāmānuja saw little reason to discard it, especially since he could find evidence for the view outside Pāñcarātra literature. But he could not in the same way introduce into his cosmology the Pāñcarātra doctrine of the four *vyūhas*, Vāsudeva, Saṁkarṣaṇa, Pradyumna and Aniruddha, for this is entirely sectarian, not found outside the Pāñcarātra fold, and Rāmānuja wished to make his philosophy as non-sectarian and catholic as possible. Accordingly although he speaks approvingly of the Pāñcarātrins (pp. 524-31), he accepts the *vyūhas* only as forms assumed by the Deity out of tenderness to His devotees for purposes of worship (pp. 525 and 526), and makes no use of the Pāñcarātra doctrine of the *vyūhas* as principles through which evolution of the universe proceeds. As a matter of fact Rāmānuja shows little interest in cosmological speculation, and is willing to obtain his information regarding the various stages of evolution of the world entirely from second-hand. He is merely concerned with pointing out that, whatever order evolution follows, it is Brahman who underlies it. In this respect he contrasts very strikingly with the philosophers of the Saṁhitās, who, as we saw, promulgated elaborate cosmological doctrines. Rāmānuja's interest is too definitely centred round the Deity for him to trouble much about the various stages through which the world passed before it arrived at its present state. Accordingly he accepts in the main the Sāṁkhyan account, especially as germs of that teaching are found in the Upaniṣads; but the religious character of his thought leads him to see God in and through the whole process.

Little interested as Rāmānuja is, in details regarding the process of creation, he shows great skill and originality in facing problems which arise in connection with the relation of the Deity to the universe, implied in creation as well as in all His other dealings with the world. Since the world with all its change and multiciplicity is real, the advaitin's easy method of getting over the difficulty by calling the world an illusion is not possible for Rāmānuja. Moreover the problem is heightened by the fact that according to Rāmānuja Brahman is highest Self, characterised by every perfection. If the Supreme Being is all-perfect, and if the world with all its imperfections is real, how are we to understand the relationship between Brahman and the world? Do not the imperfections of the world argue imperfections in Brahman, on whom it completely depends? How then do we say that He is all-perfect? Rāmānuja realises that if the religious view of Brahman is to be maintained, this problem more than any other must be faced. He accordingly defends his view regarding the relation of the Deity to the world, stated dogmatically and in general terms above, always in the light of this one problem. We shall do well, therefore, in seeking to give an account of Rāmānuja's view regarding the relation of the Deity to the world, to make this problem the basis also of our exposition.

Brahman as cause, world as effect

The fact that Brahman creates the world, as described above, establishes that Brahman stands in causal relationship to the world. In what sense Brahman, the perfect One, may stand in causal relationship to an imperfect world, is what we must consider. One fact, however, must first be made clear, although it is implied in the account of creation given above, for Rāmānuja as a monist is quite emphatic about it, viz., that when Brahman creates He does not build out of materials existing externally to, and independently of Himself, as an architect builds a house, but that He evolves the universe out of Himself. This is obviously an inheritance from the Upaniṣads, which often describe the emanation of the universe from Brahman on the analogy of the sparks which proceed from fire, or the threads which are emitted by the spider. He accordingly maintains, in opposition to the theistic Sāṁkhya, which recognises a Supreme Being but regards Him as working on given materials, that Brahman is not only the operative but also the material cause of the universe. "*Prakṛti*, i.e., the material cause, not only the operative cause, is Brahman only ; this view being in harmony with the promissory declaration and the illustrative instances. The promissory declaration is the one referring to the knowledge of all things through the knowledge of one, 'Did you ever ask for that instruction by which that which is not heard becomes heard ? ' etc. (Chānd. Up. VI. 1. 3). And the illustrative instances are those which set forth the knowledge of the effect as resulting from the knowledge of the cause, 'As by one lump of clay there is made known all that is made of clay; as by one nugget of gold, etc. . . .' (Chānd. Up. VI. 1. 4). If Brahman were merely the operative cause of the world, the knowledge of the entire world would not result from the knowledge of Brahman; not any more than we know the pot when we know the potter" (p. 398). But, it may be asked, "how then have we to understand texts . . . which declare *Prakṛti* to be eternal and the material cause of the world?" To this Rāmānuja replies, "*Prakṛti* . . . in such passages denotes Brahman in its causal phase when names and forms are not yet distinguished. For a principle independent of Brahman does not exist" (p. 399). "In addition Scripture directly states that Brahman alone is the material as well as the operative cause of the world. 'What was the wood, what the tree from which they have shaped heaven and earth? . . . Brahman was the wood, Brahman the tree from which they shaped heaven and earth. . . .'—Here a question is asked, suggested by the ordinary worldly view, as to what was the material and the instruments used by Brahman when creating; and the answer . . . declares that Brahman itself is the material and the instruments" (pp. 401 and 402).

But if Brahman is thus responsible both for the form and for the matter of the universe the problem of how the perfect Brahman can be the cause of an imperfect world arises in all its bewildering complexity. Rāmānuja imagines his opponent saying, "Perception and the other means of knowledge show this world with all its sentient and non-sentient beings to be of a non-intelligent and impure nature, to possess none of the qualities of the Lord, and to have pain for its very essence; and such a world totally differs in nature from the Brahman, postulated by you, which is said to be all-knowing, of supreme Lordly power, antagonistic to all evil, enjoying unbroken uniform blessedness. . . . The general rule is that an effect is non-different in character from its cause; as, e.g., pots and bracelets are non-different in character from their material causes—clay and gold. The world cannot, therefore, be the effect of Brahman from which it differs in character, and we hence conclude that, in agreement with the Sāṁkhya Smṛti, the *Pradhāna* which resembles the actual world in character must be assumed to be the general cause" (pp. 413 and 414).

The argument, it will be granted, is forceful, and Rāmānuja therefore examines it closely. In the first place, he will not resort to the device of some who, when thus driven into a corner, assert that Brahman is the cause and the world is really not different from Him in character, for potentially it has the same nature as Brahman. Such high-handed treatment of facts in order to support a theory Rāmānuja condemns: "it might possibly be said that as Brahman is ascertained from Scripture to be the sole cause of the world, it must be admitted that intelligence exists in the world also, which is an effect of Brahman. In the same way as the consciousness of an intelligent being is not perceived when it is in the states of deep sleep, swoon, etc., so the intelligent nature of jars and the like also is not observed, although it really exists; and it is this very difference of manifestation and non-manifestation of intelligence on which the distinction of intelligent and non-intelligent beings depends. But to this we reply that permanent non-perception of intelligence proves its non-existence. This consideration also refutes the hypothesis of things commonly called non-intelligent possessing the power of potentiality of consciousness. For if you maintain that a thing possesses the power of producing an effect while that effect is never and nowhere seen to be produced by it, you may as well proclaim at a meeting of sons of barren women that their mothers possess eminent procreative power" (p. 415). No, Rāmānuja will not escape from the difficulty of explaining how there can be any causal relation between two things so different from each other as Brahman and the world, by means of this subterfuge. He will face the objection squarely, and in order to do so begins by asking, "What sameness of character, again, of causal substance and effects, have you in mind when you maintain that from the absence of such sameness it follows that Brahman cannot be proved to be the material cause of the world? It cannot be complete sameness of all attributes, because in that case the relation of cause and effect (which after all requires *some* difference) could not be established. For we do not observe that in pots and jars which are fashioned out of a lump of clay there persists the quality of 'being a lump' which belongs to the causal substance. And should you say that it suffices there should be equality in some or any attribute, we point out that such is actually the case with regard to Brahman and the world, both of which have the attribute of 'existence' and others" (pp. 415 and 416). Rāmānuja is aware that if the objection is to be taken seriously it should not be understood in this form, in which it is so easily refuted; and he accordingly proceeds to make clear the real force of the opponent's contention. "The true state of the case is rather as follows. There is equality of nature between an effect and a cause, in that sense that those essential characteristics by which the causal substance distinguishes itself from other things persist in its effects also: those characteristic features, e.g., which distinguish gold from clay and other materials, persist also in things made of gold—bracelets and the like. But applying this consideration to Brahman and the world we find that Brahman's essential nature is to be antagonistic to all evil, and to consist of knowledge, bliss and power, while the world's essential nature is to be the opposite of all this. Brahman cannot, therefore, be the material cause of the world" (p.416).

To the objection stated thus, Rāmānuja points out that it may be replied "that even things of different essential characteristics stand to each other in the relation of cause and effect. From man, e.g., who is a sentient being, there spring nails, teeth and hair which are non-sentient things; the sentient scorpion springs from non-sentient dung; and non-sentient threads proceed from the sentient spider." This reply, however, he says, may be regarded as invalid, "for in the instances quoted the relation of cause and effect rests on the non-sentient elements only (i.e., it is only the non-sentient matter of the body which produces nails, etc.)" (p. 416). But even conceding this, Rāmānuja points out that cases may be found of causal substances which differ even in essential characteristics from their effects. "The assertion that Brahman cannot be the material cause of the world because the latter differs from it in essential nature, is unfounded; since it is a matter of observation that even things of different nature stand to each other in the relation of cause and effect. For it is observed that from honey and similar substances there originate worms and other little animals.—But it has been said above that in those cases there is sameness of nature, in so far as the relation of cause and effect holds good only between the non-intelligent elements in both!—This assertion was indeed made, but it does not suffice to prove that equality of character between cause and effect which you have in view. For, being apprehensive that from the demand of equality of character in some point or other only it would follow that, as all things have certain characteristics in common, anything might originate from anything, you have declared that the equality of character necessary for the relation of cause and effect is constituted by the persistence, in the effect, of those characteristic points which differentiate the cause from other things. But it is evident that this restrictive rule does not hold good in the case of the origination of worms and the like from honey and so on; and hence it is not unreasonable to assume that the world also, although differing in character from Brahman, may originate from the latter. For in the case of worms originating from honey, scorpions from dung, etc., we do *not* observe—what indeed we *do* observe in certain other cases, as of pots made of clay, ornaments made of gold—that the special characteristics distinguishing the causal substance from other things persist in the effects also" (pp. 417 and 418). Hence Rāmānuja declares that it is not unreasonable to conclude that the world, though differing in character from Brahman, may proceed from Him.

"But an objection is raised, if Brahman, the cause, differs in nature from the effect, viz., the world, this means that cause and effect are separate things, and that hence the effect does not exist in the cause, i.e., Brahman"; and we may as well say "that the world originates from what has no existence.—Not so, we reply. For what the preceding Sūtra has laid down is merely the denial of an absolute rule demanding that cause and effect should be of the same nature; it was not asserted that the effect is a thing altogether different and separate from the cause. We by no means abandon our tenet that Brahman the cause modifies itself so as to assume the form of a world differing from it in character. For such is the case with the honey and the worms also. There is difference of characteristics, but—as in the case of gold and golden bracelets there is oneness of substance" (pp. 418 and 419).

That the world is different in character from Brahman, who is postulated as its cause, is obvious; but that the world is one in substance with Brahman is not so evident. It is as a matter of fact the point in dispute, for does it not follow that if the world is one in substance with Brahman, then all the imperfections of the world are really the imperfections of Brahman? Rāmānuja is aware of the difficulty, and he states it in the form of an objection that he must face. "If we accept the doctrine of the oneness of substance of cause and effect, then absorption, creation, etc., of the world would connect themselves with Brahman, and the latter would thus be effected by all the imperfections of its effect ; in the same way as all the attributes of the bracelet are present in the gold also" (p. 419). It remains therefore to enquire in what sense we may say that the world is one with Brahman, its cause. It is obvious that in order to find an answer we must analyse the causal relationship which we postulate between Brahman and the world. Rāmānuja accordingly devotes several pages to a discussion of the causal principle, examining the theories propounded by various schools of thought (cf. pp. 430-4 ; 445-7), and concludes with a statement of his own view, which is that the effect is nothing but the causal substance which has passed from one state of existence to another. Thus the effect, e.g. jar, is the causal substance, clay, which has assumed another condition of existence than that of mere clay. It is one in substance with clay, and yet it has attributes which are different from those of clay in its causal state. For purposes of activity, so Rāmānuja tells us, "the material clay . . . touches (enters into contact with) an effect (*vikāra*), i.e., a particular make or configuration, distinguished by having a broad bottom and resembling the shape of a belly, and a special name *nāmadheya*), viz., *pitcher*, and so on, which is applied to that effect ; or, to put it differently, to the end that certain activities may be accomplished, the substance clay receives a new configuration and a new name. Hence jars and other things of clay are clay (*mṛttikā*), i.e., are of the substance of clay, only . . . *only* (*eva*) because the effects are not known as different substances. One and the same substance therefore, such as clay or gold, gives occasion for different ideas and words only as it assumes different configurations ; just as we observe that one and the same Devadatta becomes the object of different ideas and terms, and gives rise to different effects, according to the different stages of life—youth, old age, etc.—

which he has reached" (pp. 454 and 455). The effect therefore is one in substance with the cause in the sense that it is potentially contained in the causal substance as a state which this substance is capable of assuming. This then is the light which we derive regarding the nature of the unity which exists between cause and effect.

But before we apply this result to the case of Brahman in relation to the world, we may note a significant point in regard to the last sentence of the passage just cited, for Rāmānuja there introduces into the idea of cause the concept of growth borrowed from the organic world. He finds that the relationship between clay and jar, while illustrating his point that the effect is one in substance with the cause, fails in one important particular when considered in the light of what he is wishing to establish with regard to the relationship between Brahman and the world. For clay is only the material cause of the jar, and it requires the external agency of a potter to give it the form of a jar. Such external agency cannot, of course, exist in the case of Brahman in relation to the world. It becomes necessary, therefore, if we would understand all that is implied in regarding Brahman as the cause of the world, to pass from the mechanical or inorganic to the vital or organic realm for our illustration. "The case of the cause and the effect is thus analogous to that of the child and youth: the word 'effect' denotes nothing else but the causal substance which has passed over into a different condition" (pp. 463 4).

Applying then the result of our investigation of clay as standing in causal relation to the jar, and of the child in causal relation to the youth, it would seem that Brahman as the cause of the world must be thought to be one in substance with the world in the sense that He holds the world within Himself in potential form, and that creation is only the passing over of Brahman from one state of existence, where the world exists potentially, into another state of existence, where the world exists actually, much as a child passes over from childhood to manhood when its potentialities become actualised. The crudities of a theory of creation, according to which the Deity first exists by Himself, and then suddenly by a mere fiat of His will brings about the world, as it were, from nowhere, are thus avoided, and it is shown at the same time in what sense the world is one with Brahman. "It is in this way that we prove . . . that the world is non-different from the universal cause, i.e., the highest Brahman. Brahman only, having the aggregate of sentient and non-sentient beings for its body and hence for its modes (*prakāra*), is denoted by all words whatsoever. The body of this Brahman is sometimes constituted by sentient and non-sentient beings in their subtle state, when—just owing to that subtle state—they are incapable of being (conceived and) designated as apart from Brahman whose body they form: Brahman is then in its so-called causal condition. At other times the body of Brahman is constituted by all sentient and non-sentient beings in their gross, manifest state, owing to which they admit of being thought and spoken of as having distinct names and forms: Brahman then is in its 'effected' state. The effect, i.e., the world, is thus seen to be non-different from the cause, i.e., the Highest Brahman" (pp. 58 and 59). Rāmānuja is thus convinced that, however much the world may differ in character from Brahman, it must, if Scriptural teaching regarding Brahman as its cause be true, be one in substance with Him, in the sense that it exists potentially within Him as a state which He is capable of assuming. The world as effect is Brahman who has actualised this potentiality.

But it may be said that if the world is thus a form which Brahman assumes, all the imperfections of the world must belong to Him. To this Rāmānuja replies, as we noted, that it is not necessary for the causal substance to have the same characteristics as its effect, for a worm may arise from honey. Thus he sees no difficulty in thinking that the world is one in substance with Brahman as its cause, and yet also different from Him in character as effect.

We have spoken loosely, in the foregoing, of Brahman 'assuming' the form of the world, or of His 'passing over' from one state of existence to another. We have now to enquire what exactly this implies with regard to the change undergone by Brahman in effecting the world. To do this, we shall have to make a distinction in the nature of Brahman, and conceive Him from this point of view as having two essential aspects, viz., body and soul, the soul representing His own perfect nature and the body that part of Him which is the world.

Brahman as Soul, world as body

There is abundant evidence in the Upaniṣads, as we saw, for the view that Brahman pervades the world as the soul pervades the body. The classical formulation of the view is to be found, as already noted, in the Antaryāmin Brāhmaṇa of the Bṛhadāraṇyaka Upaniṣad. Moreover it was a common assumption, even at the time of Yājñavalkya and Ajātaśatru, that the soul is a conscious principle which is essentially different from the body which it inhabits. As speculation advanced, we saw that the later thinkers of the Upaniṣads tended increasingly, in the light of the imperfections of embodied existence, to distinguish Brahman who pervades it as something quite distinct from it and uncontaminated by the imperfections of that which He pervades. Moreover the germs of Sāṁkhyan philosophy which sets body in opposition to soul, are to be found, as we saw, in some of the later Upaniṣads and the sharp distinction which it makes between body and soul is taught in the Bhagavadgītā, as well as in Pāñcarātra literature. All this could be used profitably by Rāmānuja to show how Brahman may be one with the world without thereby being involved in its imperfections. He accordingly seizes upon this idea to explain how Brahman may be related to the change that is implied in the creation and reabsorption of the world. The difficulty to be faced is this : " it appears that Brahman is essentially free from even a shadow of all the imperfections which afflict all sentient and non-sentient beings, and has for its only characteristics absolutely supreme bliss and knowledge. How then is it possible that this Brahman should . . . actually became manifold, by appearing in the form of a world comprising various sentient and non-sentient beings—all of which are the abodes of all kinds of imperfections and afflictions ? " (p. 402). How in other words are we to understand the change whereby the perfect Brahman becomes the imperfect world ?

Rāmānuja replies : " The modification taught in our system is not such as to introduce imperfections into the highest Brahman, on the contrary it confers on it limitless glory. For our teaching as to Brahman's modification is as follows. Brahman—essentially antagonistic to all evil, of uniform goodness, differing in nature from all beings other than itself, all-knowing, endowed with the power of immediately realising all its purposes, in eternal possession of all it wishes for, supremely blessed—has for its body the entire universe, with all its sentient and non-sentient beings . . . and constitutes the Self of the Universe. Now, when this world which forms Brahman's body has been gradually reabsorbed into Brahman, each constituent element being refunded into its immediate cause, so that in the end there remains only the highly subtle, elementary matter which Scripture calls Darkness ; and when this so-called Darkness itself, by assuming a form so extremely subtle that it hardly deserves to be called something separate from Brahman, of which it constitutes the body, has become one with Brahman ; then Brahman invested with this ultra-subtle body forms the resolve, ' May I again possess a world-body constituted by all sentient and non-sentient beings distinguished by names and forms just as in the previous æon,' and modifies (*pariṇāmayati*) itself by gradually evolving the world-body in the inverse order in which reabsorption had taken place" (pp. 402-3).

The idea of Brahman modifying Himself to become manifold is not new. Rāmānuja bases his view chiefly on the Taittirīya passage which declares regarding Brahman that 'He desired, may I be many, may I grow forth.' He brooded over himself, and having thus brooded, he sent forth all whatever there is. Having sent forth he entered it. Having entered it he became *sat* and *tyat*, defined and undefined . . . real and unreal.' This certainly implies a great deal of modifying activity on the part of Brahman. But what is not found in this passage, and what Rāmānuja chiefly deserves credit for is to apply this doctrine of modification in such a way as to show how in all this modification the perfect nature of Brahman remains ever the same. He does this by bringing the sharp distinction which, as we have seen, philosophers through several centuries were in the habit of making between body and soul, to bear upon the Taittirīya doctrine of modification. "The sense of the Taittirīya text therefore is as follows. The highest self, which in itself is of the nature of unlimited knowledge and bliss, has for its body all sentient and non-sentient beings . . . in so subtle a form that they may be called non-existing; and as they are his body he may be said to consist of them (*tan-maya*).[1] Then . . . he, by a series of steps beginning with *Prakṛti* and the aggregate of souls and leading down to the elements in their gross state, so modifies himself as to have those elements for his body—when he is said to consist of them—and thus appears in the form of our world. . . . When

[1] Perhaps this word may be better translated in the light of its context as "possessed of them," i.e., the perfect Brahman possesses the elements of the world in a subtle form, his own nature being different from theirs.

the text says that the Self having entered into it became *sat* and *tyat*, the meaning is that the highest Self, which in its causal state had been the universal Self, abides, in its effected state also, as the Self of the different substances undergoing changes and thus becomes this and that " (p. 405). It is significant that thus he systematically reads into the Taittirīya doctrine of modification the distinction between body and self. Why he does so is obvious from the sentences which immediately follow. " While the highest Self thus undergoes a change—in the form of a world comprising the whole aggregate of sentient and non-sentient beings—all imperfection and suffering are limited to the sentient beings constituting part of its body, and all change is restricted to the non-sentient things which constitute another part. The highest Self is *effected* in that sense only that it is the ruling principle, and hence the Self, of matter and souls in their gross or evolved state; but just on account of being this, viz., their inner Ruler and Self, it is in no way touched by their imperfections and changes " (pp. 405 and 406).

The one Brahman, then, when considered in relation to the modification that is necessary for effecting the world, is found to disclose a distinction within itself, namely, the distinction of body and soul, the body representing the changing imperfect element in Brahman, the soul representing His unchanging essential nature, which remains ever perfect. All the modification that is undergone by Brahman in effecting the world is merely a modification, as it were, in His body, which passes from a subtle to a gross state. But this modification leaves His soul, i.e., His own essential nature, entirely untouched. In a true sense, therefore, Brahman Himself, i.e., His own essential nature, remains unmodified in all the modification that is undergone by the world in creation and reabsorption. In Rāmānuja's day, owing to the sharp distinction which philosophers were wont to make between body and soul, there could be little objection to the view that while the body or the world undergoes changes, the soul or Brahman in His essential nature, remains unchanged.

But while the distinction of body and soul is helpful as suggesting a way of thinking of Brahman in relation to the changes implied in the creation and reabsorption of the world, there are certain ideas long associated with the body in Indian thought, which compel Rāmānuja to make clear what exactly he means by regarding Brahman as possessed of a body. If we follow him in this, we shall be able to go behind Rāmānuja's metaphor of body and soul and gain a clearer understanding of his conception of the relation of Brahman to the world. As usual, he states his problem in the form of an objection raised by an opponent who declares : " It is not, we say, possible that the intelligent and non-intelligent beings together should constitute the body of Brahman. For a body is a particular aggregate of earth and the other elements, depending for its subsistence on vital breath with its five modifications, and serving as an abode to the sense-organs which mediate the experiences of pleasure and pain retributive of former works : such is in Vedic and wordly speech the sense connected with the term 'body.' But numerous Vedic texts . . . declare that the highest Self is free from *karman* and the enjoyment of its fruits, is not capable of enjoyment dependent on sense-organs, and has no life dependent on breath : whence it follows that he cannot have a body constituted by all the non-sentient and sentient beings " (p. 420). To this Rāmānuja replies, " In ordinary language the word 'body' is not, like words such as jar, limited in its denotation to things of one definite make or character, but is observed to be applied directly (not only secondarily or metaphorically) to things of altogether different make and characteristics—such as worms, insects, moths, snakes, man, four-footed animals, and so on. We must therefore aim at giving a definition of the word that is in agreement with general use. The definitions given by the Pūrvapakṣin (opponent)—'a body is that which causes the enjoyment of the fruit of actions,' etc.—do not fulfil this requirement; for they do not take in such things as earth and the like which the texts declare to be the body of the Lord. And further they do not take in those bodily forms which the Lord assumes according to his wish, nor the bodily forms released souls may assume, according to 'He is one,' etc. (Chānd. Up. VII. 262); for none of those embodiments subserve the fruition of the results of actions. And further, the bodily forms which the Supreme Person assumes at wish are not special combinations of earth and the other elements; for Smṛti says, 'The body of that highest Self is not made from a combination of the elements.' It thus appears that it is also too narrow a definition to say that a body is a combination of the different elements. Again, to say that a body is that, the life of which depends on the vital breath with its five modifications is also too narrow, viz., in respect of plants; for although vital air is present in plants, it does not in them support the body by appearing in five special forms. Nor again does it answer to define a body as either the abode of the sense-organs or as the cause of pleasure and pain; for neither of these definitions takes in the bodies of stone or wood which were bestowed on Ahalyā and other persons in accordance with their deeds. We are thus led to adopt the following definition—Any substance which a sentient soul is capable of completely controlling and supporting for its own purposes, and which stands to the soul in an entirely subordinate relation, is the body of that soul. . . . In this sense then, all sentient and non-sentient beings together constitute the body of the Supreme Person, for they are completely controlled and supported by him for his own ends, and are absolutely subordinate to him" (pp. 423 and 424) In the light of this definition we are enabled to see what exactly Rāmānuja means by regarding the world as the 'body' of Brahman. It is something which Brahman, while abiding in His own essential and perfect nature, controls and sustains for His own ends. The world is thus quite distinct from Brahman. Creation and absorption affect the world, but His own essential nature remains unmodified.

Not only does the distinction between body and soul thus help us to understand how the world may undergo change and modification in creation and re-absorption, without Brahman's essential nature being involved therein, but it also serves to show, as Rāmānuja's definition of 'body' makes clear, how completely the world is dependent on Brahman. So absolute and vital does the dependence of the body on the soul seem to Rāmānuja that, as we shall now see, he declares that the relation of body to soul is the same as the relation of attribute or mode to substance.

Brahman as substance, world as attribute or mode

Here we come upon Rāmānuja's own distinctive view of the relation in which Brahman stands to the world. That Brahman is cause, and the world is effect was, we may say, the first philosophical conception of Brahman's relation to the world. The earliest cosmogonies, it will be remembered, were concerned with the question, Whence came all this? And the answer of the Upaniṣads in the main was, Brahman is the cause. Similarly the view that Brahman is the soul and the world His body, is one which, as we have seen, can claim long descent, going back at least to a time as remote as that of the Antaryāmin Brāhmaṇa of the Bṛhadāraṇyaka Upaniṣad. Rāmānuja, we noted, adopts both these ways of thinking of Brahman's relation to the world, and defends them chiefly in the light of the fact that, while Brahman, according to him, is a perfect being, the world is characterised by imperfection. But the view which may be said to represent his own contribution to a conception of Brahman's relation to the world is that Brahman stands to the world as substance stands to attribute. In criticising the advaitin's view of substance as pure Being, we saw how Rāmānuja came to the conclusion that any substance of which we know anything in experience is always characterised by differences, and against the Bhedābhedavādin he found that these differences were real differences which nevertheless were somehow held together in the unity of the substance. Here then we find, even within the realm of everyday experience, a unity which holds together and supports real differences, and it is precisely such a unity that Brahman must be in relation to the diversity of the world, for we have found that the Scriptures teach that Brahman is one, and yet that He is the cause and the soul of the many, which are different from Him in character. Hence we may think that Brahman is the Substance of which the world is an attribute. The difference of the world from Brahman, and at the same time its complete dependence on Him, will thus be explicable. Accordingly Rāmānuja maintains, as we shall see, that the world is an attribute or mode of Brahman.

But before we do this, it is necessary to show that even the relationship which we in accordance with Scriptural teaching have postulated between Brahman and the world—viz., that Brahman is the cause and the soul of the world—ultimately reduces itself to the relation of substance to attribute, and in that finds its explanation. This is easily done with regard to causal relationship, for did not our analysis of causal connection show that the effect is nothing but the causal substance which has passed from one state or mode of existence to another? The effect jar, we saw, is nothing more than a mode or modification of the causal substance, clay; so that in the end what we find to happen when an effect is, as we say, produced by or originated from a cause is that a substance now characterised by a certain attribute, state or mode of existence assumes another attribute, state or mode of existence, which it always held potentially within itself. "A substance enters into different states in succession; what passes away is the substance in its previous states, what originates is the substance in its subsequent states. As thus the substance in all its states has being, there is nothing irrational in the *satkārya* theory" (p. 456), which is the theory just expounded, according to which the effect is nothing more than a mode of the casual substance.

Not only does the relation of effect to cause reduce itself thus to the relation of attribute or mode to substance, but so also does the relation of body to soul; for what after all is a body but a state or condition assumed by a soul? It is so completely dependent on the soul that it ceases to exist when separated from the soul, even as an attribute or mode ceases to exist except when supported by the substance to which it belongs. It thus proclaims itself to be nothing but a mode or attribute of the soul. So Rāmānuja writes, "The relation of bodies to the self is strictly analogous to that of class characteristics and qualities to the substances in which they inhere; for it is the self only which is their substance and their final cause (*prayojana*), and they are modes of the self. That the self only is their substrate appears from the fact that when the self separates itself from the body the latter perishes; that the self alone is their final cause, appears from the fact that they exist to the end that the fruits of the actions of the self may be enjoyed; and they are modes of the self appears from the fact that they are mere attributes of the Self manifesting itself as god, man or the like" (pp. 136 and 137). But to this an objection is raised. It is said that the body cannot be an attribute or mode of the soul, for if it were so, it would, even as an attribute, be apprehended only along with the substrate to which it belongs; but as a matter of fact we apprehend the body by itself, and this would never be possible if it were a mere attribute. "If it is supposed that . . . the body of a man, god, etc., stands towards the self in the relation of a mode, in the same way as . . . the generic characteristic and the quality stand in the relation of modes to the substances to which they are grammatically co-ordinated; then there would necessarily be simultaneous cognition of the generic character and the individual. But as a matter of fact this is not the case; we do not necessarily observe a human, divine, or animal body together with the self" (p. 136).

Rāmānuja has little difficulty in meeting this objection. He points out that we do apprehend the self of a human being when we apprehend his body, our reason for thinking that we do not is that the self is not an object that can be perceived by the eye. "That class characteristics and individuals are invariably observed together, is due to the fact of both being objects of visual perception; the self, on the other hand, is not such, and hence is not apprehended by the eye, while the body is so apprehended. . . . That two things are invariably perceived together, depends, as already observed, on their being apprehended by means of the same apparatus, visual or otherwise. Earth is naturally connected with smell, taste, and so on, and yet these qualities are not perceived by the eye; in the same way the eye which perceives the body does not perceive that essential characteristic of the body which consists in its being mere mode of the self; the reason of the difference being that the eye has no capacity to apprehend the self. But this does not imply that the body does not possess that essential nature" (p. 137). We must conclude, therefore, that since the body is completely dependent on the soul, and cannot exist except in relation to the latter, it is only the mode or attribute of the soul.

But to this it may be objected that one thing cannot be regarded as an attribute of another. Rāmānuja, it will be remembered, anticipated this objection, and told us that although 'attribute' is usually understood to refer only to qualities, not to things, things may also be regarded as attributes if they completely depend on something else for their existence. If we restrict the word attribute, as in general use, to abstract qualities, we shall understand Rāmānuja's meaning best if in Spinozistic fashion we speak of objects which are entirely dependent on something else for their existence as modes (or concrete attributes).

We are now ready to apply the results of our investigation to the case of the relationship between Brahman and the world. The effect, we found, was nothing but a mode of the causal substance; the body also, we have just seen, is nothing but a mode of the self. Hence it follows that all Scriptural teaching with regard to Brahman as cause and the world as effect, or of Brahman as soul and the world as body, imply in the end that Brahman is Substance and the world is His mode. "All things thus are predicative to, or modes of, *Paramapuruṣa*; hence *Paramapuruṣa* alone exists (the *substans*), adjectivated by everything else. All terms are thus connotations of Him by the rule of *Sāmānādhikaraṇya*, or the rule which expresses the inseparable relation existing between substance and attribute, or the invariable co-existence of subject and predicate."[1]

But, it may now be asked, if the world is a mode of Brahman, how can imperfection exist in the world without affecting the nature of Brahman? The answer is easy. Rāmānuja provided for it in his definition of attribute in relation to substance. "Wherever we cognise the relation of distinguishing attribute and thing distinguished thereby, the two clearly present themselves to our mind as absolutely different" (pp. 42 and 43). The difference in characteristics of the mode from the substance therefore need not alarm us, for that, Rāmānuja assures us, is

[1] Bhg. Bh. VII. 7. Govindācārya's translation, p. 236.

quite the usual characteristic of modes. What makes a thing a mode is not sameness of character with the substance to which it belongs, but as we have seen complete dependence; and that, it cannot be denied, is precisely the relation in which, according to the Scriptures, the world stands to Brahman. "From all this it follows that the entire aggregate of things, intelligent and non-intelligent, has its Self in Brahman in so far as it constitutes Brahman's body; and as thus, the whole world different from Brahman derives its substantial being only from constituting Brahman's body, any term denoting the world or something in it conveys a meaning which has its proper consummation in Brahman only: in other words all terms whatsoever denote Brahman in so far as distinguished by the different things which we associate with those terms" (p. 134).

"This being so, it appears that those as well who hold the theory of the absolute unity of one non-differenced substance as those who teach the doctrine of *bhedābheda* (co-existing difference and non-difference), and those who teach the absolute difference of several substances, give up all those scriptural texts which teach that Brahman is the universal self" (p. 134). The fact that the Scriptures proclaim "that the entire world forms the body of Brahman" (p. 135) shows that they teach that the plurality of the world, though differing from Him in character, is completely dependent on Him. and stands to Him in the relation of mode. For as genus (*jāti*) and quality (*guṇa*), so substance (*dravya*) also may occupy the position of determining attributes (*viśeṣaṇa*), in so far namely as they constitute the body of something else" (p. 135). All intelligent and non-intelligent beings are thus mere modes of the highest Brahman, and have reality thereby only" (p. 138).

Thus starting from the view that Brahman is the cause of the world, we found it necessary in the light of the modification that is required for the cause to pass into the effect, to make a distinction within the nature of Brahman in His causal aspect, and to restrict change and imperfection to one aspect of Him, which we called His body, and to regard the other aspect of Him which is unchanging and perfect and may be said to represent His own essential nature, as His soul. But even this, we found, was not entirely satisfactory owing to certain ideas associated with body. Ultimately therefore we were led to regard Brahman as the unitary Substance on whom the world completely depends for its existence, different though it is from Him in character. In this sense it is an attribute or mode of Brahman. Brahman holds the world within Himself as something quite distinct from His own essential nature, even as a substance holds within itself the mode or attribute which is quite distinct from itself; and even as a substance passes from one mode of existence to another, so the Supreme Brahman passes from a state of existence in which the world exists in a subtle form to another state in which it exists in its 'effected' form. Whether in manifest or unmanifest form, whether in creation or reabsorption, the world is distinct from Brahman, but completely dependent on Him. He is therefore the one Substance, self-dependent and supreme, and all else is but a mode of Him.

Brahman in relation to Matter (Prakṛti)

Having thus described in general terms the relation in which Brahman stands to the world, we may consider one or two special problems that arise in connection with Brahman's relation to the world. The world, we have already noted, is according to Rāmānuja composed of matter and souls. The special relationship which Brahman bears to souls will be considered in the chapter that follows. Here we must bring together Rāmānuja's teaching with regard to Brahman's relation to matter or the non-sentient world, considered from the point of view of the characteristics peculiar to *Prakṛti*.

We have already seen that *Prakṛti* is a principle which Brahman employs in creation. It is that which produces manifold and wonderful effects under the supervision of the Lord. This is the teaching of the Śvetāśvatara, the Bhagavadgītā and the Pāñcarātra Saṁhitās, and Rāmānuja accepts it. *Prakṛti* then is essentially the principle of change and differentiation. It is capable of passing from one form to another, all equally perishable and non-permanent. Accordingly it may be said to have no true being. " Non-intelligent matter, as entering into various states of a non-permanent nature, is called ' non-being.' . . . We say ' it is ' of that thing which is of a permanently uniform nature, not connected with the idea of beginning, middle and end, and which hence never becomes the object of the notion of non-existence ; while we say ' it is not ' of non-intelligent matter which constantly passes over into different states, each later state being out of connection with the earlier state " (p. 128). " By ' that which is not ' or ' which is untrue,' we have to understand . . . that which has no true being, in so far as it is changeable and perishable. . . . Of this character is all non-intelligent matter. . . . ' Non-being ' we may call it, in so far as while it is observed at a certain moment in a certain form it is at some other moment observed in a different condition " (p. 129). *Prakṛti*, then, is not non-being in the sense that it does not exist, but in the sense that it is ever changeful, and that its forms are never permanent. Even the three *guṇas* of which *Prakṛti* is ultimately composed are lost, as we saw, when it passes into its subtle state of union with Brahman during the period of absorption. Hence it is capable of complete modification, and its very nature is change.

Besides this, a characteristic which Rāmānuja associates with *Prakṛti* is that it is evil in the sense that it is the principle of pleasure and pain meted out to a soul bound to worldly existence as the result of its acts. It is hence spoken of as " the object of fruition " (p. 299). It is the sweet fruit which the embodied soul, compared in the Muṇḍaka and Śvetāśvatara Upaniṣads to a bird, eats, immersed in grief. So at any rate Rāmānuja understands the metaphor of the two birds (p. 299). The Śvetāśvatara and the Bhagavadgītā teach that *Prakṛti* is a principle whereby the soul is made to reap the fruits of its acts, and Rāmānuja bases his view chiefly on their authority. " ' There are two unborn ones, the one knowing and a lord, the other without knowledge and lordly power ; there is the one unborn female on whom the enjoyment of all enjoyers depends ' (Śvet. I. 9). ' The soul abiding in nature experiences the qualities derived from Nature, the reason being its connection with the qualities in its births in good and evil wombs ' (Bhg. XIII. 20 and 21) " (pp. 364 and 365). By the qualities which *Prakṛti* produces as the result of the deeds of souls, it further binds the souls to action and hence to worldly existence. Thus in commenting on the passage from the Bhagavadgītā above cited, Rāmānuja writes, " This soul, born in a series of retrospective births among devas, man, etc.—all variations of matter —forms—delights in *guṇa*-sated pleasures, etc., varying in their *sattvika* and other characteristics according to the incidents of such births ; and in so doing launches into activities, good or evil, in order to procure for itself such pleasures. In order then to reap the fruits of such good or evil acts, it is inevitably born again in good or evil wombs (respectively). Born, he acts again ; acting he is born again."[1] *Prakṛti* thus metes out to souls the fruits of their acts, and in so doing binds them ever more to the world of *saṁsāric* existence.

These then are according to Rāmānuja the two chief characteristics of *Prakṛti*. It is the seat of all change, and it is intrinsically connected with *karma*.

[1] Page 431 Govindācarya's translation.

In the light of these characteristics of *Prakṛti*, it is necessary to ask whether Brahman shares in them. To this Rāmānuja's answer is unmistakable. We have already seen how with great pains he showed that all change and modification is restricted to elements of the world, Brahman Himself remaining essentially unchanged. He is equally clear that Brahman does not possess in His own nature, "the evil qualities depending on *Prakṛti*" (p. 81). The three qualities of matter belong, as we saw, to its 'effected' state (p. 368), so that when *Prakṛti* is united with Brahman in the period of a *pralaya*, it has none of its own characteristics and abides in Brahman as a bare potentiality "without any distinction of names and forms" (p. 368). Brahman Himself has a divine form, peculiar to Himself, "not made of the stuff of *Prakṛti* and not due to *Karman*" (p. 256). Scriptural texts, he tells us, "deny of Brahman all connection with evil qualities and inferior bodies sprung from *Prakṛti*, and all dependence on *karman*, and proclaim His glorious qualities and glorious forms" (p. 240). And as if this were not enough to show that Brahman has none of the characteristics of matter, he compares Brahman in relation to souls and matter, to a three-coloured piece of cloth, where the thread of each colour remains ever distinct. "Of some parti-coloured piece of cloth the material cause is threads white, red, black, etc., all the same, each definite spot of the cloth is connected with one colour only, white, e.g., and thus there is no confusion of colours even in the 'effected' condition of the cloth. Analogously the combination of non-sentient matter, sentient beings, and the Lord constitutes the material cause of the world, but this does not imply any confusion of the essential characteristics of enjoying souls, objects of enjoyment, and the universal Ruler. . . . There is indeed a difference between the two cases, in so far as the threads are capable of existing apart from one another, and are only occasionally combined according to the volition of men . . . while non-sentient matter and sentient beings in all their states form the body of the highest Self, and thus have a being only as the modes of that. . . . But the two cases are analogous, in so far as there persists a distinction and absence of all confusion on the part of the constituent elements of the aggregate. This being thus, it follows that the highest Brahman, although entering into the 'effected' condition, remains unchanged—for its essential nature does not become different" (p. 142).

But if Brahman is thus quite distinct from *Prakṛti* and shares none of its characteristics, and yet maintains it as His mode, we may enquire for what purpose, if any, He keeps it in existence. Since *Prakṛti* is, as we saw, the principle of change, the principle whereby the manifoldness of this world is effected, it would seem that *Prakṛti* exists for the purpose of bringing about change and plurality. But it may be asked, why is the manifoldness of the world necessary? What purpose does it serve? It is obvious that it is only by discovering the general purpose of creation that we shall discover the ultimate reason why *Prakṛti*, which Brahman employs for creating the world, exists. But here we are faced with a difficulty. What purpose may Brahman have in creating a world? In the first place, the very idea of a Perfect Being entering upon a line of activity in order to fulfil a purpose is self-contradictory, for it argues a lack or imperfection in Him which He is seeking to overcome. In the second place, if it be said that though Brahman being perfect can have no motive of benefit to Himself for creating the world, still He may be motivated entirely by desire for the welfare of finite souls, it is only necessary to point to the pain and suffering of souls in the world to show that this cannot be His motive. Rāmānuja is aware of both these difficulties. He states them thus: "In the case of all those who enter on some activity after having formed an idea of the effect to be accomplished, there exists a motive in the form of something beneficial either to themselves or to others. Now Brahman, to whose essential nature it belongs that all his wishes are eternally fulfilled, does not attain through the creation of the world any object not obtained before. Nor again is the second alternative possible. For a being, all whose wishes are fulfilled, could concern itself about others only with a view to benefitting them. No merciful divinity would create a world so full, as ours is, of evils of all kind—birth, old age, death, hell, and so on ;—if it created at all, pity would move it to create a world altogether happy" (p. 477). It is in facing these two difficulties that Rāmānuja, following the teaching of the Vedānta-sūtras (II I. 33-35), discloses his view regarding the purpose of creation. "The motive which prompts Brahman—all whose wishes are fulfilled and who is perfect in Himself—to the creation of a world comprising all kinds of sentient and non-sentient beings dependent on His volition, is nothing else but sport, play. We see in ordinary life how some great king, ruling this earth with its seven dvīpas, and possessing perfect strength, valour, and so on, has a game at balls, or the like, from no other motive than to amuse himself ; hence there is no objection to the view that sport only is the motive prompting Brahman to the creation, sustentation, and destruction of this world which is easily fashioned by His mere will" (p. 477). The reason that sport is given as the motive of creation is confessedly to preserve the supreme perfection of Brahman. It must not, therefore, be understood in the sense of childish play, but rather in the sense of joyous and free activity, entered into by the Supreme Being as a spontaneous expression of His manifold powers. Sport, we may therefore think, implies joyousness, freedom and superabundance of energy on the part of Brahman in creating the world. There is no lack of external constraint forcing Brahman into creative activity. Hence, as we saw earlier, creation was said to follow on the mere will, or free choice, of Brahman.

But it was also noted earlier that creation not only involves will or free activity but also thought; and thought implies that the free activity entered upon by Brahman in creating the world is not meaningless, as the word sport or play might suggest. If, therefore, we would discover what meaning creation has for Brahman, we must enquire what it is that He thinks about in creating the world. We were told, it will be remembered, that what the Supreme Being considers prior to creation is " the constitution of the world previous to the *Pralaya* " (p. 333) ; and why it is necessary for Him to do so becomes obvious when we pass on to consider Rāmānuja's answer to the second objection raised above. The objection was that Brahman could have no beneficent motive in creating a world involving pain and suffering for finite souls. To this the Vedānta-sūtra (II. I. 34) replies, Not so, 'on account of there being regard,' and Rāmānuja explains, "i.e., 'on account of the inequality of creation depending on the deeds of the intelligent beings, gods, and so on, about to be created.' Śruti and Smṛti alike declare that the connection of the individual souls with bodies of different kinds—divine, human, animal, and so on—depends on the *karman* of those souls ; compare 'He who performs good works becomes good, he who performs bad works becomes bad. . . .' (Bṛ. Up. IV. 4, 5). In the same way the reverend Parāśara declares that what causes the difference in nature and status between gods, men, and so on, is the power of the former deeds of the souls about to enter into a new creation " (p. 478). In further discussion of this point, Rāmānuja writes, " If it were not admitted (that the distinctions in the new creation are due to *karman*), it would moreover follow that souls are requited for what they have not done, and not requited for what they have done " (p. 479). If then it is necessary that souls should in the new creation have a nature in accordance with their deeds in a previous creation, it is not surprising that Brahman needs to remember and have regard to the constitution of the universe in a previous creation. This not only explains the pain and suffering of souls as due to their own previous deeds, but also suggests that the purpose of creation is somehow concerned with the deeds of souls. How this is we shall see when in the next chapter we are concerned with the relation of the Deity to the individual soul. Suffice it here to have discovered that the general purpose of creation relates to the deeds of souls.

This being so, we may expect that *Prakṛti*, which Brahman employs in creating the world, finds its significance also only in relation to souls. And this is what Rāmānuja actually teaches: "all non-intelligent things, bodies human and divine, hills, oceans, etc. . . . have their root in the actions springing from the volitions of men, gods, etc. . . . and since non-intelligent matter is subject to changes corresponding to the actions of the individual souls, it may be called 'non-being,' while the souls are 'being' . . . when the works which are the cause of the distinction of things are destroyed, then all the distinctions of bodies, human or divine, hills, oceans, etc.—all which are objects of fruition for the different individual souls—pass away" (p. 128). And even more explicitly he declares that "*Prakṛti* is a non-intelligent principle, the causal substance of the entire material universe, and constituting the means for the experience of pleasure and pain, and for the final release of all intelligent souls which are connected with it from all eternity" (p. 370).

If so, it would seem that what significance *Prakṛti* has is entirely in relation to the release of souls. Its ceaseless change and all its manifold products, its evil qualities producing pleasure and pain and binding the soul to activity, are all to be explained, it would seem, in relation to souls. Brahman, we may therefore conclude, maintains *Prakṛti* with a special purpose. Its nature, quite different as it is from that of Brahman, is required for the release of souls, and hence He supports it.

But how, it may be asked, is it possible for Brahman, who is absolutely different from *Prakṛti*, to support it? Rāmānuja considers the problem of the relation of non-sentient objects to Brahman in his discussion of certain Vedānta-sūtra texts (III. 2. 26-29). He asks: "Is the relation of the two like that of the snake and its coils; or like that of light and the luminous body, both of which fall under the same genus; or like that of the individual soul and Brahman, the soul being a distinguishing attribute and for that reason a part (*aṁśa*) of Brahman?" Regarding the first alternative according to which non-sentent things are "special forms or arrangements of Brahman, as the coils are of a coiled-up snake," he writes: "If Brahman itself appeared in the form of non-sentient things—as the snake itself only constitutes the coils—both sets of texts, those which declare difference as well as those which declare the unchangeableness of Brahman, would be contrary to sense." If therefore we adopt the second alternative and "hold that the case under discussion is analogous to that of light and that in which it abides, i.e., the luminous body; the two are different, but at the same time they are identical in so far as they both are fire (*tejas*)," Rāmānuja points out that in this case "Brahma-hood (*Brahmatva*) constitutes a genus inhering in Brahman as well as in non-sentient matter, just as fire constitutes the common genus for light and luminous bodies. But on this view Brahman becomes a mere abstract generic character inhering in the Lord (*īśvara*), sentient souls and non-sentient matter, just as the generic character of horses (*aśvatva*) inheres in concrete individual horses; and this contradicts all the teaching of Śruti and Smṛti (according to which Brahman is the highest concrete entity)." Brahman must not, it would seem, be reduced to a ghostly abstraction, found in all things, and therefore found in the material world also, for according to Rāmānuja the Scriptures teach that instead of Brahman being an abstraction characterising all concrete existences, He is the most concrete of realities, of which other things are only abstractions or attributes. So he holds that this second way of understanding the relation between Brahman and material objects is likewise inadmissible, and states the third alternative mentioned above as representing the acceptable view, according to which Brahman is related to the material world as substance to attribute, or as whole to part. "We therefore hold that non-sentient matter stands to Brahman in the same relation as the one previously proved for the individual soul in Sūtra II. 3, 43, 46 viz., that it is an attribute incapable of being realised apart from Brahman and hence is a part (*aṁśa*) of the latter. The texts referring to the two as non-different may thus be taken in their primary sense; for the part is only a limited place of that of which it is a part. And the texts referring to the two as different may also be taken in their primary sense; for the distinguishing attribute and that to which the attribute belongs are essentially different. Thus Brahman's freedom from all imperfection is preserved.—Lustre is an attribute not to be realised apart from the gem, and therefore is a part of the gem; the same relation holds good between generic character and individuals having that character, between qualities and things having qualities, between bodies and souls. In the same way souls as well as non-sentient matter stand to Brahman in the relation of parts" (pp. 619 and 620).

Prakṛti, then, and all its products are supported by Brahman even as an attribute or mode is supported by a substance to which it belongs, but from which it is quite distinct, or as a part is supported by its whole. Thus the relation of *Prakṛti* and its products to Brahman is only an illustration of the relation, already formulated, of the world in general to Brahman. The world, composed of matter and souls, is quite distinct from Brahman, and their distinctness is never lost. But Brahman is one and supreme in the sense that it is on Him that matter and souls completely depend. He is therefore the one only true Substance, of which the elements of the world are eternally distinct modes. He is Perfect, but the world is imperfect. Nevertheless the relation between Him and the world is such that His perfect nature is not sullied to the slightest extent, and the distinct reality of the world is not in any way destroyed. Both it is necessary to maintain if religious experience is not a lie and a mockery, and both Rāmānuja finds himself able to support by conceiving the relation between Brahman and the world primarily on the analogy of the relation between substance and attribute.

CHAPTER III

RELATION OF THE DEITY TO THE FINITE SELF

IN discovering the relationship in which Brahman stands to the world, we have also discovered the relation in which ultimately He stands to the soul, for the world according to Rāmānuja is contsituted by material objects and souls. But the bare metaphysical description given above of the relation in which Brahman stands to the world does not suffice to disclose all that is most distinctive of Brahman's relation to souls, for souls are individual centres of thought and action, and it is necessary in the light of this their special characteristic to discover how the Deity is related to them. The intense religious experience of the Āḻvārs, and of the Vaiṣṇava sect in general through its long history, provided Rāmānuja with all the material that he could desire in this connection. But he could not draw upon it directly, for that would be to make his philosophy sectarian. In his Śrībhāṣya he introduces, as we shall see, all the essentials of his doctrine, although necessarily only in brief and summary fashion, but if we would obtain a fuller account we must turn to his Bhagavadgītā Bhāṣya.

Rāmānuja finds that the chief obstacle to the religious view of the relation between Brahman and the soul is the advaitin's doctrine that the soul is essentially the same as Brahman. We have seen that from the time of the Upaniṣads onwards, philosophers failed to state clearly the relation between Brahman and the soul. The doctrine that Brahman is to be found within one's self was so all-engrossing that, as we noted, many of the Upaniṣadic seers tended to overlook the distinction between Brahman and the soul. Even those of them who in later times spoke of Brahman and the soul as two, we saw, never consistently maintained this view. This being so, the Bhagavadgītā as well as other Vaiṣṇava works which sought to obtain support for their religious doctrines from the recognised schools of philosophic thought, perpetuated the same ambiguity. Rāmānuja was apparently one of the first who clearly saw that if the intense religious experience of his sect was to be considered valid, this ambiguity regarding the ultimate reality of the soul must cease. He accordingly sets himself in sharp opposition to the advaita view that Brahman and the soul are one, and by so doing is enabled to make a distinct contribution to a consistent philosophical formulation of the relation between the Deity and the soul, as revealed in religious experience.

Refutation of the advaita view that Brahman and the soul are one

Many are the defects which Rāmānuja finds in the advaitin's view regarding the soul's relation to Brahman. We may enumerate a few. The advaitin holds, so Rāmānuja tells us, that "the many individual souls are the reflections of the one Brahman, and their states of pain, pleasure, and so on, remain distinct owing to the different limiting adjuncts (on which the existence of each individual soul as such depends) in the same way as the many reflected images of one and the same face in mirrors, crystals, sword-blades, etc., remain distinct owing to their limiting adjuncts (viz., mirrors, etc.); one image being small, another large, one being bright, another dim, and so on." It is Brahman alone that is real; the distinction of a plurality of souls is due to faulty imagination and hence unreal (p. 436).

To this Rāmānuja asks: "To whom then does that imagination belong? Not to Brahman surely whose nature, consisting of pure intelligence, allows no room for imagination of any kind! Nor also to the individual souls, for this would imply a faulty mutual dependence, the existence of the soul depending on imagination and that imagination residing in the soul!" (p. 436).

But the advaitin may reply: "Nescience (wrong imagination) and the existence of the souls form an endless retrogressive chain; their relation is like that of the seed and the sprout. . . . And as this error of the souls has proceeded from all eternity, the question as to its cause is not to be raised (pp. 436 and 437). Well, then, Rāmānuja replies, Nescience abides in the soul. If it abides in the soul, it must abide in it either in the soul's essential form, or in its fictitiously imagined form. The first alternative is impossible because the advaitin regards the essential form of the soul as Brahman Himself, and Nescience, which is contradictory to the nature of Brahman, cannot be ascribed to Him. Nor can the second alternative be accepted, for the only other form of existence besides Brahman admitted by the advaitin is Nescience, so that the fictitiously imagined form of the soul must itself be nothing else than Nescience; and this being so, to ascribe Nescience to the soul in its fictitiously imagined form is to ascribe Nescience to Nescience, and this explains nothing. A third alternative is conceivable, namely that Nescience abides in the essential nature of the soul qualified by its fictitiously imagined aspect. But if the soul's essential nature is qualified, it can according to the advaitin be qualified only by Nescience, and if it is qualified by Nescience, it does not carry us further in trying to explain it to ascribe Nescience to what is already qualified by it. These are Rāmānuja's words: "If, as a first alternative, you should maintain that the abode of Nescience is constituted by the soul in its essential, not fictitiously imagined form, this means that Brahman itself is the abode of Nescience. If, in the second place, you should say that the abode of Nescience is the soul, viewed as different from Brahman and fictitiously imagined in it, this would mean that the non-intelligent (*jaḍa*) is the abode of Nescience. For those who hold the view of the non-duality do not acknowledge a third aspect different from these two (i.e., from Brahman which is pure intelligence, and the non-intelligent fictitiously superimposed on Brahman). And if, as a third alternative, it be maintained that the abode of Nescience is the soul in its essential nature, this nature being however qualified by the fictitiously imagined aspect, we must negative this also, since that which has an absolutely homogeneous nature cannot in any way be shown to be qualified, apart from Nescience. The soul is qualified in so far only as it is the abode of Nescience, and you therefore define nothing" (p. 437).

"Moreover," Rāmānuja points out, "the theory of Nescience abiding within the individual soul is resorted to for the purpose of establishing a basis for the distinction of bondage and release, but it really is quite unable to effect this. For if by release be understood the destruction of Nescience, it follows that when one soul attains Release and Nescience is thus destroyed, the other souls also will be released.—But Nescience persists because other souls are not released !—Well, then the one soul also is not released since Nescience is not destroyed ! But we assume a different Nescience for each soul, that soul whose Nescience is destroyed will be released, and that whose Nescience is not destroyed will remain in bondage !—You now argue on the assumption of a special *avidyā* (nescience) for each soul. But what about the distinction of souls implied therein ? (p. 438). Rāmānuja has already pointed out that that distinction can neither be ascribed to Nescience in Brahman nor to Nescience in souls.

Besides, he continues, "We further put the following question—When the Nescience abiding in the individual soul passes away owing to the rise of the knowledge of truth, does then the soul also perish or does it not perish? In the former case Release is nothing else but destruction of the essential nature of the soul; in the latter case the soul does not attain Release even on the destruction of Nescience, since it continues to exist as soul different from Brahman" (p. 439).

"It would, moreover, be necessary to define who is the imaginatively shaping agent (*kalpaka*) with regard to the soul as formed from Nescience. It cannot be Nescience itself, because Nescience is not an intelligent principle. Nor can it be the soul, because this would imply the defect of what has to be proved being presupposed for the purposes of proof; and because the existence of the soul is that which *is formed* by Nescience, just as shell-silver is. And if, finally, you should say that Brahman is the fictitiously forming agent, we have again arrived at a Brahman that is the abode of Nescience" (pp. 440 and 441).

Similarly Rāmānuja urges that the distinction between *Māyā* and Nescience must be given up. For even if Brahman possesses *Māyā*, i.e., illusive power, it cannot, without Nescience be conscious of souls. And without being conscious of others the lord of *Māyā* is unable to delude them by his *Māyā*. Moreover, if Brahman recognises all beings apart from himself as false, he does not delude them; for surely none but a madman would aim at deluding beings known by him to be unreal!" (p. 441).

For such reasons Rāmānuja finds unacceptable the advaita view that souls are related to Brahman as ultimately identical with Brahman but seemingly different, the illusion regarding their reality as individual existences being due to the limiting adjuncts produced by *Māyā* or *Avidyā* with which the unitary Brahman is associated.

Seeing that they cannot be dismissed as an illusion they must be accepted as real. Their reality is given, as Rāmānuja showed, in the fact of consciousness, for consciousness, which is ever changing, requires a substrate (pp. 56 and 57). It is also given in the fact of memory and recognition "for recognition implies a conscious subject persisting from the earlier to the later moment," for otherwise "it would be impossible for us to recognise the thing seen to-day as the one we saw yesterday, for what has been perceived by one cannot be recognised by another" (p. 57). It is implied also in inference, for inference "presupposes the ascertainment and remembrance of general propositions" (p. 509). If there were no permanent self, inference and reasoning would be impossible, "for the speaker perishes in the very moment when he states the proposition to be proved, and another person is unable to complete what has been begun by another and about which he himself does not know anything" (pp. 509 and 510). Moreover, the fact that a person is able to remember after sleep what happened before he fell asleep, Rāmānuja declares is proof that the self persisted through sleep although consciousness had come to an end (p. 60). To such empirical arguments Rāmānuja adds the testimony of the Scriptures, which abound in passages relating to the self, and which would indeed be strange if the self were a mere illusion (p. 60). The individual then is a real self.

But, it may be asked, if the individual self is accepted as real, how are we to understand Scriptural texts such as 'Thou art That,' which equate the soul with Brahman? Rāmānuja points out that in all cases of predication what is predicated is not a bare identity but a substance which is characterised by different aspects or attributes, so that the 'Thou' cannot be entirely identical with the 'That.' "In texts . . . such as 'Thou art that,' the co-ordination of the constituent parts is not meant to convey the idea of the absolute unity of a non-differenced substance; on the contrary, the words 'that' and 'thou' denote a Brahman distinguished by difference. The word 'that' refers to Brahman, omniscient, etc., the word 'thou' which stands in co-ordination to 'that' conveys the idea of Brahman in so far as having for its body the individual souls. This is in accordance with the general principle that co-ordination is meant to express one thing subsisting in a twofold form. If such doubleness of form were abandoned, there could be no difference of aspects giving rise to the application of different terms, and the entire principle of co-ordination would thus be given up" (p. 130). The text, therefore, in Rāmānuja's view, only establishes what he has shown the relationship of all things of this world to Brahman to be, viz., that they are His modes or attributes distinct from Him and not capable of being completely identified with Him. It does not intend to deny the reality of finite selves.

Besides, Rāmānuja declares that the reality of individual souls and their eternal distinctness from Brahman are taught by the Deity Himself in His incarnate form as Kṛṣṇa to Arjuna. Thus in giving the meaning of Bhagavadgītā II. 12, Rāmānuja represents Kṛṣṇa as saying: "As for me, the universal Lord (*Sarveśvara*), there is never 'nay' to my having been in all the eternity antecedent to the present. I always *was*. So is thyself and all these in thy front;—all souls under my control (*īśitavyāh*) and informers of bodies (*ksetrajñas*). Nor are all of us—myself, thyself and all—not going to be in the future. . . . As indubitably ever-existent am I—the universal Lord, the supreme spirit (*paramātma*) so also should you all, the matter-informing souls, be understood as ever-existent." And Rāmānuja comments, "It is thus evident that (1) the fact of the soul being distinct from Bhagavān Sarveśvara (God), and (2) the fact of the multeity of souls, have been declared by Bhagavān Himself. For this is an occasion when eternal truths are imparted to one with the object of removing the cover of all his ignorance. And on such an occasion, the distinctions such as *I*, *thou*, *we all*, etc., are made (thus showing that souls are many and they are different from God)" (Bhg. Bh. p. 34).

As for Upaniṣadic authority for the view that the

soul is a real self, quite distinct from Brahman, Rāmānuja finds it ready to hand in the Antaryāmin Brāhmaṇa and in the Śvetāśvatara Upaniṣad. "He who dwells in the self and within the self, whom the self does not know, of whom the self is the body, who rules the self within, He is thy self, the Ruler within, the Immortal" (Bṛ. Up. III. 7. 22); "One of them eats the sweet fruit; without eating the other looks on" (Śvet. Up. IV. 6); "There are two, the one knowing, the other not knowing, both unborn, the one a ruler, the other not a ruler" (Śvet. Up. I. 9); "Knowing as separate the self and the Mover. . . ." (Śvet. Up. I. 6). The plurality of souls Rāmānuja finds to be definitely taught in passages such as 'He is the cause, the Lord of the lords of the organs' (i.e., the individual souls) (Śvet. Up. VI. 9); 'the Master of the *Pradhāna* and the souls.' (Śvet. Up. VI. 16); and more especially, 'the Eternal among eternals, the Intelligent among the intelligent, who one, fulfils the desires of many' (Śvet. Up. VI. 13).[1]

Both reasoning based on experience and Scripture, according to Rāmānuja, lead thus to the view that finite selves are real existences, not to be dismissed as illusory manifestations of the unitary non-differenced Absolute.

The distinctive nature of the soul as an individual characterised by thought and activity

Since then the soul is a real existence not identifiable with mere consciousness nor capable of being equated without difference with Brahman, we must enquire what its distinctive attributes are, in order to discover how Brahman is related to it, considered from the point of view of its peculiar nature. In discussing Vedānta-sūtra II. 3. 19, Rāmānuja states that the essential nature of the soul is to be a knowing subject. The

[1] Quoted in Ś. Bh., pp. 468 and 469. The last quotation, i.e., Śvet. VI. 13 is found also in the Bhg. Bh., p. 35, in connection with Bhg. II. 12 above referred to.

doctrine that the self is essentially a conscious principle may be said to be Upaniṣadic in origin. From early times in the Upaniṣads we saw that the *Ātman* was identified with that within us which perceives, sees, hears and understands. Rāmānuja himself bases his view on passages such as 'He who knows, let me smell this, he is the self, etc. (Chānd. Up. VIII. 12. 4-5; I. 5; 12. 3); 'He who is within the heart, surrounded by the *Prāṇas*, the person of light, consisting of knowledge' (Bṛ. Up. IV. 5. 15), and such like (p.546). It is true that these passages are ambiguous, and may or may not refer to the individual self, as Rāmānuja understands them. Nevertheless they reveal the prevailing assumption that, whether it be the individual self or the universal Self which performs these conscious functions, that is the real self which is the knowing principle in the body. While accepting this view, Rāmānuja makes it abundantly clear, as we have seen, that the self is not mere knowledge but an individual who has knowledge as his essential characteristic. He is thus eager to emphasize the individuality of the soul as against the advaitic tendency, so prevalent hitherto in philosophic circles, to overlook all distinction between the finite self and Brahman. The same desire to preserve the individuality of the soul seems to underlie his vigorous polemic (pp. 546-53) against the idea that the self is omnipresent and all-pervading. He declares that the self is 'atomic,' that is, limited each to its body and not confused with that of any other body. According to him, the Vedānta-sūtra II. 3. 20 declares that the self is atomic and not omnipresent by pointing out that the Scripture speaks of the latter as passing out of the body, going and returning—all which movement on the part of the soul would clearly be meaningless if the soul were omnipresent (p. 546). He finds direct support (p. 548) for his view that the soul is atomic, in the passages from the Śvetāśvatara which declare that 'The individual soul is to be known as part of the hundredth part of the point of a hair divided a hundred times, and yet it is to be infinite' (V. 9): 'that lower one is seen of the measure of the point of a goad' (V. 8), and also in many Upaniṣadic passages which locate the self as abiding within the heart (p. 548). His chief objection to the view that the self is omnipresent is that if it were so, there would be "everywhere and at all times simultaneous consciousness and non-consciousness" (p. 552, II. 3. 32), but this is never the case. "On our view, on the other hand, the actually perceived distribution of consciousness and non-consciousness explains itself, since we hold the self to abide within bodies only, so that naturally consciousness takes place there only, not anywhere else" (p. 552). Moreover, he points out, as against the Vaiśeṣikas that if the self were omnipresent, all the selfs would be in permanent conjunction with all organs; and besides, the *adṛṣṭas* due to the actions of the different bodies would be entirely confused, for all selfs would then be in contact with all bodies (pp. 552 and 553). It is against all such confusion between one self and another, and hence in order to maintain the individuality of each self, that Rāmānuja seems to insist that the soul is atomic. Each individual, it would seem, has his own distinctive centre of experience.

There is still another characteristic which Rāmānuja finds to be peculiar to the soul. It is not only a knower with a unique centre of experience, but also a doer. The view may have been implied in the doctrine of *Karma*, which, as we have seen, was held even by philosophers of the earlier Upaniṣads, and according to which each soul reaped the fruit of its deeds. Although the doctrine of *Karma* would seem to require that the soul should be regarded as a free agent responsible for its own actions, the ambiguous position of the soul in the earlier systems did not lead to any clear formulation of doctrine on this point. Besides, advaitism with its doctrine of Brahman as constituted by pure Intelligence, and as the only real, could certainly not favour the view of the soul as a free agent; nor could the Sāṁkhya with its doctrine of the inactive *puruṣa*; and as we have already seen, it was precisely these two influences under which philosophers came from the time of the Bhagavadgītā onwards. By his break with advaitism and by his desire to abide by moral and religious experience, Rāmānuja is enabled to see that the self is not only a knower but also a doer; and thus the soul according to him becomes a true self or person, characterised by thought and activity. In discussing Vedānta-sūtra II. 3. 33, Rāmānuja develops the view that the self is an agent, although he is aware that works, such as the Bhagavadgītā are not very clear on the point, and often speak as though the self were inactive, all activity being due to the *guṇas* of the body. He says, "It has been shown that the individual self is a knowing subject and atomic. Now the question arises whether that self is an agent or, being itself non-active, erroneously ascribes to itself the activity of the non-sentient *guṇas*. The *prima facie* answer is that the individual self is not an agent, since the sacred texts concerned with the self declare that the self does not act, while the *guṇas* do act . . . and the Lord himself teaches that non-agency is the essential nature of the individual soul, and that it is mere delusion on the self's part to ascribe to itself agency. 'By the attributes (*guṇas*) of *Prakṛti*, actions are wrought all round.' He who is deluded by self-conceit thinks, 'I am the agent'; 'when the seer beholds no other agent than the *guṇas*'; '*Prakṛti* is said to be the cause of all agency of causes and effects, whilst the soul is the cause of all enjoyment of pleasure and pain' (Bhg. III. 27; XIV. 19; XIII. 20)."—The soul, therefore, is an enjoyer only while all agency belongs to *Prakṛti*. As against this view Rāmānuja interprets the sūtra to say that the self is "'an agent, on account of Scripture thus having a meaning.' The self only is an agent, not the *guṇas*, because thus only Scripture has a meaning. For the scriptural injunctions, such as 'he who desires the heavenly world is to sacrifice,' 'he who desires release is to meditate on Brahman,' and similar ones, enjoin action on him only who will enjoy the fruit of the action—whether the heavenly world, or release, or anything else. If a non-sentient thing were the agent, the injunction would not be addressed to another being (viz., to an intelligent being—to whom it actually is addressed)'. The term '*śāstra*' (scriptural injunction) moreover comes from *śās*, to command, and commanding means impelling to action. But scriptural injunctions impel to action through giving rise to a certain conception (in the mind of the being addressed), and the non-sentient *Pradhāna* cannot be made to conceive anything. Scripture therefore has a sense only if we admit that none but the intelligent enjoyer of the fruit of the action is at the same time the agent" (pp. 553 and 554). But if it be asked, what then about texts such as those cited above from the Bhagavadgītā, Rāmānuja declares that these texts which ascribe all activity to the *guṇas*, mean only to refer "to the fact that in all activities lying within the sphere of the *saṁsāṛa*, the activity of the self is due not to its own nature but to its contact with the different *guṇas*" (p. 554). This passage is significant as making clear Rāmānuja's position that, though activity of the kind which binds the soul to *saṁsāra* does not belong to the nature of the self, still it is the self that acts under the influence of the *guṇas*, so that the activity is always that of the self. But this does not mean, Rāmānuja tells us, that the self is always active. "The self, although always provided with the instruments of action, such as the organ of speech, and so on, acts when it wishes to do so, and does not act when it does not wish to do so. Just as a carpenter, although having his axe and other implements ready at hand, works or does not work just as he pleases" (p. 556, II. 3. 39).

The self, then, according to Rāmānuja is an individual,

a person in the true sense of the term with a unique centre of experience and characterised by thought and volition. What other characteristics it possesses we shall discover as we proceed. Suffice it here to have laid bare its fundamental qualities. Such then being its distinctive nature, we may turn to the topic of our enquiry in this chapter, viz.: the relation of the Deity to the soul. We shall find it convenient to consider the Deity's relation to the soul in the three stages in which according to Rāmānuja it is possible for the soul[1] to exist, viz.: (1) prior to world-creation, (2) in worldly existence (*saṁsāra*) and (3) in Release.

(1) *Relation of the Deity to the soul prior to world-creation*

From the account already given of Brahman as the cause of the universe, it has been made clear that the world is eternally a part of Brahman existing in Him in subtle form before He sends it out into its manifest existence. In the case of *prakṛti* we noted that the subtle form in which it existed previous to creation is one in which all its qualities were lacking. So opposed was *prakṛti* in its evolved state thought to be to the nature of Brahman that it could not be regarded as existing in a state of unity with Brahman prior to creation without first being emptied of its own distinctive nature. What then about the soul? Is the state of unity in which it exists before creation one which involves the complete suppression of its own essential nature? Rāmānuja answers with an emphatic no. "Not so, we reply. By a thing being an effect we mean its being due to a substance passing over into some other state, and from this point of view the soul also is an effect. There is, however, the difference, that the 'other condition' which is represented by

[1] According to Rāmānuja there are three kinds of souls, (*a*) eternally free souls, such as the gods; (*b*) bound souls, such as ourselves, and (*c*) released souls who have obtained salvation from the bondage of *saṁsara*. We shall concern ourselves only with the last two, the first being mythological in origin and having little or no philosophical significance.

the soul is of a different kind from that which constitutes non-sentient things, such as Ether and so on. The 'otherness' on which the soul depends consists in the contraction and expansion of intelligence; while the change on which the origination of Ether and so on depends is a change of essential nature. And change of the latter kind is what we deny of the soul." "Texts such as 'Prajāpati sent forth the creatures,' which declare the origination of the soul, really mean only to state that the souls are by turns associated with or dissociated from bodies—the effect of which is that their intelligence is either contracted or expanded. Texts again which deny the origination of the soul and affirm its permanency ('He is not born and does not die,' etc.) mean to say that the soul does not, like the non-sentient element of creation, undergo changes of essential nature" (II. 3. 15, pp. 541-3). The soul, then, exists in Brahman prior to world-creation with its intelligence in a contracted form.

When the time for creation arrives, what Brahman does is, as we have already seen, to join the soul to the material principle, and thereafter by the mutual influence of matter and soul, guided and controlled by the Supreme Being, evolution proceeds. But why it may be asked does Brahman disturb, so to speak, the sleep of the soul? What, in other words, is the motive of creation, considered from the point of view of the soul? We have already seen that when Brahman creates, He has regard to the deeds of souls, and "arranges the diversity of the creation in accordance with the different *karman* of the individual souls" (II. 1. 35, p. 479), so that souls are requited for what they have done. This seems to suggest that the whole purpose of creation is retribution, the stern adherence on the part of the Deity to the moral law. But this is not all that Rāmānuja has to say regarding the reason why Brahman creates. In commenting on Bhagavad-gītā III. 10 he writes: "In the past, this Prajāpati—

the Bhagavān--intently reflected at the time of creation, on the entities (*cit*), entangled in matter (*acit*) from an immemorial past. They were destitute of a name, of a form and of a distinction, and embosomed in Him. They were fit for fulfilling great aims, but were lying latent like inert or unintelligent substances. Prajāpati out of infinite mercy looked on them, and wishing to work out their deliverance, created them (or projected them into manifestation)" (Bhg. Bh., p. 99). If we consider this passage in the light of the text cited earlier, which declares that *Prakṛti* is "the means for the experience of pleasure and pain, and for the final release of all intelligent souls" (Ś. Bh., p. 370), it would seem that the motive of creation is that souls taught by punishment and reward may ultimately seek and win release. It is for the ultimate good of souls that the Deity sends them into worldly existence. His perfect nature requires that the evil deeds of responsible individuals should be punsihed, but in and through the operation of karmic punishment and reward is perceptible the ultimate goal towards which the Deity in his love for the soul is working. "What the Lord Himself aims at is ever to increase happiness to the highest degree and to this end it is instrumental that He should reprove and reject the infinite and intolerable mass of sins which accumulates in the course of beginning and endless æons, and thus check the tendency on the part of individual beings to transgress His laws" (pp. 488 and 489). When He creates then He creates strictly in accordance with the merits and demerits of the soul, but His reason for doing so is not retribution but the ultimate good of the soul.

Having thus considered what motive the Deity has in rousing the soul from its state of dormant intelligence we may proceed to enquire into what relation to it He enters when once the soul has begun the evolutionary process, which culminates in worldly existence. The soul prior to this process exists, as we saw, in a state of union with Brahman, such close union that it is possible to say that before creation Brahman exists as one only without a second (p. 456). But when creation begins, differentiation takes place, the soul is connected with the kind of body merited by its past deeds, and in this manner it acquires name and form or individual existence. Seeing that the soul becomes thus differentiated from Brahman and appears, as it were, as an other to Him, it is necessary for Brahman to enter into it and abide in it as its inner Self through all the changes which it now undergoes. Rāmānuja describes the process thus: "That which is denoted as 'Being,' i.e., the highest Brahman which is the cause of all, free from all shadow of imperfection, etc., resolved 'to be many'; it thereupon sent forth the entire world; introduced in this world so sent forth, the whole mass of individual souls into different bodies, divine, human, etc., corresponding to the desert of each soul—the souls thus constituting the self of the bodies; and finally, itself entering according to its wish into those souls—so as to constitute their inner Self—evolved in all these aggregates, names and forms. . . . 'Let me enter into these beings with this living Self' (*jīvena ātmanā*) means 'with this living me' and this shows the living self, i.e., the individual soul to have Brahman for its self. And that this having Brahman for its self means Brahman's being the inner Self of the soul (i.e., the Self inside the soul, but not identical with it), Scripture declares by saying that Brahman entered into it. This is clearly stated in the passage Taitt. Up. II. 6, 'He sent forth all this, whatever there is. Having sent forth he entered into it. Having entered into it he became *sat* and *tyat*.' For here 'all this' comprises beings intelligent as well as non-intelligent, which afterwards are distinguished as *sat* and *tyat*, as knowledge (*vijñāna*) and non-knowledge. Brahman is thus said to enter into intelligent being also" (p. 226). It would seem, then, that when the soul becomes differentiated from Him in passing into its 'effected' state, He enters into it and remains within it as its inner Self. What exactly this implies we shall presently see.

(2) *Relation of the Deity to the soul in worldly existence* (*saṁsāra*).

Brahman as inner Ruler.

That Brahman exists within oneself was, we may believe, an idea which Rāmānuja inherited from the philosophers of the Upaniṣads. But his own contribution lies, as we shall see, in developing this idea in the light of the perfect nature of Brahman on the one hand and the individuality of the soul on the other. Neither of these ideas was clearly or consistently upheld by philosophers. The perfections of the Supreme Being tended often, as we saw, to be forgotten in the view of Him as the Absolute, and the individuality of the soul was never clearly grasped. So long as this was so, philosophers could not grasp the full significance of the view that the Deity exists within the soul in *saṁsāra*. Rāmānuja by his consistent view of Brahman as the all-perfect Being and by his clear recognition of the individuality of the soul is enabled so to develop the doctrine of Brahman as abiding within the soul as to lay bare its full implication both with regard to Brahman's perfect nature and with regard to the soul's individuality.

Considering the latter point first, the abiding of Brahman within the soul does not mean for Rāmānuja what we pointed out it tended often to mean for earlier thinkers, that Brahman Himself is the soul in the body. Upaniṣadic sages spoke of Brahman as the conscious principle in the body, that which sees, hears, smells, thinks and understands. According to Rāmānuja the knowing principle in the body is not Brahman but the individual self. Nor again is Brahman the agent in the body, but the individual self. Thus in commenting on Vedānta-sūtra I. I. 13, which speaks of 'the self consisting of Bliss,' Rāmānuja declares that by this is meant Brahman the Highest Self, who he tells us, is clearly distinguished by the Tattirīya Upaniṣad from the individual self, who in contrast is described by it as the self consisting of Understanding (*vijṇāna*). The passage runs thus. 'Different from this self which consists of Understanding, is the other inner self which consists of Bliss' (Taitt. Up. II. 5). Rāmānuja finds in this text the necessary distinction between Brahman as He exists within the body and the individual self. Brahman exists in the body, it would seem, as mere Bliss, while knowledge and action belong to the individual self, described here as consisting of understanding. So Rāmānuja writes, "the Sūtrakāra contends that the Self consisting of bliss is the highest Self 'on account of multiplication.'—The section which begins with the words, 'This is an examination of bliss,' and terminates with the *śloka*, 'from whence all speech turns back' (Taitt. Up. II. 8), arrives at bliss, supreme and not to be surpassed, by successively multiplying inferior stages of bliss by a hundred; now such supreme bliss cannot possibly belong to the individual soul which enjoys only a small share of very limited happiness, mixed with endless pain and grief; and therefore clearly indicates, as its abode, the highest Self, which differs from all other selfs in so far as being radically opposed to all evil and of an unmixed blessed nature. The text says, 'Different from this self consisting of understanding there is the inner Self consisting of bliss.' Now that which consists of understanding (*vijñāna*) is the individual soul (*jīva*); the formative element, '*maya*' ('*consisting* of'; in *vijñānamaya*) indicates a difference (between *vijñāna* and *vijñānamaya*)[1] . . . And this interpretation is quite suitable, as the soul in the states of bondage and release alike is a 'knowing' subject. . . . But how is it then that in the *śloka* which refers to the *vijñānamaya*, 'Understanding (*vijñāna*) performs the

[1] That is, the *vijñanamaya* is not mere understanding but the *self* possessing understanding, or the individual soul.

sacrifice,' the term '*vijñāna*' only is used?—The essential nature, we reply, of the knowing subject is suitably called 'knowledge,' and this term is transferred to the knowing subject itself which is defined as possessing that nature. For we generally see that words which denote attributes defining the essential nature of a thing also convey the notion of the essential nature of the thing itself. This also accounts for the fact that the *śloka* ('*Vijñāna* performs the sacrifice, it performs all sacred acts') speaks of *vijñāna* as being the agent in sacrifices and so on; the *buddhi* (intelligence) alone could not be called an agent. For this reason the text does not ascribe agency to the other selfs (the *prāṇamaya* and so on) which are mentioned before the *vijñānamaya*; for they are non-intelligent instruments of intelligence, and the latter only can be an agent. . . . We hence conclude that He who is different from the self consisting of knowledge, i.e., the individual self, is the highest Self which consists of bliss" (pp. 212-14). Thus, according to Rāmānuja, although Brahman exists within the soul, He remains quite distinct from it. He does not take on Himself what rightly belongs to the individual self, namely, knowledge and agency in the body.

Not only the individuality of the soul but also the perfect nature of Brahman requires that Brahman though abiding in the self, must remain quite distinct from it. Thus in regard to the meaning of the passage, 'Thou art that,' Rāmānuja writes, "How, we ask . . . can Brahman, the cause of all, free from all shadow of imperfection, omniscient, omnipotent, etc., etc., be one with the individual soul, all whose activities—whether it be thinking, or winking of an eye, or anything else—depend on *karman*, which implies endless suffering of every kind?—If you reply that this is possible if one of two things is unreal, we ask—which then do you mean to be unreal? Brahman's connection with what is evil?—or its essential nature, owing to which it is absolutely good and antagonistic to all evil ?—You will perhaps reply that, owing to the fact of Brahman, which is absolutely good and antagonistic to all evil, being the substrate of beginningless Nescience, there presents itself the false appearance of its being connected with evil. But there you maintain what is contradictory. On the one side there is Brahman's absolute perfection and antagonism to all evil ; on the other it is the substrate of Nescience and the appearance of suffering which is produced thereby. Now it is a contradiction to say that Brahman is connected with all this and at the same time antagonistic to it ! " (p. 215). Such clear perception on the part of Rāmānuja of the opposition in nature between the perfections of the Supreme Being and the imperfections of the soul could not easily tolerate the view that by Brahman abiding within the self He himself becomes the self of the individual. Even as the individuality of the self required to be preserved, so the perfect nature of Brahman needs to be maintained in regard to Brahman abiding within the individual.

Rāmānuja finds that both requirements may be satisfactorily fulfilled if the Upaniṣadic conception of Brahman as existing within oneself were understood in the sense that Brahman who abides within the soul as the inner Self stands to the soul in the same relation as the soul stands to its body. And what this relationship is we have already seen. It admits of body and soul each possessing its own distinctive attributes, and yet brings the body in spite of its distinctness completely under the control of the soul. Rāmānuja's definition of body in relation to the soul was, it will be remembered, as follows: " Any substance which a sentient soul is capable of completely controlling and supporting for its own purposes, and which stands to the soul, in an entirely subordinate relation, is the body of that soul " (p. 424). In this respect we may say that Rāmānuja's view with regard to Brahman abiding as the inner Self of the soul is not so much that He abides in it as Self as that He exists within it as its inner Ruler. This is the view taught in Bṛ. Up. III. 7. 3-22, and Rāmānuja accepts it, for it suits his purpose admirably. It provides the necessary distinction between Brahman the Ruler, and the soul, the ruled, so that neither the individuality of the soul nor the perfection of Brahman is in danger of being sacrificed. "The ruling of all creatures—or their governance—is displayed by His abidance in every creature as its Soul." . . . "In the hearts of all beings, who constitute My body, I am seated as their *Ātma* (soul).—To be the *Ātma* is indeed to be in every manner the Support, the Ruler and the Master" (Bhg. Bh., p. 333, X. 19 and 20). "The individual soul being thus connected with the highest Self as its body, its attributes do not touch the highest Self, not any more than infancy, youth, and other attributes of the material body touch the individual soul. Hence in the co-ordination 'Thou art that,' the word 'that' denotes the highest Brahman which is the cause of the world, whose purposes come true, which comprises within itself all blessed qualities, which is free from all shadow of evil; while the word 'thou' denotes the same highest Self in so far as having for its body the individual souls together with their bodies. The terms co-ordinated may thus be taken in their primary senses . . . and not a shadow of imperfection such as Nescience, and so on, attaches to Brahman, the absolutely blessed. The co-ordination with the individual soul thus proves only the difference of Brahman from the soul, which is a mere mode of Brahman; and hence we hold that different from the self consisting of knowledge, i.e., the individual soul, is the Self consisting of bliss, i.e., the highest Self" (Ś. Bh., pp. 228 and 229).

We may understand therefore that when the soul enters into worldly existence (*saṁsāra*) and suffers from imperfections in accordance with its deeds, Brahman abides within it as its Self, that is, not as the knower and the agent in the body, for those are functions of the individual self, but as One who supports and rules over the soul without in any way being involved in its imperfections.

Brahman in relation to the imperfections and the individuality of souls.

To understand further the relation of Brahman to the soul in *saṁsāra,* we may enquire in what way Brahman is related to the imperfections of the soul. The imperfections are, as is evident from the passages cited above, pain and Nescience. Creatures of this world are found to "experience pain of the most dreadful kind" (p. 478), and "being engrossed by Nescience in the form of good and evil works, do not recognise their essential nature which is knowledge, but view themselves as having the character of material things" (pp. 88 and 89). How, it may be asked, if Brahman is perfect bliss, does pain afflict the individual self, which depends on Him even as completely as the body depends on the soul? Further, if Brahman has knowledge as His essential attribute, how are we to explain the Nescience which obscures the intelligence of the soul, and leads it to identify itself with the body? It is not possible to trace these evils to the body and thus save the perfect nature of Brahman, for the material principle which underlies the body is not, according to Rāmānuja, something which is independent of Brahman, but something which depends completely for all it is and does on Him. "We by no means wish to deny unevolved matter and all its effects in themselves, but in so far only as they are maintained not to have their Self in the Supreme Person. For the fact is that they constitute His body and He thus constitutes their Self; and it is only through this their relation to Him that the *Pradhāna,* and so on, are capable of accomplishing their several ends. Otherwise the different essential natures of them all could never exist—nor persist, nor act" (I. 4. 3, pp. 358 and 359). Moreover, we saw that according to Rāmānuja matter had no essential nature of its own, but acquired what nature it had entirely owing to the deeds of souls. We seem led therefore to the view that the imperfections of pain and Nescience, from which the soul suffers, are ultimately due to its own deeds. This is what Rāmāunja says: "That a soul experiences pleasures and pains caused by the various states of the body is not due to the fact of its being joined to a body, but to its *karman* in the form of good and evil deeds" (p. 428). "In the so-called *ksetrajña*-condition of the self, knowledge is, owing to the influence of work (*karman*), of a contracted nature" (p. 63). The soul's imperfections, then, whether in the form of pain or in the form of Nescience, are ultimately to be traded to *karman* or the deeds of souls, and Brahman is not responsible for them.

But it may be asked, Does not the individual self stand to Brahman even as the body stands to the soul; and does not this mean that the individual self is completely dependent on Brahman and controlled by Him? If so, how can it be that the soul's deeds, which produce evil consequences in the way of pain and Nescience, and the unending cycle of birth and death, do not implicate Brahman? Here we come upon the heart of the problem in regard to the relation of Brahman to the imperfections or evil with which the soul is afflicted in *saṁsāra*; and in seeking to solve it Rāmānuja makes still further clear his view concerning the relationship of Brahman to the individual self. He writes, "The divine Supreme Person, all whose wishes are eternally fulfilled, who is all-knowing and the ruler of all, whose every purpose is immediately realised, having engaged in sport befitting his might and greatness and having settled that work is of a twofold nature, such and such works being good and such and such being evil, and having bestowed on all individual souls bodies and sense-organs capacitating them for entering on such work and the power of ruling those bodies and organs;

and having himself entered into those souls as their inner Self abides within them, controlling them as an animating and cheering principle. The souls, on their side, endowed with all the powers imparted to them by the Lord and with bodies and organs bestowed by him, and forming abodes in which he dwells, apply themselves on their own part, and in accordance with their own wishes, to works either good or evil. The Lord, then recognising him who performs good actions as one who obeys his commands, blesses him with piety, riches, worldly pleasures and final release; while him who transgresses his commands he causes to experience the opposite of all these" (p. 498). From this it would seem that, although the soul depends on Brahman for its life, body, sense-organs and capacity to rule over its body, it has the power of free choice, so that when it acts and brings evil consequences on itself, it is alone responsible, and not Brahman. Brahman is indeed perfect, and the soul depends on Him, but not to the extent of foregoing its individuality, or involving Brahman in imperfection.

But it may be objected that to argue in this way is to make the soul quite independent of Brahman so far as action goes. It is necessary therefore to show how far the soul is, and how far it is not, independent in its actions. Rāmānuja will not consent to Brahman being reduced to a finite God, even in order to preserve the individuality of the soul. Consequently in discussing the sūtra II. 3. 40, he writes: "The activity of the individual soul proceeds from the highest self as its cause. For Scripture teaches this: 'Entered within, the ruler of creatures, the Self of all'; 'who dwelling in the self . . . rules the self from within.' Smṛti teaches the same. . . . 'The Lord, O Arjuna, dwells in the heart of all creatures, whirling, by His mysterious power, all creatures as if mounted on a machine' (Bhg. XVIII. 61)" (p. 557). Brahman then is supreme, and the soul is not entirely independent in its actions. How far then is it independent? This Rāmānuja tells us in his explanation of Sūtra II. 3. 41. "The inwardly ruling highest Self promotes action in so far as it regards in the case of any action the volitional effect made by the individual soul, and then aids that effort by granting its favour or permission (*anumati*); action is not possible without permission on the part of the highest self." For any act to be performed, then, the volition of the soul is necessary as well as the permission of Brahman, so that although in one sense it may be said that the act proceeds from Brahman in as much as it is allowed by Him, still it is based on the volition of the individual soul, and therefore it is the latter that is responsible for it. "The case is analogous to that of property of which two men are joint owners. If one of these wishes to transfer that property to a third person he cannot do so without the permission of his partner, but that that permission is given is after all his own doing, and hence the fruit of the action (reward or anything) properly belongs to him only" (p. 557). Or, to borrow a parable from the New Testament, the action of the prodigal son in taking his share of the goods from his father and in wasting it in riotous living is one for which the son alone is responsible, although the father permitted it. So also it would appear that though without Brahman's permission the soul is impotent to act, the responsibility for the act always rests upon the soul who wills it. Thus it would seem that the evils from which the soul suffers in *saṁsāra* are due to its own deeds. Although Brahman is supreme and has absolute power over the soul, His control is not of a kind which deprives the soul of its individuality.

Having in this way discovered how Brahman is related to the deeds which bring pain and Nescience to the soul, we may next enquire what these evils suffered by the soul reveal with regard to the nature of Brahman. That souls are responsible for the deeds which bring about the afflictions from which they suffer may be granted, but it may be said that since it is ultimately Brahman who sends these afflictions, He cannot be freed from the accusation of having an evil nature. Rāmānuja denies this by pointing out that the evils suffered by the soul do not argue that Brahman is hard-hearted or pitiless, "For by pity we understand the inability, on somebody's part, to bear the pain of others, coupled with a disregard of his own advantage. When pity has the effect of bringing about the transgression of law on the part of the pitying person, it is in no way to his credit; it rather implies the charge of unmanliness (weakness)" (p. 488). The afflictions suffered by the soul thus reveal, not any mercilessness on the part of Brahman but His perfect nature, which cannot tolerate the transgression of the moral law. Nor can this be objected to on the ground that if Brahman must act in accordance with the moral law He is not infinite and supreme, for Rāmānuja makes it clear that the moral law is not external to the Deity, but one which He Himself has framed in accordance with His own will. "The divine Supreme Person, all whose wishes are eternally fulfilled, who is all-knowing and the ruler of all, whose every purpose is immediately realised . . . (has) settled that work is of a two-fold nature, such and such works being good and such and such being evil" (p. 488). Good and evil then mean nothing more than what pleases or displeases the Supreme Person (p. 487), so that ultimately the moral law is determined by Him as what He wills, and not He by it. The evils which the soul suffers, therefore, far from implying any imperfection in Brahman, bespeak His perfect moral nature which cannot tolerate evil, and which therefore metes out punishment to the soul in accordance with its deeds. "The Lord, then, recognising him who performs good actions as one who obeys his commands, blesses him with piety, riches, worldly pleasures and final release; while him who transgresses his commands he causes to experience the opposites of all these" (p. 488). The stern law of *Karma*, according to which the soul undergoes sufferings in accordance with its deeds, is thus only an expression of the moral will of Brahman.

While it may be conceded that the evils suffered by the soul in *saṁsāra* reflect the moral nature of the Supreme Being who in strict justice apportions pleasure and pain to souls, it may be said the Deity is thus disclosed to be stern justice not tempered with mercy, and hence He must from this point of view be judged to suffer from a defect. Rāmānuja has already shown that it is impossible for the Deity to be merciful at the expense of tolerating sin. He must "control and subdue it" (p. 488). But this does not mean, he declares, that the Deity has no love for the erring soul, for as already noted what Brahman aims at is that by means of punishment He may lead the soul to supreme happiness. His strict justice represented by the law of *Karma*, is therefore not an end in itself, but only a means which the Deity in His mercy adopts for the good of the soul. In and through all the evils suffered by the soul in *saṁsāra*, then, is discernible the perfect and loving nature of the Deity.

But why, it may be asked, if Brahman is moved by love for the soul, does He permit it to do evil? Rāmānuja is convinced that such "allowance of the action on the part of one able to stop it does not necessarily prove hard-heartedness" (p. 558), for it would seem that the soul, being a true individual, cannot be deprived of its privileges to act as it chooses. As Piḷḷai Lokācārya[1] tells us, the soul being a free agent, cannot be forced into goodness. "Even the all loving Father, the Great Īśvara, does not force His presence on the soul, not yet ripe to receive Him. With infinite patience He waits and watches the struggle of the soul in *saṁsāra*, since the struggle

[1] A follower of Rāmānuja of the thirteenth century (A.D. 1213).

is necessary for the full unfoldment (*vikāṣa*) of the faculties of the soul."[1] If the Lord permits the soul to do evil, then, it is only because He respects its individuality. The soul educated by means of the law of *Karma*, must of its own accord forsake evil and choose the good. Consequently in spite of the love which the Deity has for the soul, He allows it to do evil, if it so desires.

Another difficulty is raised. It is said, " there is a Scriptural text—' He (the Lord) makes him whom He wishes to lead up from these worlds do a good deed, and the same makes him whom He wishes to lead down from these worlds do a bad deed ' (Kauṣ. Up. III. 8)—which means that the Lord Himself causes men to do good and evil actions." Rāmānuja rejoins, " The text quoted, we reply, does not apply to all agents, but means that the Lord, wishing to do a favour to those who are resolved on acting so as fully to please the highest Person, engenders in their minds a tendency towards highly virtuous actions, such as are means to attain to Him ; while on the other hand, in order to punish those who are resolved on lines of action altogether displeasing to Him, He engenders in their minds a delight in such actions as have a downward tendency and are obstacles in the way of attainment of the Lord " (p. 558). His leading some to do good and others to do evil does not then argue any partiality on the part of Brahman, but is determined entirely by the deserts of the souls concerned.

We may therefore conclude that when considered in relation to the evils suffered by the soul, Brahman is found to be eminently moral and gracious. The evils are due entirely to the action of responsible individuals, and although Brahman has absolute power over them, He will not deprive them of the power to act in accordance with their own wishes. His perfect nature demands that sin should not be tolerated. Accordingly He punishes the sinner ; but in so doing He is only

[1] Tattva-Traya, p. 2 in the Translation by M. N. Paul.

seeking in His infinite mercy to lead the soul to a state of supreme happiness.

In finding thus a solution to the problem of evil as it characterises the soul, we have indeed found a solution to the problem of evil in general, for whatever evil charaterises the material world exists as we saw entirely for the sake of souls. Consequently for him who has overcome evil deeds, the world can offer no evil. He will find the world to be essentially blissful, of the same nature as that of Brahman Himself. "The individual souls . . . which are under the influence of *karman*, are conscious of this world as different from Brahman, and, according to their individual *karman*, as either made up of pain or limited pleasure. But as this view depends altogether on *karman*, to him who has freed himself from Nescience in the form of *karman*, this same world presents itself as lying within the intuition of Brahman, together with its qualities and *vibhūti*, and hence as essentially blissful. To a man troubled with excess of bile the water he drinks has a taste either downright unpleasant or moderately pleasant, according to the degree to which his health is affected; while the same water has an unmixedly pleasant taste for a man in health." Moreover such a man will see the whole world as designed by the Deity ultimately for his happiness, and therefore He will rejoice in it. "As long as a boy is not aware that some plaything is meant to amuse him, he does not care for it; when on the other hand he apprehends it as meant to give him delight, the thing becomes very dear to him. In the same way the world becomes an object of supreme love to him" . . . (p. 306). Evil then is evil only for him who is engrossed in evil deeds. It ceases to exist for one who has overcome evil deeds and sees the spiritual purpose of all creation. Accordingly evil is not ultimate. It represents only a temporary phase in the evolution of moral persons.

By throwing the blame for evil ultimately on the

souls themselves, Rāmānuja seeks to preserve the perfection and love of the Supreme Being. The chief difficulty of the theory is to explain how souls which are eternally parts of the Supremely perfect Brahman, ever came to desire what is evil. Rāmānuja adopts the device of his predecessors to get over the difficulty by declaring that *karman* is beginningless; but this is no solution for it is merely to accept evil desires on the part of souls as somehow an ultimate fact. Nevertheless it is to Rāmānuja's credit that he sought systematically to maintain the perfection of Brahman as against the imperfections of the world. The solution that he offers to the problem of evil is not new, for the view that *karman* explains all the sufferings of *saṁsāra* is, as we saw, common to most of his predecessors. But his merit lies in attempting to make clear the exact relation in which the perfect Brahman stands to the deeds of souls. This could not satisfactorily be done by earlier philosophers, who neither consistently upheld the perfect nature of Brahman nor fully recognised the individuality of the soul; and without making clear the relation of Brahman to the deeds which explain the evils of *saṁsāra*, it is obviously impossible with any success to maintain, as Rāmānuja does, that Brahman is not responsible for the evils of *saṁsāra*, and that in and through them all the gracious Deity is working out the ultimate good of souls. In relation to the evils of the world then Brahman appears to be perfect and loving, and the soul, which is responsible for evil, as dependent on Him, but not in such a way as to be deprived of its capacity for self-determination.

The soul as a part of Brahman

Seeing that the soul is allowed by the Deity to act in accordance with its own desires it is necessary to consider afresh from the point of view of this distinctive quality of the soul—as a self-determining individual the general relationship of souls as attributes, modes or parts of the Supreme Being, predicated in the last chapter. Rāmānuja finds no reason to modify the conclusion there established. He considers this problem in discussing sūtras II. 3. 42-52. "The Sūtras have declared that the individual soul is an agent, and as such dependent on the highest Person. The following question now arises: Is the individual soul absolutely different from Brahman? Or is it nothing else than Brahman itself in so far as under the influence of error? or is it Brahman in so far as determined by a limiting adjunct (*upādhi*)? or is it a part (*aṁśa*) of Brahman?" (p. 559). Let us see what can be said in support of each of these positions.

(*a*) The individual soul is absolutely different from Brahman. That the soul is different from Brahman is indicated by the fact that the soul is as we saw an individual having a consciousness and will of its own. Moreover scriptural texts such as "There are two, the one knowing, the other not knowing, both unborn, the one strong, the other weak (Śvet. Up. I. 9) declare their difference" (p. 559). Further, to say that two different things are one is to "convey a contradiction—as if one were to say 'Water the ground with fire'—and must therefore be understood in some secondary metaphorical sense" (cf. 559). To say that the soul, though different from Brahman, is related to Him as part to whole is also impossible, "for by a 'part' we understand that which constitutes part of the extension of something. If, then, the soul occupied part of the extension of Brahman all its imperfections would belong to Brahman. Nor can the soul be a part of Brahman, if we take 'part' to mean a piece (*khaṇḍa*); for Brahman does not admit of being divided into pieces, and moreover, the difficulties connected with the former interpretation would present themselves here also. That something absolutely different from something else should yet be a part of the latter cannot in fact be proved" (pp. 559 and 560). So much then may be said for the view that the soul as agent is neither one with Brahman nor a part of Him, but entirely different from Him.

(*b*) The soul is nothing other than Brahman under a delusion. In support of this view it may be claimed that "this is the teaching of texts such as 'Thou art that,' 'this self is Brahman.' Those texts, on the other hand, which declare the difference of the two merely restate what is already established by perception and the other means of knowledge, and therefore are shown, by those texts the purport of which it is to teach non-duality not established by other means, to lie—like perception and the other means of knowledge themselves—within the sphere of Nescience" (p. 560). According to this interpretation then the soul is identical with Brahman, its difference from Him being entirely illusory.

(*c*) The soul is Brahman determined by an *upādhi*. This may be maintained on the ground that "Scripture teaches the self to be Brahman," and also on the ground that the soul cannot be merely the product of illusion in Brahman, as was claimed under (*b*), "for on that view the distinction of bondage and release and so on, would be impossible" (p. 560). This view, therefore, though similar to (*b*) in regarding the soul as one with Brahman, distinguishes itself from it by claiming that the soul is Brahman under a real determination.

(*d*) The soul is a part of Brahman. This is the view which Rāmānuja adopts as being the teaching of sūtra II. 3. 42. "Against all these views the Sūtra declares that the soul is a part of Brahman, since there are declarations of difference and also 'otherwise,' i.e., declaration of unity. To the former class belong all those texts which dwell on the distinction of the creator and the creature, the ruler and the ruled, the all knowing and the ignorant, the independent and the dependent, the pure and the impure, that which is endowed with holy qualities and that which possesses qualities of an opposite kind, the Lord and the dependent. To the latter class belong such texts as 'Thou art that' and 'this self is Brahman.' . . . In order, then, that texts of both these classes may be taken in their primary, literal sense, we must admit that the individual soul is a part of Brahman" (pp. 560 and 561). The defninciency of the first view which we expounded is the same as that of the second, in that each in its own way is one-sided, basing itself on one set of texts to the neglect of its opposite. Consequently it cannot be maintained that the soul is entirely different from Brahman as the first does, nor that it is entirely identical with Him as the second does. With regard to the third, Rāmānuja writes, "Nor finally is there any good in the theory of the soul being Brahman in so far as determined by a limiting adjunct. For this view also is in conflict with the texts which distinguish Brahman as the ruling and the soul as the ruled principle, and so on. One and the same Devadatta does not become double as it were—a ruler on the one hand and a ruled subject on the other—because he is determined by the house in which he is, or by something else" (p. 562). So Rāmānuja concludes, "In order to be able to account for the two-fold designation (viz., that the soul is different from Brahman and yet also that it is one with Him) we must . . . admit that the soul is a *part* of Brahman" (p. 562).

Rāmānuja finds support for this doctrine in the Chāndogya passage which declares, "One part (quarter) of it are all beings, three feet (quarters) of it are the Immortal in heaven (Chānd. Up. III. 12. 6), and in Bhagavadgītā XV. 7 which says 'An eternal part of myself becomes the individual soul (*jīva*) in the world of life' (pp. 562 and 563).

But what, it may be asked, is to be understood by regarding the soul as a 'part' of Brahman? The category of part and whole as ordinarily employed has a distinctively quantitative significance which, as Rāmānuja is aware, cannot apply in the case of souls in their relationship to Brahman. He sees the absurdities into which we shall be led if in this connection we understand 'part' in a quantitative sense, i.e., if by "'part' we understand that which constitutes part of the extension of something." He says, "If, then, the soul occupied part of the extension of Brahman, all its imperfections would belong to Brahman" (559), just as, for instance, a defect in the foot of an organism is a defect of the organism itself. "Nor can the soul be a part of Brahman if we take 'part' to mean a piece (*khaṇḍa*); for Brahman does not admit of being divided into pieces" (p. 559). The quantitative significance of the word 'part,' then, must be excluded, and the word must be understood in a qualitative sense. "The individual soul is a part of the highest Self; as the light issuing from a luminous thing such as fire or the sun is a part of that body; or, as the generic characteristics of a cow or horse, and the white or black colour of things so coloured, are attributes and hence parts of the things in which those attributes inhere; or as the body is a part of an embodied being. For by a part we understand that which constitutes one place (*deśa*) of some thing, and hence a distinguishing attribute (*viśeṣaṇa*) is a part of the thing distinguished by that attribute. Hence those analysing a thing of that kind discriminate between the ***distinguishing*** element or part of it; and the ***distinguished*** element or part. Now although the distinguishing attribute and the thing distinguished thereby stand to each other in the relation of part and whole, yet we observe them, to differ in essential character. Hence there is no contradiction between the individual and the highest Self—the former of which is a *viśeṣaṇa* of the latter—standing to each other in the relation of part and whole, and their being at the same time of essentially different nature. . . . For as the luminous body is of a nature different from that of its light, thus the highest Self differs from the individual soul which is a part of it. It is this difference of character—due to the individual soul being the distinguishing element and the highest Self being the substance distinguished thereby—to which all those texts refer which declare difference. Those texts, on the other hand, which declare non-difference are based on the circumstance that attributes which are incapable of separate existence are ultimately bound to the substance which they distinguish" (II. 3. 45, pp. 563 and 564).

Thus by regarding the soul as a part of Brahman Rāmānuja makes it clear that he means nothing more than that souls are attributes or modes of Brahman—the view already expounded in connection with the relationship of the world to Brahman. But from this it must not be thought that souls are merely adjectival to Brahman with no individuality of their own. This would seem to be the view of those who declare that the soul is merely Brahman as determined by an *upādhi*; and, as we saw, Rāmānuja explicitly rejects this view by pointing out that it fails to distinguish sufficiently between Brahman, the Ruler, and the soul, the ruled. "One and the same Devadatta does not become double as it were—a ruler on the one hand and a ruled subject on the other" (p. 562). The view of the soul as an attribute of Brahman is not then to be understood in a sense in which its individuality is destroyed. Rāmānuja, as we noted, provided for the necessary distinction in his analysis of the substance-attribute relationship, whereby he held that an attribute is not always only an abstract quality but that even objects which in a sense have an individuality of their own, such as a staff or a bracelet, may be regarded as attributes of the man to whom they belong. The soul then is an attribute of Brahman only in this sense, viz.: that it belongs to Him and is completely dependent on Him for its existence, not in the sense that it has no distinct individuality of its own.

Having thus restated, in the light of the individuality which the soul as a free agent possesses, the relationship in which it stands to Brahman, we may proceed to enquire in what various ways the qualities of perfection and love, which we found to characterise the nature of the Deity, express themselves in relation to man. We shall consider this question in relation to the conditions which the soul must fulfil for Release or salvation, for Release being according to Rāmānuja, as according to his predecessors, the chief end of man, it is in connection with it that the Deity's nature in relation to men is fully revealed.

The nature of Brahman as reflected in the conditions to be fulfilled by the soul, for Release

In the Upaniṣads we saw that the predominant idea was that Release from *saṁsāra* was to be obtained by knowledge. He that knows Brahman is freed from all fetters. But what exactly was the relation of this knowledge to conduct was not clearly determined. Some philosophers seemed to think that the mere knowledge that one was oneself Brahman sufficed to produce liberation, and that accordingly the Brahman-knower need not trouble himself about good and evil deeds. So long as Brahman was thought to be merely a conscious principle ,which pervades all things, there was no perceivable connection between Him and conduct ; questions of good and bad conduct were therefore not quite relevant in connection with the realisation of Brahman. But we saw that some of the later Upaniṣads ascribed many perfections to the Supreme Being, and ever more increasingly asserted that Brahman may not be known by one who has not ceased from evil conduct. Rāmānuja builds his view on them as providing the necessary place for moral conduct, which, as we have tried to show, his cult had always emphasized throughout its history. The moral basis upon which Ghora-Āṇgirasa, and following him Vāsudeva, founded the cult was so firm that even the later alliance of the cult with advaitism, for which morality can have no real significance, did not suffice to uproot this basis, and accordingly, as we saw, the

Vaiṣṇava religion always emphasized ethical requirements as necessary to be fulfilled by the devotee. Rāmānuja is a true Vaiṣṇava in emphasizing right conduct as obligatory on one who would obtain Release. Anxious as he is to build his view on Upaniṣadic doctrine regarding the way of obtaining Release, he speaks of knowledge as that which ultimately produces Release, but knowledge he interprets, as we shall see, in the sense of *bhakti* or devotion which his cult had always regarded as necessary for Release; and he makes right conduct a means to the attainment of this redeeming knowledge, even as the later Upaniṣads had done. In this way he is able to secure both the doctrines fundamental to his sect, viz., that the Deity requires virtuous living and grants Release only to him who has whole-hearted devotion. The ethical and loving nature of Brahman thus reflects itself in the conditions pertaining to conduct and devotion obligatory on one who is seeking Release.

The ethic of Rāmānuja is fundamentally that of the Gītā. The one who aspires after Release must fulfil many practical requirements. It is first of all necessary for him to perceive his own essential nature. This according to Rāmānuja is chiefly the lesson of Bhagavadgītā II. 12-72. Since the root of all evil is Nescience, whereby the soul identifies itself with the body and gives itself to the pursuit of bodily ends, it is necessary for it to see that its own true nature is quite distinct from that of the body. "Knowing *ātma* to be that which is distinct from body, uncontaminated with qualities pertaining to bodies, and to be that which is eternal; keeping the mind imperturbable under the varying conditions of pleasure and pain, gain and loss . . . and destitute of any wish for reward. . . . In this-wise wilt thou escape sin" (Bhg. Bh. II. 38, pp. 10 and 11). One must meditate on oneself as not only different from the body but as having qualities similar to Brahman. "The individual self is, in such meditation, to be conceived (not as the ordinary self, but) under that form which it has to attain (i.e., the pure form which belongs to it in the state of Release)"; "the character of such meditation, therefore, is that it is a meditation on the highest Self as having for its body the individual self, distinguished by freedom from evil" (Ś. Bh. III. 3. 52, p. 675).

Having thus freed himself from the mistaken notion of the bodily self as constituting his true nature, and having recognised his kinship with the Perfect Brahman, the individual is to give himself to the pursuit of all the duties binding on him in his station in life, without any tinge of selfishness or desire for personal gain. "This is the state, or condition of work-performance in an unselfish or disinterested manner, based on the knowledge of the eternal *ātma*. This method has for its aim the achievement of true wisdom. It is Brāhmī or that which leads to Brahm" (Bhg. Bh. II. 72, p. 82). "All daily (*nitya*) and incidental (*naimittika*) rites prescribed in Śāstras shall be performed. . . . As for fructiferous rites (*kāmya*) even those shall be performed in the manner prescribed for the several castes (*varṇa*) and orders of life (*āśrama*), and according to one's ability; but resigning their specific fruits" (Bhg. Bh. II. 41, pp. 64 and 65). The Deity is "pleased and conciliated by the different kinds of acts of sacrifice and worship duly performed by the devotee day after day. This is what the text 'they seek to know through the sacrifice' really means. The conclusion therefore is that in the case of householders knowledge has for its prerequisite all sacrifices and other works of permanent and occasional obligation. 'As a horse.' As the horse, which is a means of locomotion for man, requires attendants, grooming, etc., so knowledge, although itself the means of Release, demands the co-operation of the different works. Thus the Lord Himself says, 'The work of sacrifice, giving, and austerities is not to be relinquished, but is indeed to be perfomed; for sacrifices, gifts and austerities are purifying to the thoughtful.' 'He from whom all beings proceed . . . worshipping Him with the proper works man attains to perfection' (Bhg. XVIII. 5.46)" (Ś. Bh. III. 4. 26, pp. 699 and 700).

Not only such sacrificial rites, but also the duties connected with each *āśrama*, have to be performed (Ś. Bh. III. 4. 32, p. 702). Those who do not stand within any *āśrama* should devote themselves to "practices not exclusively connected with any *āśrama*, such as prayer, fasting, charity, propitiation of the Deity, and so on" (III. 4. 36, p. 704). But "Better than to be outside the *āśramas* is the condition of standing within an *āśrama*. The latter state may be due to misfortune; but he who can should be within an *āśrama*, which state is the more holy and beneficial one" (III. 4. 39, p. 705). Those who have fallen from the *āśrama* state owing to a lapse from chastity are not qualified for knowledge of Brahman (III. 4. 42 and 43, pp. 706 and 707).

The duties obligatory on the four castes are prescribed in the Śāstras, and Rāmānuja following the teaching of the Gītā declares that these duties should be faithfully performed by the devotee. "Duties varying according to the qualities born of the natures of Brāhmaṇas, etc., are assigned by the Śāstras; i.e., the Śāstras define that such are the qualities possessed by the Brāhmaṇas, etc., such the duties proper to their station, and such their occupations, etc." (Bhg. Bh. XVIII. 41, p. 547), "every man devoted to his own duty obtaining *Saṁsiddhi* = *Paramapada* = the final state of perfection" (Bhg. Bh. XVIII. 45, p. 551).

He who conforms to these religious and social duties laid down in the Śāstras will, Rāmānuja declares, be characterised by the virtues which the Gītā enumerates as belonging to the man of 'Divine' nature—virtues such as fearlessness, purity of heart, charity, self-restraint, penance, uprightness, harmlessness, veracity, gentleness, modesty, and the like (Bhg. Bh. XVI. 1-3, pp. 484-486); and he who does not conform to them will be characterised by the vices enumerated as belonging to a man of 'demoniac' nature (Bhg. XVI. 4).

All these, viz.: the knowledge of oneself as different from the evil nature of the body and as akin to the pure nature of Brahman, and the fulfilment of religious and social duties inculcated in the Śāstras,[1] without any expectation of reward, are among the requirements which the Deity enjoins on the individual who would attain Release The soul that would obtain salvation must renounce the evil nature of the body and apply itself to carrying out His will

But such mere disinterested performance of one's religious and social duties does not suffice The Deity is not a mere moral governor of the universe. He is above all characterised by love. Consequently what He requires more than all else is whole-hearted devotion, a devotion which demands the centering of one's thoughts entirely on Him in all one's service. "Do the work that is before thee, and all other Śruti-and-Smṛti-enjoined works, such as the daily (*nitya*), and occasional (*naimittika*) duties, apportioned to the several castes (*varṇas*) and orders (*āśramas*), so that while discharging them I may be in thy memory daily. This is the most expedient method by which thou canst succeed in keeping thy *manas* and *buddhi* set on me, and thus remembering me at the last moment, thou shalt reach me according to thy wish. There is no doubt about this" (Bhg. Bh. VIII. 7, pp. 267 and 268). "Whatsoever mundane calling thou mayst be engaged in, out of necessity to live; whatsoever thou mayst be eating as thy food, whatsoever daily and occasional Veda enjoined duties thou mayst be fulfilling, such as *homa* (fire-sacrifices), *dāna* (gifts), *tapas* (austerities), deliver them all unto me. . . . That is to say, do all acts as if the doer, the enjoyer, and the worshipper were all offered up in me" (Bhg.

[1] These are the Vedas, the Dharma-Śāstras, Itihāsas and Purāṇas, according to Rāmānuja (cf. Bhg. Bh. XVI. 24, p. 497).

Bh. IX. 27). "Thus, then, in conclusion, thou shalt carry on all thy worldly duties required for thy bodily subsistence, and scriptural duties—viz., daily, casual, etc., rites—as if all was done to please me, as done by one who is essentially my liege and done, being actuated to do so, by myself. Thou shalt ever in love be engaged in singing my praises, in my services, in bowings, etc. Thou shalt contemplate that the universe is under my rule and guidance, and subsists as essentially my appendage. Thou shalt ponder and reflect over the multitude of my lovable attributes. Occupying thyself daily, thus, in devotion of the aforementioned description, thou shalt reach myself" (Bhg. Bh. IX. 34, p. 316).

Although Rāmānuja describes the devotion that is required of the individual as chiefly contemplative, involving the centering of one's thoughts on the Deity, it is a devotion which requires the dedication of one's will, for, as we saw, it involves the performance of all one's duties. Besides, it may lead to ecstatic emotional experience, as in the case of the Āḻvārs. Thus in commenting on Gītā IX. 14, Rāmānuja writes, "Overwhelmed with intense love for me, they [i.e., the worshippers who seek Release] discover that it is impossible to support existence for even an infinitesimal part of a moment without being engaged in singing my names, or in holy exercises, or falling prostrate before me. They repeat and call upon my names—which connote the several distinguishing attributes of my nature—their frames quivering and hairs bristling with joy, thrilled in holy excitement at such recollections, their voices tremulous and convulsed with holy joy, uttering broken speech, and constantly repeating in yearning notes such names as Nārāyaṇa, Kṛṣṇa, Vāsudeva, etc. With equal zeal are they assiduous in the performance of holy duties and worship, as helps to which, in firm determination, they employ themselves in the laying out of gardens and construction of temples, etc. They stretch themselves on the ground like a fragile reed, regardless of dust, mire or pricking pebbles, all the eight members of the body . . . falling prostrate in united concerted devotion and worship. Ever and incessantly praying to be eternally united to me, they ever meditate on me and worship me, with the vivid fervent appeal that in holy service they may realise their true *ātma*-nature of abasement and abnegation (*dāsya*)" (pp. 298 and 299).

Such devotion, whereby the individual is engaged in the performance of his duties and in ecstatic worship, with mind wholly centred on the Deity is what is required of him who would obtain Release. Performance of one's duty and devotion to the Deity are hence the prime requisites.

When all one's conduct and all one's devotion are offered thus whole-heartedly to the Deity, He grants to the soul, it would seem, a mystic realisation of Himself when the soul sees God face to face. It is this realisation of Brahman through whole-hearted devotion which according to Rāmānuja the Upaniṣadic seers meant when they declared that he who knows Brahman obtains Release. In seeking thus to find a basis in the Upaniṣads for this fundamental doctrine of his cult, and in equating *bhakti* or devotion with knowledge, Rāmānuja gives to *bhakti* a predominantly meditative significance, on the one hand, and, on the other, regards the redeeming knowledge taught by the Upaniṣads as neither something purely intellectual nor something accomplished once and for all, but as a meditative devotion practised continually throughout one's life and culminating in a mystic intuition of the Deity. Thus he writes: "the knowledge which the Vedānta-texts aim at inculcating is a knowledge other than the mere knowledge of the sense of sentences, and denoted by '*dhyāna*,' '*upāsanā*' (i.e., meditation), and similar terms. With this agree scriptural texts such as 'Having known it, let him practise meditation' (Bṛ. Up. IV. 4, 21) . . . all these texts must be viewed as agreeing in meaning with the injunction of meditation contained in the passage quoted from the Bṛ. Up. and what they enjoin is therefore meditation " (Ś. Bh., p. 13). " ' Meditation ' means steady remembrance, i.e., a continuity of steady remembrance, uninterrupted like the flow of oil ; in agreement with the scriptural passage which declares steady remembrance to be the means of release, ' on the attainment of remembrance all the ties are loosened ' (Chānd. Up. VII. 26. 2). Such remembrance is of the same character (form) as seeing (intuition) ; for the passage quoted has the same purport as the following one, ' The fetter of the heart is broken, all doubts are solved, and all the works of that man perish when He has been seen who is high and low ' (Muṇḍ. Up. II. 2. 8). And this being so, we conclude that the passage ' the Self is to be seen ' teaches that ' Meditation ' has the character of ' seeing ' or ' intuition.' " " With reference to remembrance, which thus acquires the character of immediate presentation (*pratyakṣatā*) and is the means of final release, scripture makes a further determination, viz., in the passage Ka. Up. II. 23, ' That Self cannot be gained by the study of the Veda (' reflection '), nor by thought (' meditation '), nor by much hearing. Whom the Self chooses, by him it may be gained, to him the Self reveals its being.' This text says at first that mere hearing, reflection, and meditation do not suffice to gain the Self, and then declares, ' Whom the Self chooses, by him it may be gained.' Now a ' chosen ' one means a most beloved person ; the relation being that he by whom that Self is held most dear is most dear to the Self. That the Lord (*Bhagavān*) Himself endeavours that this most beloved person should gain the Self. He Himself declares in the following words, ' To those who are constantly devoted and worship with love I give that knowledge by which they reach me ' (Bhg. X. 10), and ' To him who has knowledge I am dear above all things, and he is dear to me ' (VII. 17). Hence he who possesses remembrance, marked by the character of immediate presentation (*sākṣātkāra*), and which itself is dear above all things since the object remembered is such; he, we say, is chosen by the highest Self, and by him the highest Self is gained. Steady remembrance of this kind is designated by the word 'devotion' (*bhakti*); for this term has the same meaning as *upāsanā* (meditation)" (Ś. Bh., pp. 15 and 16). Rāmānuja here makes it quite clear that the knowledge which brings about Release is one which involves a relationship of love between the soul and the Deity. It is only to him to whom the Deity is most dear that this redeeming knowledge is granted.

But, once more, since the Deity is not merely love but also perfection, this blissful vision of the Deity is not granted except to one who has become purified by devout works and strenuous discipline. "That of such steady remembrance sacrifices and so on are means will be declared later on (Vs. III. 4. 26)" (p. 16). "Sacrifices and similar works being performed day after day have the effect of purifying the mind, and owing to this, knowledge arises in the mind with ever increasing brightness" (III. 4. 35, p. 703). "Hence in order that knowledge may arise, evil works have to be got rid of, and this is effected by the performance of acts of religious duty not aiming at some immediate result (such as the heavenly world and the like); according to the text 'by works of religious duty he discards all evil.' Knowledge which is the means of reaching Brahman, thus requires the works prescribed for the different *āśramas*" (pp. 18 and 19). "The Vākyakārā also declares that steady remembrance results only from abstention, and so on; his words being, 'This (viz., steady remembrance = meditation) is obtained through abstention (*viveka*) freeness of mind (*vimoka*), repetition (*abhyāsa*), works (*kriyā*), virtuous conduct (*kalyāṇa*), freedom from dejection (*anavasāda*), absence of exultation (*anuddharṣa*); according to feasibility and scriptural statement.' The Vākyakāra also gives definitions of all these terms. Abstention (*viveka*) means keeping the body clean from all food, impure either owing to species (such as the flesh of certain animals), or abode (such as food belonging to a *Cāṇḍāla* or the like), or accidental cause (such as food into which a hair or the like has fallen). . . . Freeness of mind (*vimoka*) means absence of attachment to desires. . . . Repetition means continued practice. . . . By works (*kriyā*) is understood the performance, according to one's ability, of the five great sacrifices. . . . By virtuous conduct (*kalyāṇāni*) are meant truthfulness, honesty, kindness, liberality, gentleness, absence of covetousness. . . . That lowness of spirits or want of cheerfulnes which results from unfavourable conditions of place or time and the remembrance of causes of sorrow, is denoted by the term 'dejection'; the contrary of this is 'freedom from dejection.' . . . 'Exultation' is that satisfaction of mind which springs from circumstances opposite to those just mentioned; the contrary is 'absence of exultation.' Over-great satisfaction also stands in the way (of meditation). . . . What the Vākyakāra means to say is therefore that knowledge is realised only through the performance of the duly prescribed works, on the part of a person fulfilling all the enumerated conditions" (pp. 16-18).

It is not surprising that all this careful discipline of the mind and will is required before redeeming knowledge can be granted to the soul, for, as we saw earlier, the Deity cannot tolerate evil of any kind. He is the Perfect One, free from all evil; accordingly he who would realise Him must rid himself of all evil, and do His bidding as embodied in the duties laid down in the Śāstras. Nor is it surprising that this redeeming knowledge is granted only to him who has whole-hearted devotion or to whom the Deity is most dear, for, as we saw earlier, the Supreme Being is characterised by love for the soul, and consequently it is most natural for Him to seek for the love of the soul in return. His predominantly loving nature is indicated by the complete devotion which He requires of the soul, all other conditions being only instrumental in producing such attachment to Him on the part of the soul. The Deity's perfect nature, characterised above all by love, is therefore what is revealed in the conditions which it is necessary for the soul to fulfil in order to obtain Release.

The Manifold operation of Divine grace

That the Deity is eminently loving Rāmānuja finds to be the teaching of many passages in the Gītā. In his interpretation of them, as in his interpretation of many other devotional passages[1] in the Gītā, he seems chiefly to draw upon the rich religious experience of the Āḷvārs. In commenting on Gītā IX. 26, he describes the Deity as appreciating thus the gift brought to Him by the worshipper in love. "Though I, as such, am naturally in the enjoyment of supreme felicity, yet do I enjoy the offering brought me, as if I came in possession of a treat so rare as to be beyond the most distant expectation of a desiring heart. It is thus declared in the Mokṣa Dharma—'Whatsoever acts are consecrated to the Deva (God) with single-pointed devotion, the Deva Himself, forsooth, accepts them all on His head'" (pp. 308 and 309). Then again in interpreting Gītā IX. 2, he writes: "I reckon that when to a loving devotee . . . I deliver my own self entirely, even that is no sufficient compensation for the love he has borne (for me). I reckon, too, that even when I have given my own self to them I have done little or nothing for him. That is how I think of my beloved lovers" (p. 289). Similarly Rāmānuja explains Gītā VII. 18, which says 'the *jñānī* is to be known as my very soul,' to mean "As for the *jñānī*, I deem him as my own self, i.e., my very life depends on him. If it be asked how,

[1] Cf., e.g., Bhg. Bh. IV. 8 VI. 47; VII. 1, 18; VIII. 14; IX. 13, 14 26, 34; X. 9 and 10, etc.

the reason is that in the same manner that he cannot live without me—his highest goal—I cannot live without him " (p. 246).

Since the Deity is thus full of love for the soul struggling in *saṁsāra*, He seeks to redeem it by His grace. The Vaiṣṇava religion had, throughout its history spoken of the gracious Deity as helping man in various ways, and especially in his efforts after Release. The Āḻvārs spoke touchingly of Divine grace which stoops to rescue even the meanest and the most unworthy. Rāmānuja accordingly advocates the doctrine, especially as it is not without a basis even in the Upaniṣads, his favourite text in this connection being Ka. Up. II. 23, 'That Self cannot be gained by the study of the Veda, nor by thought, nor by much hearing. Whom the Self chooses, by him it may be gained; to him the Self reveals its being' (S. Bh., p. 15).

But, as we saw, the Deity is according to Rāmānuja not only love, but He is also one who is free from all evil, and requires that the soul that would find Him must free itself from evil and do such actions as please Him. Moreover we noted how anxious Rāmānuja was to preserve the individuality of the soul. Both these factors contribute to his view regarding the manner in which grace functions in rescuing the soul from *saṁsāra*. Grace cannot operate, it would seem, so as to deprive man of his individuality or to lead the Deity to compromise with evil.

Rāmānuja describes by means of a parable the factors which are involved in the soul's ultimate realisation of Brahman. He says, " take the case of a young prince who, intent on some boyish play, leaves his father's palace and, losing his way, does not return. The king thinks his son is lost; the boy himself is received by some good Brahman who brings him up and teaches him without knowing who the boy's father is. When the boy has reached his sixteenth year and is accomplished in every way, some fully trustworthy person tells him, ' Your father is the ruler of all these lands, famous for the possession of all noble qualities, wisdom, generosity, kindness, courage, valour and so on, and he stays in his capital, longing to see you, his lost child. Hearing that his father is alive and a man so high and noble, the boy's heart is filled with supreme joy; and the king also, understanding that his son is alive, in good health, handsome and well instructed, considers himself to have attained all a man can wish for. He then takes steps to recover his son, and finally the two are reunited " (Ś. Bh., p. 199). Two points are worthy of notice in this parable. Firstly, the boy has reached his sixteenth year [signifying maturity], is in good health, handsome, well instructed by a good Brahman, is accomplished in every way, has heard of his father from a reliable source and is filled with joy [at the prospect of being reunited with his father]. Secondly, the father takes steps to recover him and the two are reunited. The first would seem to imply that he who would realise Brahman must have attained a certain maturity, possess spiritual health [i.e., be free from the evil qualities of the body], be well instructed in the Vedas in the recognised orthodox manner, have performed all the rites and duties laid down in the Śāstras [i.e., be ' accomplished in every way '], have obtained instruction regarding Brahman from approved [' fully trustworthy '] sources, and desire to be reunited with the Deity. The second would signify that he cannot, however, of his own accord reach Brahman, for Release is always a gift of God's grace and involves the Deity taking the necessary steps to this end. Since grace functions then only when the soul has elaborately prepared itself by Vedic instruction, performance of Śāstric duties, intellectual knowledge of Brahman, and desire for Release, there can be no talk of the Deity either over-riding the individuality of the soul or permitting a violation of His Laws. This is the view consistently maintained throughout the Śrī Bhāṣya. Rāmānuja there makes it clear that the saving knowledge, which is the work of grace, is not possible except to one who has undergone thorough preparation involving Vedic knowledge and sacrifice. It is therefore not possible for the Śūdra. "It is impossible that the capability of performing meditations on Brahman should belong to a person not knowing the nature of Brahman and the due modes of meditation, and not qualified by the knowledge of the requisite preliminaries of such meditation, viz., recitation of the Veda, sacrifices, and so on. Mere want or desire does not impart qualification to a person destitute of the required capability. And this absence of capability is due, in the Śūdra's case, to absence of legitimate study of the Veda. The injunctions of sacrificial works naturally connect themselves with the knowledge and the means of knowledge (i.e., religious ceremonies and the like) that belong to the three higher castes, for these castes actually possess the knowledge (required for the sacrifices), owing to their studying the Veda in agreement with the injunction which prescribes such study for the higher castes; the same injunctions do not, on the other hand, connect themselves with the knowledge and means of knowledge belonging to others (than members of the three higher castes). And the same naturally holds good with regard to the injunctions of meditation on Brahman. And as thus only such knowledge as is acquired by study prompted by the Vedic injunction of study supplies a means for meditation on Brahman, it follows that the Śūdra for whom that injunction is not meant is incapable of such meditation" (I. 3. 32, p. 338). Nor may the Deity for this reason be accused of partiality for the higher castes, for caste is determined by the body (II. 3. 47), and that a soul is born in one body rather than another is, as we saw, always determined by its own deeds. The Deity then in restricting the possibility of saving knowledge to the higher castes is only observing His law that the soul shall be dealt with in accordance with its deeds. Both the individuality of the soul and the moral consistency of Brahman are thus preserved in the operation of Divine grace.

That grace is not arbitrary, but acts in accordance with the law of *Karma*, Rāmānuja has told us in connection with the passage Kauṣ. Up. III. 8, which declares that the Lord 'makes him whom He wishes to lead up from these worlds do a good deed, and the same makes him whom He wishes to lead down from these worlds do a bad deed.' He said that this meant that "the Lord, wishing to do a favour to those who are resolved on acting so as fully to please the highest Person, engenders in their minds a tendency toward highly virtuous actions, such as are means to attain to Him; while on the other hand, in order to punish those who are resolved on lines of action altogether displeasing to Him, He engenders in their minds a delight in such actions as have a downward tendency and are obstacles in the way of the attainment of the Lord" (Ś. Bh. II. 3. 41, p. 558). If he favours or disfavours a particular soul, then, it is always in accordance with His law that souls shall be dealt with in the light of what they deserve.

If grace must thus always act in regard to the principle of *Karma*, does it not mean, it may be asked, that it is unable to triumph over *Karma*? We have already suggested an answer to this question and it may be restated here in order to make clear Rāmānuja's doctrine of grace.

The question labours under a misapprehension regarding Rāmānuja's view of the law of *Karma*. As we have already noted, the law of *Karma* is according to Rāmānuja not a principle external to the Deity, but expresses His own mode of action. Nor is it in any way opposed to grace, for it is, as we saw, itself only a means of grace, a means which the Deity in love to the soul adopts for leading it to a state of supreme happiness. "What the Lord Himself aims at is ever to increase happiness to the highest degree, and to this end it is instrumental that He should reprove and reject the infinite and intolerable mass of sins" (Ś. Bh., pp. 488 and 489). Accordingly there can be no real opposition between the law of *Karma* and the principle of grace, any more than there can be any real opposition between the act of a mother who finds it necessary to show her pleasure and her displeasure to her child, in order that by this means she may lead the child to its own happiness, and the love that she bears for the child. If she shows pleasure and displeasure, it is because of her love, not in spite of it. The pleasure and pain that things cause, Rāmānuja declares is never due to themselves, but entirely due to the Deity who is thus showing favour or disfavour to the soul, in order that by this means it may obtain what is ultimately satisfying to it. Thus he interprets the passage (Bṛ. Up. IV. 5, 6) which states, 'Verily, a husband is dear, not for the love of the husband, but for the love of the Self a husband is dear. Everything is dear, not for the love of everything, but for the love of the Self everything is dear.' He says this text must be understood as follows: "A husband, a wife, a son, etc., are not dear to us in consequence of a wish or purpose on their part, but they are dear to us for the wish of the Self, i.e., to the end that there may be accomplished the desire of the highest Self—which desire aims at the devotee obtaining what is dear to him. For the highest Self pleased with the works of His devotees imparts to different things such dearness, i.e., joy-giving quality as corresponds to those works. . . . Things are not dear, or the contrary, to us by themselves, but only in so far as the highest Self makes them such" (p. 390). "The fact is, that not even non-sentient things are, essentially or intrinsically, bad; but in accordance with the nature of the works of those beings which are under the rule of *karman*, one thing, owing to the will of the Supreme Person, causes pain to one man at one time and pleasure at another time, and causes pleasure or pain to one person and the opposite to another person " (p. 609). If then the law of *Karma*, whereby pleasure and pain are meted out to souls, is nothing else than the method whereby the Deity in love to souls is leading them to their own happiness, there can be no question of grace overcoming or not overcoming the law of *Karma*, for the latter is only an expression of God's grace.

This again, we may remark, is a noteworthy contribution which Rāmānuja has to offer. The law of *Karma* was recognised by previous philosophers, but what exactly was the relation of this law to the Deity was left undetermined. The suggestion was indeed made in the Gītā, as we noted, that rebirth is for the perfecting of the soul; but the full implications of this view could not be realised so long as perfection was not consistently maintained as a fundamental characteristic of the Deity. For, it is obvious that if perfection is not ultimate there can be little meaning in saying that the law of *Karma* with its painful process of birth and rebirth is for the perfecting of souls. By systematically upholding perfection as a characteristic of Brahma, Rāmānuja is enabled to relate the law of *Karma* directly to the Deity and regard it as an expression of His own perfect nature, and, what is more, to see in it the manifestation of God's love.

Besides working on the soul by means of karmic pleasure and pain, does grace operate, we may ask, in any other manner? Rāmānuja's treatment of the question in the Śrī Bhāṣya, to which we are for the time being confining ourselves, is very meagre. In a sense it may be said that the Scripture, " which in tender regard to man's welfare is superior to a thousand parents " (p. 662), and the ' works ' prescribed in the Śāstras, which " produce and help to perfect the knowledge of Brahman " (p. 19), are means of Grace. They owe their origin to the Deity (I. 3. 28, pp. 332

and 333), and, as we have already seen, it is necessary to be led by them to the final realisation of Him. More especially grace functions, it would seem judging from the Kauṣītaki passage above mentioned, as a positive power leading the good soul onwards: "The Lord, wishing to do a favour to those who are resolved on acting so as fully to please the highest Person, engenders in their minds a tendency towards highly virtuous actions, such as are means to attain to Him" (p. 558). Whether this tendency which the Deity engenders within the soul is resistible is not stated, but from the context in which this text occurs, and in which the responsibility of the soul for its deeds is upheld, it would seem that it is not a power which works in a manner to deprive the soul of its individuality. Finally, the crowning act of grace is, as already noted, the redeeming knowledge of Brahman, whereby the soul casts off its Nescience and obtains Release.

But how, it may be asked, is it possible for grace to produce such knowledge as will wipe out the effect of all past deeds? Here again we come upon the question of the relation of grace to the law of *Karma*, and when it is remembered that according to Rāmānuja *Karma* is not an independent force but is merely the manner in which the Deity expresses His approval or disapproval of the deeds of souls, the problem readily solves itself. When the soul has pleased the Deity by its devotion, His displeasure arising from its past deeds is counteracted, and when the counteraction is complete the soul obtains Release. Rāmānuja will not admit that the law of *Karma* is suspended, for being as it is the mode in which the Deity acts, it can never cease to be. Nevertheless, he declares that even as the effect of one force is counteracted by another, so the effect of devotion on the part of the soul has the effect of counteracting the tendency of past deeds to produce displeasure in the Deity. In this connection he writes: "When a man reaches knowledge, the non-clinging and destruction of all sins may be effected through the power of knowledge. For Scripture declares the power of knowledge to be such that 'to him who knows this, no evil deed clings,' and so on. Nor is this in conflict with the text stating that no work not fully enjoyed perishes; for this latter text aims at confirming the power of works to produce their results; while the texts under discussion have for their aim to declare that knowledge when once sprung up possesses the power of destroying the capability of previously committed sins to produce their own evil results and the power of obstructing that capability on the part of future evil actions. The two sets of texts thus refer to different matters, and hence are not mutually contradictory. There is in fact no more contradiction between them than there is between the power of fire to produce heat and the power of water to subdue such heat. By knowledge effecting the non-clinging of sin we have to understand its obstructing the origination of the power, on the part of sin, to cause that disastrous disposition on the part of man which consists in unfitness for religious works and inclined to commit further sinful actions of the same kind. By knowledge effecting the destruction of sin, on the other hand, we understand its destroying that power of sin after it has once originated. That power consists fundamentally in displeasure on the part of the Lord. Knowledge of the Lord, which, owing to the supreme dearness of its object is itself supremely dear, possesses the characteristic power of propitiating the Lord—the object of knowledge—and thus destroys the displeasure of the Lord, due to the previous commission of sins on the part of the knowing Devotee; and at the same time obstructs the origination of further displeasure on the Lord's part, which otherwise would be caused by sins committed subsequently to the origination of such knowledge." But from this it must not be thought, so Rāmānuja warns us, that the man who has obtained saving knowledge may deliberately commit sin after the origination of such knowledge. "What Scripture says about sin not clinging to him who knows can however be understood only with regard to such sins as spring from thoughtlessness; for texts such as 'he who has not turned away from evil conduct' (Ka. Up. I. 2, 24) teach that meditation, becoming more perfect day after day, cannot be accomplished without the Devotee having previously broken himself off from evil conduct" (IV. I. 13, pp. 722-4). Saving grace then never works in such a way as to annul the law of *Karma*. The soul by its knowledge or devotion propitiates the Lord, whose displeasure on account of its past sins is thus counteracted. The fact that the soul remains in the body even after it has obtained saving knowledge is a proof to Rāmānuja that the law of *Karma* is operative throughout, and that the good and evil deeds which had begun to be effective are working themselves out, and that Release does not take place till all such deeds have worked themselves out in accordance with the law of *Karma*. Thus in commenting on Vedānta-sūtra IV. I. 15, he asks himself "whether all previous good and evil works are destroyed by the origination of knowledge, or only those the effects of which have not yet begun to operate." He answers, "Only those previous works perish the effects of which have not yet begun to operate; for the text 'For him there is delay as long as he is not delivered from the body' (Chānd. Up. VI. 14. 2) expressly states when the delay of the body's death will come to an end (the body meanwhile continuing to exist through the influence of the *anārabdhakārya* works). There is no proof for the ex.stence of an impetus accounting for the continuance of the body's life, other than the Lord's pleasure or displeasure caused by good or evil deeds" (pp. 724 and 725). Rāmānuja declares that the soul which has obtained saving knowledge may even have to go through several bodily existences if the deeds which have begun to operate are such as necessitate it.

"If those good and evil works are such that their fruits may be fully enjoyed within the term of one bodily existence, they come to an end together with the current bodily existence; if they require several bodily existences for the full experience of their results, they come to an end after several existences only. . . . All those works, on the other hand, good and evil, which were performed before the rise of knowledge and the results of which have not yet begun to operate —works which have gradually accumulated in the course of infinite time so as to constitute an infinite quantity—are at once destroyed by the might of the rising knowledge of Brahman" (IV. 1. 19, p. 727). The law of *Karma* is thus not violated by the Deity in any way in granting Release to the devotee. The soul's knowledge or devotion counteracts the effect of previous sins producing displeasure in the Deity, and all those deeds which have begun to operate work themselves out completely in accordance with the law of *Karma* before He grants it Release.

From a philosophic point of view Rāmānuja's attempt systematically to uphold the law of *Karma* in relation to grace is significant; for this law secures, as already noted, the moral consistency and perfection of Brahman on the one hand, and the moral responsibility and individuality of the soul on the other. Both we said, Rāmānuja was anxious to maintain; and by regarding the law of *Karma* as not in any way opposed to grace, but as only a means whereby the grace of the Deity is leading the soul to its own ultimate happiness, he is enabled to conceive of grace as functioning always in accordance with the law of *Karma*, and hence always in such a manner as neither to detract from the moral consistency and perfection of Brahman nor to deprive the soul of its individuality.

So far in our treatment of Rāmānuja's doctrine of grace we have confined ourselves to the Śrī Bhāṣya. His teaching in the Bhagavadgītā Bhaṣya is not fundamentally different, but it reveals a difference in one important particular, which must here be noted. From the references to the Bhagavadgītā Bhāṣya given above in connection with the conditions which the soul must fulfil if it would obtain Release, it is obvious that the position that the Deity in His grace grants Release only to one who has fulfilled the necessary conditions of knowledge, duty and devotion is maintained by Rāmānuja in the Bhagavadgītā Bhāṣya also. " Thus, then, in conclusion, thou shalt carry on all thy worldly duties required for thy bodily subsistence, and scriptural duties, viz., daily, casual, etc., rites—as if all was done to please me, as done by one who is essentially my liege, and done, being actuated to do so, by myself. Thou shalt ever in love be engaged in singing my praises, in my services, in bowings, etc. Thou shalt contemplate that the universe is under my rule and guidance, and subsists as essentially my appendage. Thou shalt ponder and reflect over the multitude of my lovable attributes. Occupying thyself daily, thus, in devotion of the aforesaid description thou shalt reach myself " (Bhg. Bh. IX. 34, p. 316). The soul therefore has many conditions to fulfil if it would obtain Release. Indeed even devotion, which the Deity requires as the supreme condition of Release, is possible only to one who has through effort achieved merit : " Those whose self-acquired merits have led them to come to me as their asylum, whose bonds of sin have been broken down and who partake of the divine nature, are noble-souled (*mahātmās*) (IX. 13, p. 293). " It is only to one who is entirely cleansed of all his sins that I become the object of love. It is only such a person who would converge all the strength of his intellect (*buddhi*) to me as his sole aim " (XII. II, p. 387). Since grace functions in accordance with the law of *Karma*, there is little possibility of the soul which fails to fulfil the necessary conditions obtaining Release.

Although this seems in the main to represent his view, the religion of devotion to which he belonged seems to lead him in the Bhagavadgītā Bhāṣya to assert that the Deity requires nothing from the soul beyond complete surrender (*prapatti*). In the Śrī Bhāṣya, as we saw, Rāmānuja maintained that the knowledge of Brahman is not possible for the Śūdra, for the Śūdra had not received Vedic instruction or performed the necessary religious rites. The Gītā however maintains that all beings are alike to the Deity and that He requires nothing beyond whole-hearted devotion from His worshipper (IX. 29-34). Moreover the Āḻvārs, some of whom, as we saw, were outcastes, had sung of the condescending grace of Him who had stooped to save them, however mean and vile. Rāmānuja accordingly declares that Release is possible to all without considerations of caste, provided there is complete devotion. "Be it the divine, the human, the animal, or the stationary kingdoms, be they high or low, in point of kind (or caste), in point of look (colour, etc.), in point of nature (character, etc.), or in point of enlightenment, as Refuge to all, independent of such distinctions, I am equal. Inferiority as regards kind (caste), look, nature or understanding in any person does not, because of it, warrant that he is hateful to me or fit to be rejected as unworthy to come to me as his Refuge. No one on the other hand claiming superiority of caste, etc., is because of it specially entitled to claim me as his Refuge, or has warrant to be particularly dear to me. Save the ground that he elects me as his Refuge, not any qualifications (as caste, colour, etc.), will constitute a claim for my acceptance of Him" (IX. 29, p. 311). "By putting trust in me, even women, the Vaiśyas (or the trading class who, by the very nature of their calling commit sin) or the Śūdras (the low servile class) though sin-born, do yet go to the supreme state" (IX. 32, p. 314).

The Deity overlooks not only caste but also the devotee's sinful condition. This again is a doctrine not unknown to the Gītā (cf. IX. 30; XVIII. 66), and abundantly attested to in the experience of the Āḷvārs. So Rāmānuja writes, " People are born of several castes, each caste having its own rules of conduct. . . . Even if they should transgress those laws, they are deserving of being accounted as righteous men, if in the manner aforesaid they do but worship me with a worship exclusively devoted to me." " But if it be objected that transgression of customary laws (of caste) must impede the further and further development of the flow of God-devotion . . . the answer is—Through love of me, loving for love's sake, and ecstatically transported by that love as he is, he is soon shorn of all sin, the humours of *rajas* and *tamas* are rooted out, and he speedily becomes a holy soul (*dharmātma*)." "The great virtue of loving devotion is such that all the army of opposition is destroyed, and having reached the eternal position of non-obstructiveness the devotee becomes speedily deeply imbued with love for me " (IX. 30 and 31, pp. 312 and 313).

The answer to the question how exactly the sinner becomes through loving devotion transformed into a ' holy soul ' is left ambiguous. Is it devotion itself that does this work, or is it grace, which is brought about through devotion ? Whichever it is, the devotee comes, it would seem, under the influence of a power which hastens for him the work of Release by warding off obstacles and imbuing him with love. That the Deity himself does this work, Rāmānuja considers to be the teaching of Gītā VIII. 14, ' Whoso with undivided mind, and constantly ever ponders on myself, to such a Yogi, Pārtha, ambitious of eternal union, I am easy.' Regarding the meaning of this text Rāmānuja writes that the Deity intends to say, " I am again happily accessible to him (i.e., the Yogi) thiswise—I, on my part, would not be able to bear separation of them (my lovers) from me ; and therefore I myself elect him (*vṛṇe*). I carry to fruition the meditation he adopts for reaching me ; I ward off for him the obstacles which may hamper him in his progress in meditation; I generate in him the intense love and affection for me" (p. 273). The Deity would thus appear to take a very active part in leading the soul to salvation; the soul indeed playing a part, but only a subordinate one.

Accordingly Rāmānuja asks himself how an individual may overcome his bodily nature, and he says that the answer is found in Gītā XV. 4. 'Let Him, the primal *Puruṣa* alone be sought as the Refuge—He from whom is the old will derived.' He interprets this to mean, "By the mere step taken (*iyata*), viz., of having taken Him as Refuge, all those instincts of old will awaken in him. Instincts are impulses which are means to dispel all ignorance, etc. They are called old because they are the instincts of the ancient mokṣa seekers (*mumukṣ*), for they of old sought me alone as their Asylum and became released from bondage" (p. 468). Here Rāmānuja appears to advocate the view that all that is necessary for salvation is to flee to the Deity for Refuge and He will awaken in the soul such tendencies as will lead it to Release. This becomes even more obvious in his interpretation of the next stanza of the Gītā, which enumerates various qualities which the seeker after Release must possess, and Rāmānuja writes, "To those who claim me as their Saviour (or Protector) all the several stages of the aforesaid character-forming are effected through my sole agency. Those states are easily traversed till perfection is reached" (p. 469). Salvation would thus seem to be due to the 'sole agency' of the Deity Himself.[1]

Although the view that salvation is entirely the work of God, while all that the soul has to do is to surrender itself to Him, is thus to be found in the Bhagavadgītā Bhāṣya, in the main Rāmānuja's position is that the

[1] Cf. also, "having through my mere grace alone fully overcome, with its cause, the obstacles to the attainment of high devotion . . . thou shalt become my eternal servant" (Śaraṇāgati-gadya, Bradmavādin, Vol. I, p. 230).

soul has also an active part to play. Thus, as we have already pointed out, he enumerates several conditions which the soul must fulfil if it would gain Release. Indeed, in connection with Gītā XVIII. 66, where we should most expect an exposition of the doctrine of *Prapatti* or the absolute surrendering of oneself to the Deity and leaving the work of salvation to be done by Him, Rāmānuja reveals his bias that the soul cannot leave all to the Deity but must set itself to do its duty. The text reads, 'Renouncing all *dharmas*, hold me as thy sole Refuge. I will deliver thee from all sins, Grieve not.' Rāmānuja interprets 'renouncing' to mean performing one's duty without attachment to fruit of action or to self, and the words 'I will deliver thee from all sins' to mean that the Deity will remove the obstruction caused by previous sins, as taught for instance in the Śrī Bhāṣya. Regarding the latter point Rāmānuja writes, "Śrī Bhagavān consoles Arjuna in his grief which may be supposed to be caused by the reflection that Bhakti-Yoga is one which has to be practised by a person whose sins have entirely ceased and who dearly loves the Lord, but the sins that obstruct at the very outset of the undertaking of Bhakti-Yoga are endless, and it is impossible to exhaust them by expiatory duties . . . and hence Arjuna reflected on his unfitness to launch on Bhakti-Yoga, and cried out in his helplessness. To console Arjuna in this predicament, the Lord may be understood to have counselled him thus: The endless sins hoarded up in the long past are barriers to Bhakti-Yoga being commenced; and to perform, in the short time thou livest, all the expiatory ceremonies prescribed . . . is out of the question. Therefore give up these Dharmas and adopt me in lieu therefore, so as to enable thee to launch on Bhakti-Yoga—adopt me sole, me the most merciful, me the Asylum of the cosmos, demanding no price whatever for admission, me the ocean of compassion for those who depend on me. If thou comest to me thus, I will untrammel thee from all the fetters of the sins described, which obstruct thy embarking on Bhakti-Yoga" (pp. 546 and 545). Rāmānuja thus makes it clear that the Deity will remove only the obstruction caused by sins of previous births. The soul is responsible for the present living of the good life. In this way he seems generally to maintain the responsibility of the soul for carrying out fully its share of work in regard to Release, although he also provides a basis in the Bhagavadgītā Bhāṣya as we saw for the view that all that the Deity requires of the soul is that it should unconditionally surrender itself to Him, the work of salvation being done primarily by the Deity Himself.

The ambiguity in Rānānuja's teaching on this point became a subject of bitter controversy between the two schools which claim to follow him—the Vaḍagaḷai or Northern School and the Teṇgaḷai or Southern. The former hold[1] that *Prapatti* is only one among several ways leading to God, that it should be resorted to only by those who find it impossible to follow the other ways of salvation, that the other modes duly practised aid *Prapatti*, and that an element of human effort is always involved in it. The Southern School, on the other hand, holds that *Prapatti* is the only way of salvation, that these other modes actually disqualify the soul for *Prapatti*, and that no effort is needed on the part of the soul, for God Himself completes the work of salvation. The characteristic difference between the two schools is indicated by their nicknames. The Northern is called the 'monkey school' (*Markaṭa Nyāya*) because it teaches that the soul must co-operate with the Deity in salvation, as the young monkey clings to its mother who carries it to safety; while the Southern is called the 'cat school' (*Nārjāra Nyāya*) because it teaches that the soul need do nothing for salvation beyond passively

[1] See J.R.A.S., 1910, article on the Aṣṭadaśa Bhedas by Mr. A. Govindācārya.

submitting to the Deity, as the kitten remains passive while its mother carries it about in its mouth.

It must be said that the general trend of Rāmānuja's teaching is certainly in favour of the Northern School. Anxious as he is throughout to emphasize the need to conform to Scriptural injunctions, and insistent as he is on the individuality of the soul, it seems hardly likely that the Teṇgaḷai view, which seems to deprive the soul of its individuality, could have won his approval. We may conclude therefore that according to him the grace of the Deity in leading the soul to Release operates in such a manner as neither to detract in any way from His moral consistency and perfection nor to deprive the soul of its individuality.

One more topic remains to be dealt with in connection with the grace of the Deity in relation to the soul in *saṁsāra*. We have seen that grace operates as the law of *Karma* meting out pleasure and pain, expresses itself in the Scriptures which inform us about Brahman and prescribe rites and duties which prepare the soul for saving knowledge, functions within the soul by engendering in it such tendencies as lead it to Release and obstructing such as hinder it in its struggle upwards, and finally grants it the saving knowledge which produces Release. But this is not all. The love of the Deity manifests itself, according to Rāmānuja, in His assuming numerous forms so as to delight the hearts of his worshippers. In this respect his teaching is essentially the same as that of the Pāñcarātrins, who it will be remembered recognised five forms of the Deity—*Para, Vyūha, Vibhava Antaryāmin,* and *Arcā* forms. The doctrine being sectarian Rāmānuja does not systematically expound it ; but it is quite evident, as we shall see, that he recognised all these five forms. The *Para* form is the one in which the Deity exists in the heavenly world with Śrī and a host of eternal beings (cf. Bhg. Bh. Preface, pp. 7 and 8) ; but the forms which concern us here are those which the Deity assumes for the sake of the souls in *saṁsāra*. These are firstly the *Vyūhas* which are assumed by the Deity for the sake of worship. Rāmānuja speaks with approval of this doctrine in establishing that the Vedānta sūtras do not mean to reject the Bhāgavata system (II. 40-43). He says in that connection that we have to understand " ' by the *vyūha* ' the fourfold arrangement or division of the highest Reality as Vāsudeva, Saṁkarṣaṇa, Pradyumna and Aniruddha," and that by " worship of the *Vyūha* one attains to the ' Subtile ' called Vāsudeva, i.e., the highest Brahman." " Saṁkarṣaṇa Pradyumna and Aniruddha are thus mere bodily forms which the highest Brahman voluntarily assumes. Scripture already declares ' not born he is born in many ways,' and it is this birth consisting in the voluntary assumption of bodily form due to tenderness towards its devotees—which the Bhāgavata systems teaches ; hence there lies no valid objection to the authoritativeness of that system " (Ś. Bh., pp. 525-6).

Not only does the Deity in His mercy assume the *vyūha* forms in order to aid the devotee in his worship of Him, but He also incarnates Himself. We have already seen how important a part the belief in incarnation played in the Vaiṣṇava religion. The motive given for incarnation in the Bhagavadgītā and the Anugītā was primarily to uphold righteousness (*dharma*) ; but we noted that as Vaiṣṇava theology developed, and the Deity was removed further and further away from the heart of His worshippers, the theory was advanced that the Deity incarnates Himself for the sake of showing Himself as it were to His devotee. This is the view of the Pāñcarātrins, and it is also Rāmānuja's view. " The highest Brahman whose nature is fundamentally antagonistic to all evil and essentially composed of infinite knowledge and bliss—whereby it differs from all other souls—possesses an infinite number of qualities of unimaginable excellence, and, analogously, a divine form suitable to its nature and intentions, i.e., adorned with infinite, supremely excellent and wonderful qualities—splendour, beauty, fragrance, tenderness, loveliness, youthfulness, and so on. And in order to gratify His devotees He individualises that form so as to render it suitable to their apprehension—He who is a boundless ocean as it were of compassion, kindness and lordly power, whom no shadow of evil may touch—He who is the highest self, the highest Brahman, the supreme soul Nārāyaṇa." "This essential form of His the most compassionate Lord by His mere will individualises as a shape human or divine or otherwise, so as to render it suitable to the apprehension of the devotee and thus satisfy him" (Ś. Bh., pp. 240 and 241). Rāmānuja accepts the view of Gītā IV. 7 and 8 that the Deity incarnates Himself when 'virtue wanes and vice waxes' for 'protecting the virtuous, destroying the wicked and for firmly re-installing *dharma*.' Nevertheless his own predominant view of the motive of incarnation is that of the Pāñcarātrins. Thus in commenting on verse 8 cited above he says that the virtuous (*sādhus*) are the "eminent Vaiṣṇavas who are seeking me out as their shelter. They are those who feel that without seeing me—whose names and wonderful works transcend the powers of speech and mind—they cannot live and move, cannot support their very being. . . . For the protection of these holy men—lest they, in their agony at not seeing me, pine away—I grant them the privilege to be able to see me and my doings, and hold converse with me, and so on" (Bhg. Bh. IV. 8, p. 141). The passage is also significant as revealing the influence of the religion of the Āḻvārs on Rāmānuja. The Āḻvārs we saw dwelt with great feeling on the incarnations of Viṣṇu. Especially the cowherd Kṛṣṇa-Avatāra aroused in them feelings of great intimacy and affection. Love-sick for Kṛṣṇa they paled and pined away. Such deep devotion cannot exist for a remote transcendent Deity. To satisfy the longing soul the Deity must assume a form suitable to its apprehension.

The Āḻvārs worshipped the Deity in His various incarnations and Rāmānuja is without doubt thinking of these saints when he declares that the Deity incarnates Himself in order that He may show himself to His worshippers, who would otherwise pine away at not seeing Him. Accordingly Rāmānuja asserts, " The object of incarnations is to relieve the earth of its burden, but at the same time no less is the Lord's intention thereof that He should be within reach of even people of our description. To fulfil this purpose, He manifested Himself on earth so as to be actually an object for all men's sights to see, and performed such other wonderful acts as to captivate the hearts and the eyes of all creatures high and low " (Bhg. Bh. Preface, p. 9). Rāmānuja's view then is that the Deity assumes incarnate forms primarily to manifest Himself to His worshippers.

Rāmānuja makes it clear that when the Deity incarnates Himself, He is not compelled to do so by *Karma* but assumes bodies entirely from free choice. " As for taking birth it is in His case by free will, whereas in the case of the creatures, it is impelled by *karma* " (Bhg. Bh. IV. 6, p. 140). He is also insistent that in incarnating Himself the Deity does not lay aside His own essential nature ; " in order to fit Himself to be a refuge for gods, men, etc., the supreme Person, without, however, putting aside His true nature, associates Himself with the shape, make, qualities and works of the different classes of beings, and thus is born in many ways " (Ś. Bh. I. 3. 1, p. 297). " Never divesting myself of my essential attributes of suzerainty, that of being birthless, of being exhaustless, or being the Lord of all, etc., I go into birth. . . ." (Bhg. Bh. IV. 6, p. 138). Moreover, Rāmānuja declares that " the bodily forms which the Supreme Person assumes at wish are not special combinations of earth and the other elements " (Ś. Bh., p. 423). " In the Mahābhārata also the form assumed by the highest Person in His *avatāras* is said not to consist of *Prakṛti*, ' the body of the highest Self does not consist of a combination of material elements'" (Ś. Bh., p. 241). Thus Rāmānuja is anxious to maintain the perfections of Brahman even in all His incarnations.

Besides the *Vibhava* or incarnate forms which the Deity in His grace assumes from time to time to be accessible to His worshippers, He also abides according to Rāmānuja as the *Antaryāmin* in the heart of the devotee for purposes of meditation. Thus in commenting on Sūtra I. 3. 13 he quotes the Chāndogya passage which runs, 'Now in that city of Brahman there is the palace, the small lotus, and in it that small ether. Now that which is within that small ether that is to be sought for, that is to be understood' (VIII. 1. 1). Regarding this passage Rāmānuja writes, "The text at first refers to the body of the devotee as the city of Brahman, the idea being that Brahman is present therein as object of meditation; and then designates an organ of that body, viz., the small lotus-shaped heart as the palace of Brahman. It then further refers to Brahman—the all-knowing, all powerful, whose love towards His devotee is boundless like the ocean—as the small ether within the heart, meaning thereby that Brahman who for the benefit of His devotees is present within that palace should be meditated upon as of minute size and finally—in the clause 'that is to be searched out' enjoins as the object of meditation that which abides in that Brahman, i.e., on the one hand its essential freedom from all evil qualities, and on the other the whole treasure of its auspicious qualities, its power of realising its wishes and so on. The 'that' (in 'that is to be searched out') enjoins as the objects of search the small ether, i.e., Brahman itself as well as the qualities abiding within it" (Ś. Bh., p. 316).

Not only does the Deity out of boundless love for the soul abide as *Antaryāmin* "for the purpose of devout meditation, in the heart of the devotee" (Ś. Bh., p. 326), but He also exists in His *Arcā* form in idols, to aid the worship of His followers. Rāmānuja does not explicitly mention this form of the Deity, but he accepts the teaching of Gītā IX. 26, and declares that the Deity appreciates even the smallest offering, be it leaf, flower or fruit, if offered to Him in love (Bhg. Bh., p. 308). Besides, in connection with Gītā IV. 11, 'In the way they resort to me (*prapadyante*) in that way do I serve them,' he writes, "Not only by the method of incarnations, in the form of devas, men, etc., I am saviour to those who seek me as their Refuge, but any other method or form, which it may be their pleasing option to select. Whatever that is, to that I adapt myself. By whatever conception they choose to seek me I manifest myself to them in that mode"; and Rāmānuja explains the "I serve" of the text to mean "I appear to them" (*darśayāmi*), and adds, "In short, albeit my nature is such as even Yogis find it to be transcending thought and speech, yet to all who are of my ways, I suit myself in a manner that I am to them not only a visible demonstration, but they may enjoy me by every one of their sense faculties and in all diverse ways" (Bhg. Bh., pp. 143 and 144). Moreover we know from his life that Rāmānuja presided at the great Śrīraṅgam Temple and consecrated many images for the purposes of worship. And of this unsurpassable grace which leads the Deity to enter and abide in an idol in order that He may thus win the love of the devotee Piḷḷai Lokācārya writes, "This is the peculiar privilege of the devotee when he can, as if force the Lord of the Universe to dwell in a particular image of gold, silver or stone. This is the greatest grace of the Lord, that being free He becomes bound, being independent He becomes dependent for all His service on His devotee. . . . In other forms the man belonged to God but behold the supreme sacrifice of Īśvara, here the Almighty becomes the property of the devotee. . . . He carries Him about, fans Him, feeds Him, plays with Him—yea, the Infinite has become finite, that the child soul may grasp, understand and love Him" (Tattva Traya, pp. 82 and 83).

These, then, the *Vyūha, Vibhava, Antaryāmin* and *Arcā* forms are, according to Rāmānuja as according to the Pāñcarātrins, assumed by the Deity out of infinite compassion for the souls in *saṁsāra*, so that souls may by means of these forms be aided in their worship and meditation of Him, and finally be released from the bonds of worldly existence.

If the Deity in His grace by means of Karmic pleasure and pain, by Vedic revelation, by Śāstric duty, by inward inspiration and outward manifestation of Himself in several forms seeks to lead the soul to Himself, it is only because the soul is a true individual and the Deity is a consistently perfect Being; grace, however boundless, cannot operate in any cataclysmic fashion which would either override the individuality of the soul or detract from the moral consistency and perfection of Brahman. If then through all these elaborate means the Deity seeks out of his great love for souls to lead them to Release, we must enquire what exactly is this condition to which He is leading them, and in what relationship He stands to them in this final state.

(3) *Relation of the Deity to the soul in Release*

We have sought in the foregoing to point out that by breaking away from advaitism, Rāmānuja was enabled consistently to maintain on the one hand that Brahman is highest Person characterised by every perfection and above all by love, and on the other that the soul is a true individual. Both these views, we saw, he tried systematically to uphold in his account of the numerous ways in which the Deity relates Himself to the soul in *saṁsāra*. The same two tenets are maintained by him in regard to the relation in which the Deity stands to the soul in Release.

In our account of views prior to Rāmānuja we have shown that there are abundant traces in them of the doctrine that the soul continues to exist in Release, enjoys perfection and bliss, and even becomes like Brahman. But this view was essentially impossible on the advaita hypothesis which these writers accepted, and according to which the soul in Release becomes unified without difference with Brahman. In accepting both positions, earlier philosophers were unable, as we pointed out, to present any consistent view regarding the state which the soul attained in Release. Rāmānuja sets himself in sharp opposition to the advaita view, and by doing so is enabled to give very clear and consistent formualtion to the view that the soul persists in Release.

Refutation of the advaita view

As against the advaita doctrine Rāmānuja says that if Release meant " a mere return into the substance of Brahman," it would not be anything beneficial to man, " for to be refunded into Brahman as an earthen vessel is refunded into its own causal substance, i.e., clay, means nothing else but complete annihilation " (S. Bh. I. 4. 21, p. 392).

Moreover, he declares, the advaitin's view " cannot stand the test of being submitted to definite alternatives. Is the soul's not being such, i.e., not being Brahman, previously to its departure from the body, due to its own essential nature or to a limiting adjunct, and is it in the latter case real or unreal ? In the first case the soul can never become one with Brahman, for if its separation from Brahman is due to its own essential nature, that separation can never vanish as long as the essential nature persists. And should it be said that its essential nature comes to an end together with its distinction from Brahman, we reply that in that case it perishes utterly and does not therefore become Brahman. The latter view, moreover, precludes itself as in no way beneficial to man, and so on. If, in the next place, the difference of the soul from Brahman depends on the presence of real limiting adjuncts, the soul is Brahman even before its departure from the body, and we therefore cannot reasonably accept the distinction implied in saying that the soul becomes Brahman only when it departs. For on this view there exists nothing but Brahman and its limiting adjuncts, and as those adjuncts cannot introduce difference into Brahman which is without parts and hence incapable of difference, the difference resides altogether in the adjuncts, and hence the soul is Brahman even before its departure from the body. —If, on the other hand, the difference due to the adjuncts is not real, we ask—what is it then that becomes Brahman on the departure of the soul?—Brahman itself whose nature had previously been obscured by Nescience, its limiting adjunct!—Not so, we reply. Of Brahman whose true nature consists in eternal, free, self-luminous intelligence, the true nature cannot possibly be hidden by Nescience" (I. 4. 22, p. 393).

For these reasons, then, the soul cannot be regarded as becoming merged in Brahman on attaining Release. On the other hand, Rāmānuja urges that, since the soul is by its very nature a distinct individual, it must persist as a self-conscious being in the state of Release; otherwise Release cannot be Release, but is identical with death. "To maintain that the consciousness of the 'I' does not persist in the state of final release is again altogether inappropriate. It in fact amounts to the doctrine—only expressed in somewhat different words—that final release is the annihilation of the self. The 'I' is not a mere attribute of the self so that even after its destruction the essential nature of the self might persist—as it persists on the cessation of ignorance; but it constitutes the very nature of the self. . . . Moreover, a man who suffering pain, mental or of other kind . . . puts himself in relation to pain —'I am suffering pain'—naturally begins to reflect how he may once for all free himself from all these manifold afflictions and enjoy a state of untroubled ease; the desire of final release thus having arisen in him he at once sets to work to accomplish it. If, on the other hand, he were to realise that the effect of such activity would be the loss of personal existence, he surely would turn away as soon as somebody began to tell him about 'release.' . . . Nor must you maintain against this that even in the state of release there persists pure consciousness; for this by no means improves your case. No sensible person exerts himself under the influence of the idea that after he himself has perished there will remain some entity termed 'pure light!'" (Ś. Bh., pp. 69 and 70). Whatever Release means, then, Rāmānuja assures us that it is not a state where the individuality of the soul is forfeited.

The character of the released soul and what it reveals regarding the nature of Brahman

This being so, we may next consider briefly what kind of character the soul possesses in the state of Release. According to Rāmānuja the released soul, laying aside the limitations arising from *karman*, manifests itself in its own essential nature. His chief authority for this view is the passage from the Chāndogya Upaniṣad (VIII. 12, 3), which says, 'Thus does that serene being, having risen from the body and having approached the highest light, manifest itself in its own form' (Ś. Bh., p. 755). In this connection he writes: "The subject matter of the whole section shows that by the self manifesting itself in its own form there is meant the self as possessing the attributes of freedom from all evil and sin and so on. For the teaching of Prajāpati begins as follows: 'the self which is free from sin, free from old age, from death and grief, from hunger and thirst, whose desires and thoughts spontaneously realise themselves.' . . . The manifestation of the true nature of the soul when reaching the highest light therefore means the manifestation of that self which has freedom from sin and so on for its essential attributes—that nature being in the *saṁsāra* state obscured through Nescience. . . . Intelligence, therefore, bliss and the other essential qualities of the soul which were obscured and contracted by *Karman*, expand and thus manifest themselves when the bondage due to *Karman* passes away and the soul approaches the highes light " (S. Bh. IV. 4. 3, pp. 757 and 758).

Further, we are told that the released soul obtains whatever it wishes, and even meets its relatives by its mere will (IV. 4. 8). It enters as many bodies as it pleases, not impelled by *Karma*, but entirely by its own will (IV. 4. 15). It enjoys all the different worlds in which Brahman's power is manifested (IV. 4. 18). It finds itself on an equality with all other freed souls for all distinctions of rank, caste and the like are entirely due to the body (I. 4. 22, p. 395; I. 1. 1, p. 101). And, more than all this, it enjoys that beatific vision of the Deity for which it longed while in *saṁsāra*, and by which it sees all things in Him and Him in all things; " when the meditating devotee realises the intuition of this Brahman, which consists of absolute bliss, he does not see anything apart from it, since the whole aggregate of things is contained within the essence and outward manifestation (*vibhūti*) of Brahman " (I. 3. 7, pp. 305 and 306). Such intuition of the highest Self belongs, we are told, to the natural state of the soul, and follows in Release, when Nescience is destroyed (I. 2. 12, p. 271). So Rāmānuja states that " the highest Brahman which is free from all change and of an absolutely perfect and blessed nature —this, together with the manifestations of its glory, is what forms the object of consciousness for the released soul " (IV. 4. 19, p. 768).

Freedom from evil of every kind, the attainment of all its desires, and uncontracted intelligence expressing itself in blissful devotional contemplation of the Deity constitute accordingly the characteristics of the released soul; and since according to Rāmānuja the "special condition into which the soul passes on having . . . approached the highest light is a manifestation of its own true nature, not an origination of a new character" (IV. 4. 1, p. 756), it appears that these qualities belong to the essential nature of the soul, and that consequently the evil qualities which it possesses in *saṁsāra* are foreign to it. "'As the lustre of the gem is not created by the act of polishing, so the essential intelligence of the self is not created by the putting off of imperfections . . . thus knowledge and the other attributes of the self are only manifested through the putting off of evil qualities; they are not produced, for they are eternal'" (IV. 4. 3, p. 758). That the soul should have these characteristics for its essential nature, and that Release should consist in the full manifestation of these perfections, serve to show that in Release the soul becomes most truly itself. Release is for it self-realisation, not self-annihilation. It means for the soul achievement of true individuality. At the same time they reveal also the nature of Brahman as possessed of the same two characteristics which we have found it always to disclose, viz., perfection and love. The perfect nature of Brahman is revealed in the fact that perfections belong to the essential nature of the soul, which as His mode, is entirely dependent on Him for its essential nature. It is also manifest in the fact that till the soul is purged of all evil it is unable to obtain unbroken communion with Him. His love shows itself in the fact that it is to the achievement of its own true individuality whereby it is enabled to attain all its desires, that the Deity leads the soul. It also reveals itself in the fact that it is a life of complete devotion[1] to Himself that He has set as the ultimate goal for finite beings. So eager He is, it would seem, to obtain their love. The highest state, then, being one in which individuals freed from all

[1] That is, intuition, which by Rāmānuja is equated with *bhakti* and *upāsanā* (see Ś. Bh., pp. 15 and 16).

evil render to Him their complete devotion, thus reveals the Deity to be Himself free from evil and full of love.

The relation of Brahman to the released soul

Though the soul achieves individuality in Release and remains as a distinct self, its individuality is not, according to Rāmānuja, such as to annul the supremacy of Brahman and to reduce Him to one among a number of equally independent selves. Rāmānuja holds that the released soul becomes like Brahman in nature in that it is characterised by uncontracted intelligence (p. 100) and in that it is free from all evil (p. 759). Nevertheless, he maintains, it always remains only a mode of Brahman, and never an independent Substance such as Brahman is. " The soul having reached Brahman and freed itself from the investment of Nescience sees itself in its true nature. And this *true nature* consists herein that the souls have for their inner Self the highest Self while they constitute the body of that Self and hence are *modes* (*prakāra*) of it. This is proved by all those texts which exhibit the soul and Brahman in co-ordintaion —' Thou art that,' etc. . . . The consciousness of the released soul therefore expresses itself in the following form : ' I am Brahman, without any division.' Where the texts speak of the soul's becoming equal to, or having equal attributes with, Brahman, the meaning is that the nature of the individual soul—which is a mere mode of Brahman—is equal to that of Brahman, i.e., that on putting off its body it becomes equal to Brahman in purity " (IV. 4. 4, p. 759). Further, " The exalted qualities of the soul—freedom from evil and sin and so on—which manifest themselves in the state of Release no doubt belong to the soul's essential nature ; but that the soul is of such a nature fundamentally depends on the supreme Person, and on Him also depends the permanency of those qualities ; they are permanent in so far as the Lord Himself on whom they depend is permanent" (IV. 4. 20, p. 769). Thus Rāmānuja makes it quite clear that, though souls in Release become like Brahman in character, they are entirely dependent on Him for all they have and are.

This reveals itself in the two important particulars in which released souls differ from Brahman. They are atomic (IV. 4. 14, p. 764) and hence strictly finite, while Brahman, as already said, is the inner Self of all and hence universal and all pervading. Moreover, they do not have creative and ruling power over worlds; this belongs exclusively to Brahman. Such, Rāmānuja says, is the teaching of sūtra IV. 4. 17: 'with the exception of world-energy,' etc. Regarding it he writes, "The doubt here presents itself whether the power of the released soul is a universal power such as belongs to the Supreme Person, extending to the creation, sustentation, and so on, of the worlds; or is limited to the intuition of the Supreme Person. . . . To this the Sūtra replies, 'with the exception of world-energy.' The released soul, freed from all that hides its true nature, possesses the power of intuitively beholding the pure Brahman, but does not possess the power of ruling and guiding the different forms of motion and rest belonging to animate and inanimate nature. How is this known?—'From subject-matter.' For it is with special reference to the highest Brahman only that the text mentions ruling and controlling power over the entire world. 'That from whence these beings are born, that through which they live when born, that into which they enter at death, endeavour to know that; that is Brahman' (Taitt. Up. III. 1. 1). If such universal ruling and controlling power belonged to the released soul as well, it would not be used—as the text actually uses it—for defining Brahman; for all definition rests on special individual attributes" (pp. 766 and 767). Brahman then has powers peculiar to Himself, viz., infinitude and omnipotence, and the released soul, though sharing in the perfections of His nature, is atomic and completely dependent on Him.

This being so, the doubt arises that "if the powers of the released soul altogether depend on the Lord, it may happen that He, being independent in all His doings, may will the released soul to return into the *Saṁsāra*" (p. 770). Rāmānuja assures us that this will never happen, for not only does Scripture tell us so but also because the Deity, being perfect and all-loving, will not allow the devotee whom He has redeemed, and whom He dearly loves, ever again to suffer the miseries of *Saṁsāra*. "We know from Scripture that there is a Supreme Person whose nature is absolutely bliss and goodness; who is fundamentally anatogonistic to all evil . . . who is all-knowing, who by His mere thought and will accomplishes all His purposes; who is an ocean of kindness as it were for all who depend on Him; who is all-merciful . . . and with equal certainty we know from Scripture that this Supreme Lord, when pleased by the faithful worship of His devotees . . . frees them from the influence of Nescience which consists of *karman* accumulated in the infinite progress of time and hence hard to overcome; allows them to attain to that supreme bliss which consists in the direct intuition of His own true nature; and after that does *not* turn them back into the miseries of *Saṁsāra*." "Nor indeed need we fear that the Supreme Lord when once having taken to Himself the devotee whem He greatly loves will turn him back into the *Saṁsāra*" (IV. 4. 22, pp. 770 and 771); and as if fearing lest it be thought that the Deity forces the soul to stay in the state of Release against its will, Rāmānuja declares that the soul also, having once attained Release, never wishes to return to *Saṁsāra*. "As, moreover, the released soul has freed itself from the bondage of *karman*, has its powers of knowledge fully developed, and has all its being in the supremely blissful intuition of the highest Brahman, it evidently cannot desire anything else nor enter on any other form of activity, and the idea of its returning into the *Saṁsāra* therefore is altogether excluded" (p. 771). The non-return of the soul to *saṁsāra* is thus not only in accordance with the will of the Deity, but also in accordance with the soul's own desires. Hence not even in the state of Release is the will of the finite individual over-ridden.

The Deity, then, we may conclude, grants to the souls, whom He has redeemed the perfections of His nature—knowledge, bliss and freedom from evil. These are also the perfections of their own nature. Consequently in Release, souls become most truly themselves. And yet there is no conflict between the individuality of finite selves and the Universality and supremacy of Brahman, for they form the body or modes of Brahman, while He is the inner Self on whom they completely depend. He loves them dearly, and so never sends them back into *saṁsāra.* They enjoy blissful vision of Him and wish for nothing else. Souls thus co-operating with the will of the Supreme Being, dwell eternally in loving contemplation of Him, revealing within themselves the perfections of His nature, while He animates and sustains them, and bears infinite love for them.

Thus in all His relationship to the soul, whether prior to world-creation, in *saṁsāra*, or in the state of Release, Brahman appears as a perfect Being filled with love for the soul. He holds it in existence prior to world-creation ; aiming at its happiness, He sends it into *saṁsāra* with a body suitable to its deserts ; and He abides in it as an animating and cheering principle. He seeks in His grace to lead it from sin, suffering and Nescience to a life of perfection, bliss and complete devotion to Himself, and to this end He sends pleasures and pains, prescribes duties, gives information about Himself in the Vedas, engenders in it, if it so deserve, such tendencies as may aid it in this direction, and assumes various finite forms in order to be accessible to it. Finally in due time He grants it Release, when, its evil nature having perished, it lives in and through Him, enjoying blissful and loving contemplation of Him, exhibiting within itself perfections akin to His, and being the object of His eternal love.

Concluding Statement

Now that we have considered the relation of Brahman to souls and to the world, we are ready for a summary statement of Rāmānuja's conception of the Deity. Brahman is not mere Thought but highest Self. He has for His essential attributes thought, bliss and freedom from evil. He is characterised by every perfection, and above all by love. The world and all that is therein are real and completely dependent on Him. He is their cause in the sense that He holds them within Himself in subtle form prior to world-creation, and then by His will sends them out into gross existence. They form His body in the sense that, though animated, sustained and controlled by Him for His own ends, their change and imperfections do not in any way affect His own essential nature. They are His attributes or modes in the sense that, though distinct from Him, they can have no existence apart from Him. Of the constituent elements of the world, matter exists entirely for the sake of souls, Brahman not sharing in its evil nature, but employing it in order to mete out to them pleasure and pain in accordance with their deeds so that He may lead them to Himself. Souls are true individuals whom He loves, and who share the perfections of His nature, but who owing to their own deeds are imperfect. In His grace He seeks to lead them to a life of perfection and complete devotion to Himself, and when they have once attained it He will never allow them to be separated from Him again.

This in brief is the conception which Rāmānuja seeks systematically to uphold. The whole, as is readily observable, centres round the idea of the Deity as a personal Being filled with every perfection and abounding in love. This is the view which in essence found early expression, as we saw, in portions of the Gītā and in the Nārāyaṇīya section of the Mahābhārata. It tended to be much confused in formulation in the Gītā as well as in later Vaiṣṇava philosophical works owing to affiliation with advaitism. The Āḻvārs rediscovered it in the ardour of religious experience, and sang of a God who is boundless in mercy and loves the soul even as a lover his beloved. Such love demands the personality of the Supreme Being on the one hand, and the reality of the soul on the other. It is these that in opposition to the advaitin Rāmānuja seeks systematically to maintain in the light of concepts derived chiefly from the Upaniṣads. The Deity, Rāmānuja tells us, is a personal Being characterised by every perfection, and the world is created by Him out of love for souls, so that He may, by means of experiences undergone by them in it, wean them as responsible individuals from evil, and redeem them to a life of complete devotion to Himself. Rāmānuja's contribution lies in clearly grasping this view, so truly representative of the devotional spirit of the religious sect to which he belonged, in finding support for it in the Upaniṣads and the Vedāntasūtras, and in systematically upholding it in the light of the difficulties with which it is faced, such for example as the relation of God's perfection to the imperfections of the world, and the relation of God's grace to the soul's individuality. With such problems he persistently grapples, never allowing his mind's eye to be removed from the perfection and love of Brahman on the one hand and the individuality of the soul on the other. What he gives is not empirical proof—for that, he warns us, is impossible—but an intellectual picture whereby we may conceive of the Supreme Being as holding all things together, supporting and ruling them as Self in relation to body, or as Substance in relation to attribute; that is, a unity which holds together and supports real differences without however being implicated in their imperfections. Perhaps it is not possible for us in seeking to obtain an intelligible conception of the Supreme Being to pass beyond such pictorial thought. Nevertheless it is valuable as providing religion with an intelligible conception of the Deity in relation to the universe, and more especially in relation to the finite self, as an all-perfect Person characterised above all by love.

BIBLIOGRAPHY[1]

UPANIṢADS.

Translations.

R. E. Hume. The Thirteen Principal Upaniṣads, Oxford, 1921.
F. Max Müller. Sacred Books of the East, Vols. 1 and 15.

System.

P. Deussen. Philosophy of the Upaniṣads; trans. by A. S. Geden, 1906.
A. Berriedale Keith. The Religion and Philosophy of the Veda and Upaniṣads, Vol. 2 (Harvard Oriental Series, Vol. 32), 1925.
R. Gordon Milburn. The Religious Mysticism of the Upaniṣads, 1924.
R. D. Ranade. A Constructive Survey of the Upaniṣadic Philosophy, Poona, 1926.

Concordance.

G. A. Jacob. A Concordance of the Principal Upaniṣads and the Bhagavadgītā, Bombay, 1891.

BHAGAVADGĪTĀ.

Translations.

L. D. Barnett. The Bhagavadgītā, London, 1905.
W. D. P. Hill. The Bhagavadgītā, Oxford, 1928.
K. T. Telang. S.B.E., Vol. 8, 1898.

PAÑCARĀTRA AND PURĀṆIC LITERATURE.

Historical Introduction.

L. D. Barnett. Hindu Gods and Heroes, London, 1922.
R. G. Bhandarkar. Report on the Search for Sanskrit MSS. in the Bombay Presidency during the year 1883-4, Bombay, 1887.

Vaiṣṇavism, Śaivism and Minor Religious Systems, Strasburg, 1913.
H. T. Colebrooke. Miscellaneous Essays, London, 1837.
Epigraphia Indica and Record of the Archæological Survey of India.
E. W. Hopkins. The Great Epic of India, Yale, 1901.
A. Berriedale Keith. Indian Mythology (The Mythology of all Races, Vol. 6), Boston, 1917.
S. Kṛṣṇasvāmi Aiyaṅgār. Early History of Vaiṣṇavism in South India, Madras, 1920.
A. A. Macdonell. A History of Sanskrit Literature, London, 1899.
Vedic Mythology, Strasburg, 1897.

[1] Arranged in accordance with the main divisions followed in this work. Books placed for convenience under one division often apply to more than one division.

Macdonell and Keith. Vedic Index of Names and Subjects, London, 1912.
J. Muir. Original Sanskrit Texts, London, etc., 1858.
H. C. Raychoudhery. Materials for the Study of the Early History of the Vaiṣṇava Sect, Calcutta, 1922.
E. J. Thomas. Vedic Hymns, London, 1923.
S. Sörensen. Index to the Names in the Mahābhārata, London, 1904, etc.

Translations.

P. C. Ray. The Mahābhārata. Śānti Parva and Aśvamedha Parva.
K. T. Telang. The Anugītā—S.B.E., Vol. 8, 1898.
M. N. Dutt. Viṣṇu Purāna, The Wealth of India, Vol. I, Calcutta, 1892, etc.
Śrīmad Bhāgavatam, The Wealth of India, Vols. 2 and 3, Calcutta, 1892, etc.
H. H. Wilson. Viṣṇu Purāṇa, London, 1840.

System.

G. A. Grierson. The Nārāyaṇīya and the Bhāgavatas, Bombay, 1909.
G. N. Mallik. The Philosophy of the Vaiṣṇava Religion, Punjab, 1927.
F. Otto Schrader. Introduction to the Pāñcarātra and Ahirbudhnya Saṁhitā, Madras, 1916.
P. T. Śrīnivāsa Aiyaṅgār. Outlines of Indian Philosophy, Benares and London, 1909.

THE ĀLVĀRS.

Lives.

A. Govindācārya. The Holy Lives of the Āzhvārs, Mysore, 1902.
S. Kṛṣṇasvāmi Aiyaṅgār. Ancient India, Madras, 1911.

Hymns.

Text (selections)—Nityānusandhānam Series, edited by M. B. Śrīnivāsa Aiyaṅgār, Madras, 1898, etc.

Translations (Selections).

J. S. M. Hooper. Hymns of the Āḷvārs (Heritage of India Series), 1929.
N. Kūrattāḷvār Aiyaṅgār. A Free Translation of the Tiruvāimoḷi of Śaṭhakopā (Penukonda Āḷvār Sannidhi Series, No. 4), Trichinopoly, 1925.
Viśiṣṭādvaitin, Vol. 1.

RĀMĀNUJA.

Life.

A. Govindācārya. The Life of Rāmānujācārya, Madras, 1906.
S. Kṛṣṇasvāmi Aiyaṅgār. Śrī Rāmānuja, Madras, 1908.
T. Rājagopālācārya. The Vaiṣṇavite Reformers of India, Madras, 1909.

Translation of Writings.

A. Govindācārya. Bhagavadgītā Bhāṣya.
J. J. Johnson. Vedānta-tattva-sāra[1] (in the Paṇḍit, New Series, Vols. 9-12), Benares, 1887-90.
G. Thibaut. Śrī Bhāṣya, S.B.E., Vol. 48, 1904.
Śaraṇāgati gadya[1]—Brahmavādin, Vol. 1, 1895.
Vedārtha saṁgraha—Brahmavādin, Vols. 1 and 2, 1895-7.

[1] Ascribed to Rāmānuja.

System.

V. S. Ghate. The Vedânta, Poona, 1926.
Mādhva. Sarvadarśana Saṁgraha, trans. by E. B. Cowell and A. E. Gough, 1878.
Piḷḷai Lokācārya. Artha Pañcaka; trans. by A. Govindācārya in J.R.A.S., 1910.
Tattva Traya; trans. by M. N. Paul, Allahabad.
M. Raṅgācārya. Introduction to his Translation of the Śrī Bhāṣya, Madras, 1899.
Śrīnivāsa. Yatīndramata Dīpikā; trans. by A. Govindācārya, Madras, 1912.
G. Thibaut. Introduction to Vol. 34 of S.B.E., 1890.
Vedānta-Deśika (or Veṇkata-nātha) Saṁkalpa Sūryodaya; trans. by K. Nārāyaṇācārya and D. Raghunāthasvāmi Aiyaṇgār, Śrīraṇgam, 1917.

GENERAL WORKS.

S. N. Das Gupta. A History of Indian Philosophy, Cambridge, 1922.
J. N. Farquhar. An Outline of the Religious Literature of India, London, 1920.
S. Rādhākṛṣnan. Indian Philosophy, 2 vols., George Allen & Unwin, Ltd.

ENCYCLOPÆDIA.

Hastings' Encyclopædia of Religion and Ethics.

PERIODICALS.

Brahmavādin.
Indian Antiquary.
Journal of the Royal Asiatic Society.
Viśiṣṭādvaitin.

INDEX